Armageddon Now!

The Premillenarian Response to Russia and Israel Since 1917

DWIGHT WILSON

Baker Book House
Grand Rapids, Michigan

ISBN: 0-8010-9512
Second printing, March 1981

Printed in the United States of America

Acknowledgments

No matter how independently conceived or carried out, every historical study is the product of a community of scholars. That fact is particularly true of this study. Special thanks are due to Page Smith for graciously guiding this disciple at the University of California, Santa Cruz, where the studies resulting in this book were pursued, and also to John Dizikes of UCSC for fortifying my ambition to chase my own peculiar interests. I would be remiss if I were not to formally acknowledge my obvious intellectual debt to Ernest R. Sandeen and Samuel S. Hill, Jr.

Librarians are either the most helpful people in the world, or perhaps simply the people whom I most ask for help. Whatever the case, the UCSC Interlibrary Loan Librarian, Joan Hodgson, has given efficient, courteous service to a multitude of requests. The staff of the Biola Library, including Arnold D. Ehlert, Jan Mayer, Gerald Gooden, and Robert Bamattre, rendered not only competent service but red-carpet treatment. Each of the following librarians provided service far beyond expectations: Walter Osborn, Moody Bible Institute; Jewell Carter, Golden Gate Baptist Theological Seminary; and Stuart Compton, Simpson College. My thanks also to the library staffs of the Pacific School of Religion, the Graduate Theological Union, San Francisco Theological Seminary, Central Bible College, Bethany Bible College, the University of Utah, Stanford University, and the University of California, Berkeley.

Without the encouragement of my wife, Kathryn, these studies would never have begun. She has graciously shouldered some of my responsibilities without complaint, proofread the early drafts, and provided beautiful companionship.

Acknowledgments

The Shepherd Boy and the Wolf

A mischievous lad, who was set to mind some sheep, used, in jest, to cry "Wolf! Wolf!" When the people at work in the neighboring fields came running to the spot he would laugh at them for their pains. One day the wolf came in reality, and the boy this time called "Wolf! Wolf!" in earnest; but the men, having been so often deceived, disregarded his cries, and the sheep were left at the mercy of the wolf.

—Aesop

Contents

1

Introduction

One of the persistent, dynamic minorities of American society is a few million people who refer to themselves as premillennialists or premillenarians—Christians who believe in an imminent, personal return of Jesus Christ to establish an earthly kingdom which will last a millennium. Other twentieth-century ideologies have had expectations—for example, a Third Reich that would last a thousand years or a dialectically determined proletarian state that would gradually wither away as it purified itself from the depravity of capitalistic greed. But this group of dedicated True Believers expectantly awaits the inevitable establishment of the final kingdom of the arch-Messiah Himself. This is a study of one of the identifying characteristics of their thought, a characteristic which has developed a special significance in view of the rise of Soviet Russia and the establishment of Israel in this century. This significance has been intensified by the coalescence of these two phenomena during the Cold War and especially by the position Israel has assumed as an issue in East-West relations since 1967.

Of interest to the student of minorities in America will be the social attitudes of this fast-growing religious minority which has roots in the colonial era and the nineteenth century. Those interested in foreign affairs will observe the deep emotional folkways that contribute to that nebulous body of public opinion which looks over the shoulders of those who formulate governmental policies. Scholars in religious studies will see the motivating core of this wing of the Evangelical movement, and it is to be hoped that premillenarians themselves will come to a new consciousness of their own roots and to a re-evaluation of the evolution of contemporary premillenarian thought.

The number of American premillenarians may be conservatively estimated at eight million. Of the over twelve million Southern Baptists more than half may be counted as premillenarians, and the largest entirely premillenarian denomination, the Assemblies of God, lists over a million followers. To these may be added various smaller sects and a scattering of believers in the larger denominations. In a technical sense, the ideas here discussed are specifically associated with the futurist school of the premillenarians, but there are those apart from the futurist persuasion who also subscribe to these particular beliefs about Russia and Israel. On the other hand, there are premillenarians such as the Seventh Day Adventists who do not await the restoration of Israel. However, because of its general currency among the conservative, Evangelical wing of American Protestantism, we will use the term *premillenarian* to designate those who hold these beliefs about Russia and Israel. The prevailing view of eschatology in Protestant theology is postmillennialism—the belief that Christ will return *after* a millennium (literal or figurative) that has been ushered in by the extension of Christianity. Another view, amillennialism, holds that the millennium is not a literal thousand years and has in fact already begun. Both of these schools emphasize the fact that the millennium is mentioned only once in Scripture (Rev. 20). Premillennialism is usually associated with a pessimistic social outlook that expects a degeneration of social conditions prior to the end, whereas postmillennialism is associated with a modernistic, liberal optimism which expects a betterment of the human condition.

The sources from which this analysis is basically drawn are premillenarian books and periodicals which are primarily the food of the laity rather than the clergy. Hence, it usually excludes formal theological treatises and scholarly premillenarian journals such as *Bibliotheca Sacra,* even though they parallel the popular material in content. The author is a third-generation premillenarian who has spent his whole life in premillennialist churches, has attended a premillennialist Bible college, and has taught in such a college for fourteen years. His experience has shown that the literature under study has direct correlation with the content of sermons and Sunday school lessons and with the body of popular opinion within those churches. These sources include *The Pentecostal Evangel,* the weekly journal of the largest premillenarian denomination, the Assemblies of God; *The Alliance Witness,* the journal of a smaller sect, the Christian and Missionary Alliance; the publications of the two leading educational institutions of the movement, Moody Bible Institute's *Moody Monthly* and Biola College's *The King's Business;* and independent publications such as *The Sunday School Times, Christian Life,* and *Christianity Today.* Specialized periodicals such as *Prophecy Monthly* and *Our Hope* (together with its successor *Eternity*) have also been used, as has the official journal of the National Association of Evangelicals, the *United Evangelical Action.* To some, these publications may appear as representative of a radical Protestant view, but seen from within the movement itself, they are a rather moderate expression. These sources could be supplemented by a multitude of similar (and more radical) publications of smaller denominations, independent churches, and popular evangelists, as well as by scores of radio and television programs.

As the year 2000 approaches there will undoubtedly be increased interest in premillenarian ideas and even more hazardous speculation that this third millennium will be the Thousand Year Kingdom of Christ. There has been no significant speculation in this regard as yet, because the quarter century that remains makes the year 2000 too far removed to induce a sense of crisis or terror; but as it approaches, the cry of impending doom may be expected to swell. To the extent that this cry is reinforced by continuing crises in the Middle East there will grow an ever more deafening roar of "Armageddon Now!"

Before Balfour and Bolsheviks

> *The Jews in London are collecting money in order to purchase Palestine at this moment: the Jews in America have collected enormous sums to build the temple again in Jerusalem.*
>
> —John Cumming, *Signs of the Times,* 1855

> *Russia will burst forth, overcome all resistance, march to Palestine; and, unsuccessful in achieving the evil thing it had set its heart upon, God will avenge his own by the most terrific judgments.*
>
> —John Cumming, *The End,* 1855

In retrospect, the first week of November, 1917, included two epochal events for the premillennialist—the rebirth of God's chosen people and the awakening of the Russian giant. On November 2, 1917, the British Foreign Secretary, Arthur Balfour, publicly announced that "His Majesty's Government view with favor the establishment in Palestine of a national home for the Jewish people and will use their best endeavors to facilitate the achievement of that object. . . ." The Balfour Declaration was viewed by the premillennialists as the beginning of the restoration of Israel to Palestine, the opening scene of the end-time saga which would culminate in the early reign of Christ for the millennium. This unveiling of the divine drama was enthusiastically applauded by the premillennialists.

Like the rest of the world, the premillennialists were not quite so immediately aware of the significance of the second event—the Bolsheviks' November revolution in Russia. But as they progressively became conscious of the new role of the red superstar on the stage of history, they began to boo and hiss the villain, even though they saw as God-given the giant's part in the Biblical drama that had been prophetically written. Their perception of Russia's position resulted from a theology that was based upon a literalistic interpretation of the Bible and had developed during the nineteenth century. The various millennial currents were most effectively solidified in *The Scofield Reference Bible.*[1] The significance of the *Scofield Bible* cannot be overestimated. As Ernest R. Sandeen has observed, it is "perhaps the most influential single publication in millenarian and Fundamentalist historiography."[2] Total publication to date exceeds three million copies.[3] Editor C. I. Scofield's initials were the basis of a common pun: "C. I. and I don't see eye-to-eye." This was indicative of the fact that Scofield was considered the accepted standard from which to depart. A glance at Scofield's notes on the subjects of Israel and Russia will provide a peek into the premillennialists' mind and help us to understand their response to the events of 1917.

Most prophecies of Israel's restoration to Palestine were interpreted by Scofield as being yet unfulfilled. Among these prophecies are Ezekiel 37 (the "Dry Bones" chapter); Deuteronomy 30:5-7 ("God will bring thee into the land which thy fathers possessed"); Isaiah 11:11, 12 ("the Lord shall set his hand again the second time to recover the remnant of my flock out of all countries"). In a note at Romans 11:26, Scofield summarizes his view: "According to the prophets, Israel regathered from all nations, restored to her own land and converted, is yet to have her greatest earthly exaltation and glory." Until this restoration occurs the world will continue in "the Times of the Gentiles"—a term which Scofield defines in a note at Revelation 16:19: " 'The Times of the Gentiles' is that long period beginning with the Babylonian captivity of Judah, under Nebuchadnezzar, and to be brought to an end by the destruction of Gentile world-power by the 'stone cut out without hands' (Dan. 2:34, 35, 44), i.e. the coming of the Lord in glory (Rev. 19:11, 21), until which time Jerusalem is politically subject to Gentile Rule (Lk. 21:24)." Until this destruction of Gentile power, "the Gentile nations are permitted to afflict Israel in chastisement for her national sins, but invariably and inevitably retribution falls upon them."[4] It is regrettable that this view allowed premillennialists to expect the phenomenon of anti-Semitism and tolerate it matter-of-factly.

One of the nations destined to receive inevitable retribution is Russia. Ezekiel 38 and 39 pronounce doom upon something called Gog: "Son of man, set thy face against Gog, the land of Magog, the chief prince of Meshech and Tubal, and prophesy against him, And say, Thus saith the Lord God; Behold, I am against thee."[5] In a note at Ezekiel 38:2 Scofield identifies Gog:

> That the primary reference is to the northern (European) powers, headed up by Russia, all agree. The whole passage should be read in connection with Zech. 12:1-4; 14:1-9; Mt. 24:14-30; Rev. 14:14-20; 19:17-20. "Gog" is the prince, "Magog," his land. The reference to Meshech and Tubal (Moscow and Tobolsk) is a clear mark of identification. Russia and the northern powers have been the latest persecutors of dispersed Israel, and it is congruous both with divine justice and with the covenant . . . that destruction should fall at the climax of the last mad attempt to exterminate the remnant of Israel in Jerusalem. The whole prophecy belongs to the yet future "day of Jehovah" (Isa. 2:10-22; Rev. 19:11-21), and to the battle of Armageddon (Rev. 16:14; 19:19, *note*), but includes also the final revolt of the nations at the close of the kingdom-age (Rev. 20:7-9).[6]

Apparently the defeat of Russia was associated with the battle of Armageddon, which Scofield explains in a note at Revelation 19:17: "Armageddon (the ancient hill and valley of Megiddo, west of Jordan in the plain of Jezreel) is the appointed place for the beginning of the great battle in which the Lord, at His coming in glory, will deliver the Jewish remnant besieged by the Gentile world-powers under the Beast and False Prophet (Rev. 16:13-16; Zech. 12:1-9)."

In the premillennial scheme as developed by Scofield, Israel is to be restored to Palestine, and Russia is to lead a confederacy of nations in an invasion of Palestine. This simplistic twofold scheme has continually governed the premillennialists' response to both nations throughout this century. This system of eschatology was the culmination of developments throughout the nineteenth century and had many roots even further back.

According to Peter Toon in his study of Puritan eschatology, the belief in the restoration of Israel was widely held even among the Puritans of the seventeenth century. Most Puritans subscribed to the idea of a large-scale conversion of Jews to Christianity before the end of time, and in turn believed that there would also be a return of the Jews to Palestine. Sir Henry Finch in *The World's Great Restauration, or The Calling of the Jews* (1621) explained that the Euphrates River would dry up for the Jews to pass through on their return to Palestine, and that they would be opposed by Gog and Magog (equated with the Turks), but the Jews would win as God fought for them.[7] This interest in the restoration of the Jews was reinforced by the horrors of the Thirty Years War in Germany, which led men to imagine that they were living in the last days.[8] Toon cited the great jurist Hugo Grotius for the observation that eighty books concerned with the millennium had been published in England by 1649. A writer of the second quarter of the seventeenth century, Joseph Mede, Professor of Greek at Cambridge, is designated by Toon as the "father of premillennialism," and John Milton and Isaac Newton are listed among his indebted successors.[9]

The radical Puritans, known as the Fifth Monarchy Men, believed that the millennium or Fifth Monarchy—the successor to the four kingdoms of Daniel's prophecy—would soon be established.[10] They interpreted the prophetic symbols as contemporary figures in British political life and pictured themselves as the instruments of God that would tear down the existing structure in order that God might establish this new kingdom of heaven. This is a curious contrast to the twentieth-century premillennialists who tend to be pessimistic, fatalistic, nonpolitical, and nonactivist. John Tillinghast argued that "the present worke of God is, to bring downe lofty men, to lay men low, and to throwe down Antichrist."[11] King

Charles I was adversely identified by various writers as the little horn of Daniel 7:8, as one of the ten horns of the Beast of Revelation 17:12-15, and as the king of the north of Daniel 11:15-19.[12] As far as Israel was concerned, Tillinghast's interpretation led him to identify the 1,290 days of Daniel 12:11 as the years between 366, when the Jewish Temple was supposedly destroyed, and 1656, when he expected the Jews to be converted and return to Palestine.[13] Similarly, John Canne predicted that the Jews in 1655 would both defeat the Turks, who controlled Palestine, and return to their homeland, where they would be converted in 1700. Mary Cary forecast the conversion *and* return for 1656.[14] Such speculation among English Puritans declined after the restoration of the monarchy. The American, Increase Mather, in a 1669 work entitled *The Mystery of Israel's Salvation Explained and Applyed,* affirmed the following beliefs:

> That after the Jews are brought into their own land again, and there disturbed with Gog and Magog (not John's, but Ezekiel's Gog and Magog, at the battle of Armageddon) who shall think with great fury to destroy the converted Israelites. . . .
>
> The Jews who have been trampled upon by all nations, shall shortly become the most glorious nation in the whole world, and all other nations shall have them in great esteem and honor. Isa. 60:1, 3. . . .
>
> That the time will surely come, when the body of the twelve Tribes of Israel shall be brought out of their present condition of bondage and misery, into a glorious and wonderful state of salvation, not only spiritual but temporal.[15]

Eschatological interests continued to concern the American Puritans in the eighteenth century, but the focus was not premillennial.

America's first major postmillennial thinker was Jonathan Edwards. His views paralleled those of Daniel Whitby (1638-1725), the founder of modern postmillennialism. This scheme became the standard American interpretation from which the twentieth-century premillennialists would dissent. The restoration of Israel continued to be a prevailing theme even of the postmillennialist literature. Whitby's 1703 work, *Paraphrase and Commentary on the New Testament,* included "A Treatise of the Millennium: Shewing That It Is Not a Reign of Persons Raised from the Dead, but of the Church Flourishing Gloriously for a Thousand Years

After the Conversion of the Jews, and the Flowing-in of All Nations to Them Thus Converted to the Christian Faith."[16] Edwards speculated in his *History of Redemption* that within a century and a half the Mohammedans might be overthrown and the Jews converted. Contemporary signs convinced him that the millennium was at hand.[17]

It is difficult to show a direct continuity from the seventeenth-century Puritan radicals to the present-day premillennialists, but Ernest R. Sandeen has magnificently demonstrated the development since the Napoleonic era in his ground-breaking work, *The Roots of Fundamentalism: British and American Millenarianism, 1800-1930*. Sandeen describes the significance of that early era:

> The identification of the events of the 1790s with those prophesied in Daniel 7 and Revelation 13 provided biblical commentators with a prophetic Rosetta stone. At last a key had been found with which to crack the code. There could now be general agreement upon one fixed point of correlation between prophecy and history. After 1799, in Egyptology as in prophecy, it seemed as though there were no limits to the possibility of discovery.[18]
>
> As the unbelievable events of the 1790s unfolded, students of . . . apocalyptic literature became convinced (in a rare display of unanimity) that they were witnessing the fulfillment of the prophecies of Daniel 7 and Revelation 13. The Revolution brought the cheering sight of the destruction of papal power in France, the confiscation of church property, and eventually the establishment of a religion of reason; the final act occurred in 1798 when French troops under Berthier marched on Rome, established a republic, and sent the pope into banishment. Commentators were quick to point out that this "deadly wound" received by the papacy had been explicitly described and dated in Revelation 13. Although prophetic scholars had previously been unable to agree on what dates to assign to the rise and fall of papal power, it now became clear, after the fact, that the papacy had come to power in 538 A.D.[19]

This interpretation assumes that the two beasts in Daniel and Revelation are identical and that the forty-two months of Revelation 13 figuratively represent 1,260 years, 538-1798. This is an example of one of those necessary shifts to symbolism—days equal years—an uncomfortable equation for literalists.

In the work of Lewis Way, Sandeen has found evidence that belief in Israel's restoration was a "firmly established plank in the millenarian creed" in the nineteenth century. In 1811 Way discovered the existence of a grove of trees in Devonshire whose owner had designated in his will that "these oaks shall remain standing, and the hand of man shall not be raised against them till Israel returns and is restored to the Land of Promise."[20] An even earlier work, which Sandeen describes as among the first evidences of the prophetic revival, contained extensive discussion of the idea. This study by George Stanley Faber entitled *A Dissertation on the Prophecies, That Have Been Fulfilled, Are Now Fulfilling, or Will Hereafter Be Fulfilled, Relative to the Great Period of 1260 Years; The Papal and Mohammedan Apostacies; the Tyrannical Reign of Antichrist, or the Infidel Power; and the Restoration of the Jews* appeared in London in 1804. By 1811, the second American edition had been published. The Antichrist was identified as Napoleon;[21] he would be destroyed in Palestine;[22] the drying-up of the Euphrates predicted in Revelation 16:12 meant the fall of the Turks;[23] the "kings of the east" of Revelation 16:12 signified the restoration of the ten lost tribes of Israel.[24] All these developments could not be "very far distant."[25] Faber followed the pattern of the radical Puritans in apportioning appropriate Biblical roles to contemporary good fellows and evildoers—but on the international scene.

Similar concerns were the subject of another work by Faber which was published in Boston in 1809—*A General and Connected View of the Prophecies Relative to the Conversion, Restoration, Union, and Future Glory of the Houses of Judah and Israel; the Progress, and Final Overthrow, of the Antichristian Confederacy in the Land of Palestine; and the Ultimate General Diffusion of Christianity.* Faber pictured Napoleon as the Antichrist at the head of a revived Roman Empire,[26] and cited as supporting evidence the fact that the Jews of Frankfort hailed the emperor as their messiah.[27] Opposed to Napoleon and instrumental in restoring Israel to Palestine were the "ships of Tarshish" (Isa. 60:9) and the "isles of the sea" (Isa. 24:15). Asserting that they were necessarily a Gentile, Protestant, maritime power, Faber attempted to make the identification specific:

> Is then *England* the great *maritime power,* to which the high office of converting and restoring a large part of his ancient people is reserved by the Almighty? . . . *England* may, or may not. . . . This however I may *safely* say, that, the more true piety increases among us, the more likely will it be that *England* is *the great maritime power* in question.[28]

Russia, England's ally in the Napoleonic wars, was assigned a role in this end-time scenario; she was the "king of the north" of Daniel 11, whom Faber depicted as benevolent. He observed that Russia had risen "in the inconceivably short space of a little more than a century from barbarous insignificance to immense power and influence,"[29] and that "it will be a tremendous instrument in the hand of God."[30] In commenting on Revelation 16:17-21, he said: "The necessary conclusion seems to be, if I be right in supposing *the northern king* to be *Russia,* that *the hail-storm* of *the seventh veil* means *some dreadful invasion of the papal Roman Empire and her northern allies* during the time that *Antichrist* is engaged in prosecuting his conquests in Palestine and Egypt."[31] At the battle of Armageddon the "tremendous instrument" of Russia would prove ineffective; but when Antichrist attacked "the maritime power," the Word of God would oppose and defeat him.[32] The identity of Gog and Magog in Ezekiel 38 Faber found inscrutable. He readily dismissed the Turks as a possibility,[33] and finally discharged the Russians too: "The Russians and Muscovites seem to be colonies of *Rosh* and *Meshech* or (as the name may be pronounced) Mosch; but I know not, that we have any reason for supposing that they are here intended."[34] He then gave himself some good advice which, in this context, he took to heart: "But let us forbear to speculate on this obscure subject, further than we have the express warrant of Scripture."[35] His caution, however, did not prevent him from identifying the "merchants of Tarshish," who oppose Gog, as that same "great maritime nation" that resisted Antichrist, an obvious reference to England again.[36]

The Napoleonic empire passed from the scene, but interest in the restoration of the Jews continued. The first of a series of prophetic conferences was held at the Albury Park estate of Henry Drummond in 1826. Drummond was a wealthy banker and member of Parliament (1810-13, 1847-60) whose patronage supported many prophetic endeavors; he also wrote and edited works on prophetic themes. Twenty laity and clergy were invited to discuss prophecy in general and the second advent and the restoration of the Jews in particular. In the discussions the only appeal allowed was to the authority of Scripture. The prophetic conference was to be a means of theological development of the premillennial movement for the next century, until it was supplanted by the Bible institute movement in the twentieth century. One of the leading figures of the Albury conferences was Edward Irving, a popular London preacher of the 1820s and the founder of the Catholic Apostolic Church. The conclusions reached by the conferences included the beliefs that the present age would end in a cataclysmic judgment and the Jews would be restored to Palestine, that "the 1260 years of Daniel 7 and Revelation 13 ought to be measured from the reign of Justinian to the French Revolution," and that "the vials of wrath (Revelation 16) are now being poured out and the second advent is imminent."[37] Also, the widespread influence of premillenarian John Darby and the rapid growth of his Brethren movement in the 1830s are further indication of the breadth of interest in Jewish restoration.

The belief in the restoration of Jews was not confined to those of premillennial views nor to those of inferior social status. The idea was pervasive in Britain, and as Sandeen observes, "There can be no question that the millenarian movement played a significant role in preparing the British for political Zionism."[38] Attendants at Edward Irving's services included members of Parliament and cabinet ministers. Samuel Taylor Coleridge was certainly not a premillennialist. Nevertheless, believing that the millennium had begun with Constantine and would culminate in a perfected earth, Coleridge awaited the return of the Jews to Palestine. He claimed that his views were not based on Daniel or the Apocalypse, but on "undisputed" passages: "I fully agree with Mr. Irving as to the literal fulfillment of all the prophecies which respect the restoration of the Jews (Deuteron. xxv.1-8)."[39]

Lord Shaftesbury was a vigorous promoter of Jewish settlement in Palestine. In his view such settlement would develop the land between the Mediterranean Sea and the Euphrates River. As a millennialist, he believed that Palestine actually belonged to the Jews and should be returned to them, ideally as Christian converts. Because Jerusalem's first Anglican bishop was Jewish, it appeared to him, as well as others, that the restoration had already begun.[40]

In nineteenth-century America general religious interest in Palestine was much more extensive than was premillenarianism. From early in the century there was manifest a missionary interest in the area, both to Jews and Arabs. By mid-century an enthusiasm for scientific research and archaeological study had also developed, partly as a by-product of the religious interest. Fascination was stimulated too by British Romanticism as epitomized by the young Jewess, Rebecca, in Sir Walter Scott's *Ivanhoe*. Along with a multitude of other reforms American romantic utopianism in the Jackson Era expressed concern for Jewish homelessness. In 1840 out of humanitarian concern President Van Buren intervened with the Turkish government on the behalf of Jews in Palestine, and by the latter part of the century, most of the diplomatic exchanges between Turkey and the United States were concerned with the protection of American Jews in Palestine. In 1897, the advent of political Zionism was given at least respectful attention, and prior to World War I, Christian groups more often than not were sympathetic toward Zionism. This can best be explained as sympathy for the underdog rather than as a captivating concern for Jewish welfare or restoration. Remnants of these extensive nineteenth-century interests still exist today, but compared to the intensive attention of premillenarians, they have been only passing fancies.[41]

A variety of millennial groups developed in the United States in the early nineteenth century. "America in the early nineteenth century was drunk on the millennium."[42] A postmillennial view was expressed by the moderator of the General Assembly of the Presbyterian Church in a speech in London to the Evangelical Alliance in 1846: "I really believe that God has got America within anchorage, and that upon that arena, He intends to display his prodigies for the millennium."[43] The Mormons taught a premillennial eschatology; but although they believed in the restoration of the Jews to Palestine, their primary thrust was the building of their own New Jerusalem. William Miller, the founder of the modern Adventist movement, predicted the second advent of Christ in 1843. His error produced a general disillusionment with premillennial teachings, and even made the faithful thereafter a bit shy of date-setting. As Sandeen again has so aptly observed, "It took a long time for Americans to forget William Miller."[44] The founder of the utopian Oneida community, John Humphrey Noyes, who came to believe that the second advent had occurred in A.D. 70, described the general mood of the era:

> It is certain that in 1831, the whole orthodox church was in a state of ebullition in regard to the Millennium. A feeling of expectation on this point lay at the bottom of the triumphant march of revivals which shook the land for several years from that time. The Millerites have since met with unbounded ridicule; but it should be remembered that all that portion of the churches who were spiritual, who believed in revivals, and who were zealous and successful in laboring for them had a fit of expectation as enthusiastic and almost as fanatical as the Millerites.[45]

In the 1850s premillennialism recovered from the setback suffered as a result of Miller's errors—and accordingly, writers began to risk works on prophetic themes again. Jacob J. Janeway, a theology professor at the Presbyterians' Western Seminary, published in 1853 *Hope for the Jews: or The Jews Will Be Converted to the Christian Faith; and Settled and Reorganized as a Nation in the Land of Palestine.* Janeway believed the Jews would be restored "under the reign of the promised Messiah."[46] The issue of the preconditions for the restoration was to become an item for discussion over the years. Janeway contended that if the Jews returned in their present state of unbelief they would have no peace or security. He discussed their historical persecution, and then by way of contrast the renewed interest in returning, mentioning that "a society of Jews has been formed in London, with the view of stirring up their countrymen, in all lands, to seek a re-possession of the land."[47]

For those so predisposed, crises—foreign or domestic—stimulate apocalyptic concern. Even as far back as the late Roman Empire the patriarch Proclus (434-47) was interpreting the *Rosh* and *Meshech* of Ezekiel 38:2 (ARV) as the invasion of the empire by the Huns.[48] Likewise the Crimean War, just as the Napoleonic wars before, accelerated the production of prophetic materials. A preacher of the Scottish National Church, John Cumming, published in 1855 two works which became the seedbed for many premillenarian volumes. One bibliographer claims that Cummings' works "outsold those of any other writer of his day."[49] One, published in Philadelphia, was entitled *Signs of the Times; or Present, Past, and Future* and took as its title-page text Luke 21:25: "And there shall be signs in the sun, and in the moon, and in the stars, and upon the earth distress of nations with perplexity." The other book, published in London, was emphatically entitled *The End* with a somewhat less dramatic subtitle, *The Proximate Signs of the Close of This Dispensation.*

Cumming calculated the year 1864 to be the date of fulfillment of various prophecies. He almost affirmed it would be the end of the world: "I do not prophesy; I do not foretell the future; I only forth tell what God has said; but I do feel, that if 1864 be not the close of the age that now is, and the commencement of a better one, it will be a time unprecedented since the beginning—portentous, startling, and terrible to the enemies of God; but glorious, holy and full of joyous scenes to the people of God."[50] The 1260 days (years) of Daniel were identified as the era of papal power which began in 530 when Justinian gave the pope civil power and ended in 1790 with the supposed decline of the papacy. Daniel's 1290 days brought Cumming to 1820 which corresponded exactly, according to him, with Daniel's prediction of the end of the Persian Empire (i.e., the Turks). The Turks were also identified as Daniel's "little horn." The corresponding decline of the Catholics and the Moslems proved to Cumming the validity of his system; and as a consequence, Daniel's 1335 days led him to the end in 1865.[51] He then cited the prediction of the church father Lactantius that the world would come to an end after 6000 years of existence, supported the idea from Jewish traditions, and offered calculations that terminated the 6000 years at 1862, saying, "Just as the six days have their seventh, the 6000 years will have their seventh thousand, or what we call the millennium."[52]

One of the "signs of the times" was "The Moslem and His End," but an even greater portent was "The Jew, His Ruin and Restoration." Pointing out that only in the past thirty years had Jews been allowed to live in Jerusalem, Cumming saw this as the sign of the "budding of the fig tree" (Matt. 24:32) which pointed to the end. Anti-Semitism and the condition of the Jews were depicted as the fulfillment of God's curse (Deut. 28) because of Israel's sin. Cumming observed, "Palestine is at this moment an illustration and specimen of a land that God Almighty has cursed, a desert attesting the truth of God's word, yet pregnant with a glorious Eden."[53] After the fall of the Moslems, the "drying up of the Euphrates," the Jews would emigrate from all nations, including the "land of Sin"—China. Cumming predicted the nations would assist the Jews:

> We may expect that the nations of the earth will begin, on the eve of that movement among the Jews, to discuss in their cabinets the restoration of the Jews. There are books recently written, which urge on the nations to help them to their own land. The Jews in London are collecting money in order to purchase Palestine at this moment: the Jews in America have collected enormous sums to build the temple again in Jerusalem. All these things are signs of the times, and indications of the approaching change.[54]

Rumors of the rebuilding of the Temple are a recurring theme in popular prophetic writings down to the present. Cumming did not divulge his source, but assured his readers that an American, a Mr. Noah, was collecting a million dollars for the purpose.[55] Cumming attributed all this international involvement to divine intervention: "It is the breath from on high touching the fig tree."[56] The inherent destiny of it all, however, did not preclude Cumming's being concerned with the ethics of the situation. He recounted rumors of a Jew attempting to bribe the western powers to return Palestine to the Jews after the fall of the Turkish Sultan, and then made an astute moral observation that is extremely rare among prophetic writers:

> . . . The prediction does not mean that every power employed to accomplish it is good. The prediction of the Crucifixion does not imply that those who crucified the Lord of glory did what was right.[57]

Lecture VII of *The End* was entitled "The Russian and Northern Confederacy" and began with a quotation of the entire thirty-eighth chapter of Ezekiel. At great length Cumming established the identity of the great northern power that was "doomed to perish ultimately in Palestine amid tremendous scenes." His argument is particularly significant because it is evidently the source for a multitude of later writers on the subject. He cited Pliny, the Roman writer, for the information that "Hierapolis, taken by the Scythians, was afterwards called Magog." The Jewish historian Josephus was quoted: "The Scythians were called by the Greeks Magog." No sources were given for the assertion that *Caucasus* is derived from the words *Gog* and *chasan* and means "Gog's fortified place." According to Josephus the Moscheni inhabiting the Moschi mountains east of the Black Sea were founded by Meshech. To Herodotus was attributed the information that the Muscovites came from Pontus in Asia Minor. It was claimed that the Araxes River was called *Rosh* in Arabic and that *Russian* was derived from *Rosh.* From these rather obscure historical premises Cumming made an illogical leap: "We arrive at the conclusion that Rosh, Meshech, Tubal, find their descendants at this moment in the northern and southern parts of Russia."[58]

Russia's allies in this great end-time confederacy were similarly revealed:

> Now it happens that Xenophon, Pliny, Strabo, Cicero, Josephus, and the modern Bochart, all state that Gomer's three sons settled in the territories of Asia Minor; but as a matter of history the sons of Gomer soon extended beyond these. . . . Advancing again along the Danube, these same descendants of Gomer peopled what is now called Germany, the name being derived from Gomer. . . . Some of the descendants of Gomer again spread into Gaul. . . .[59]

After having identified the Biblical names geographically, Cumming added a time element:

> Now the prophecy of Ezekiel is that Gomer—that is, Germany, which is the great or the father-nation of all the rest—will be added to the prince of Rosh, Meshech, and Tubal; and that this combination of Germany and Russia will be the chief part of the great confederacy or conspiracy of the last days, that will go forth to cleave its way, as this chapter indicates, to the land of Palestine, there and then to perish for its crimes under the judgments of God.[60]

That much has proved to be standard premillenarian fodder clear down to the present day, but each era has given to it a contemporary flavor just as Cumming did.

> I do not say our existing complications are the fulfilment;

> because one does not like to dogmatize; but is it not remarkable that here the prediction is that Rosh, Meshech, Tubal, or Russia in all its divisions, and the descendants of Gomer, or the Germans, should coalesce, and form as one this great confederacy? Does it not look as if the fulfilment were taking place before our eyes? Is not Prussia practically allied to Russia? . . . I may ask, is it not at least, as the most sceptical before me will admit, a remarkable coincidence, that the prediction in Ezekiel, that Rosh, Meshech, Tubal, Gomer and all his bands, should be united together in one great confederacy, is at this moment a historical fact?[61]

Cumming then identified the leader of the resistance to this conspiracy, the "merchants of Tarshish," as England.[62] Unfortunately, all opposition was to be in vain for "Russia will burst forth, overcome all resistance, march to Palestine."[63]

There was a large streak of fatalism in Cumming: "There is not a soldier fallen in the Crimea who has not first finished his mission."[64] But he did not apply this concept to nations, moralizing that "because Russia is now fulfilling a prophecy, Russia is not therefore doing right or fulfilling her duty."[65] "God predicts in His word what He does not applaud in His law."[66] Again it should be emphasized how extremely rare in the apocalyptic tradition is such an obvious insight. Cumming's fatalism certainly did not make him a pacifist, however. He was extremely happy that England's projected role would be both "right in the light of duty" and "indicated in the light of prophecy."[67] "I have no sympathy therefore with those who think that war is and can be never a nation's duty."[68] "We are told that God will bless them that bless Israel," said Cumming, expressing what was to become a monotonous theme among premillennialists supporting the restoration. God "has promised a special blessing upon them that pity His ancient people, and try to do them good instead of trying to do them harm." Cumming particularly castigated anti-Semitic fatalism: "There is a very stupid notion abroad, that because God has predicted that the Jews for 18 centuries shall be a scoff, a by-word, and be spit upon, and be treated as the offscouring of the earth, they therefore do well to treat the Jew with cruelty." Cumming demanded morality of all—Russians, Jews, and anti-Semites—not a passive, fatalistic resignation to the predictions of prophecy.[69]

By 1861, when Cumming wrote *The Great Preparation,* the international scene had changed: British-French rivalry now influenced his interpretation. Gomer, Russia's ally in the final conspiracy, was no longer identified as merely extending into Gaul, but was specifically identified as including France as well as Germany.[70] In retrospect, he observed that Russia's aggression in 1854 had been premature, but this did not thwart his confidence as he generalized: "Every Russian looks eastward. He calculates on taking Constantinople on his march, and occupying Palestine."[71] Specifically, he quoted Peter the Great: "I look upon Russia as called on to establish her rule over all Europe, and its invasion of east and west as a decree of Divine Providence."[72] His calculations on the end of the age were slightly modified, and he hazarded yet another date. If his beginning dates were correct (he acknowledged they might be wrong), "the affliction of the Jews will cease about the end of 1867, the Jews will be restored, the Gentile oppression will come to an end; Jerusalem will be no longer trodden under foot but repossessed."[73]

Except for his inclination to set dates, John Cumming is probably the best nineteenth-century example of the kind of writer that developed the ideas which contributed to the mind-set of the twentieth-century premillennialist. His failures in date-setting may account for the preference of later writers for terms such as *imminent* and *soon* rather than specific dates. The most infamous date-setter of all was Michael Baxter, a British preacher who also toured the United States. From 1861 to 1908 he made various errors, including identifying Louis Napoleon as the Antichrist and predicting the second advent between 2:30 and 3:00 p.m., March 12, 1903.[74]

The late nineteenth century reflected a broad shift in premillenarian thinking from a historicist position to a futurist position. The historicists believed that the "days" of Daniel's prophecies symbolized years, and consequently identified the prophecies as fulfilled within history (this explains the penchant for setting dates). The futurists, on the other hand, looked for the fulfillment of prophecies in the future; the period of history between the first and second advent of Christ was just a parenthesis during which God's time-clock had been stopped. The clock would start again when the church was taken out of the world (the rapture) prior to the second advent. Generally, the futurists' eschatology paralleled the teaching of John Nelson Darby, the founder of the Brethren movement, but scholars have been unable as yet to show for all futurists a direct relationship to that movement.

Reflecting this new emphasis was *Maranatha: Or, The Lord Cometh,* a work by James H. Brookes, pastor of the Walnut Street Presbyterian Church in St. Louis. He was a friend and teacher of C. I. Scofield and had a strong influence on the premillennial movement. His chapter on the "Return of the Jews" was basically an interpretation of Daniel's prophecy. As a matter of fact, he called this prophecy a "remarkable revelation . . . concerning the destiny of the Jews."[75] Brookes pleaded for a literal interpretation of Scripture and pointed out that the Promised Land of Israel was an *unconditional* promise.[76] The history of Israel, he said, corresponded to the seventy weeks in the vision of Daniel 9. He argued, however, that the term *weeks* was a mistranslation, which should have been rendered "heptads" or "sevens"—in this case, "sevens" of years.[77] Sixty-nine of these seventy "weeks" of years covered the period from 453 B.C. to A.D. 29, that is, from the command to rebuild Jerusalem to the rejection of Jesus as the Messiah and His crucifixion.[78] The last "week" of seven years is a future period of tribulation for the Jewish people just prior to the second advent of Christ.[79] This is basically the same analysis that is noted in *The Scofield Reference Bible* at Daniel 9:24. In contrast to Jacob J. Janeway in *Hope for the Jews,* Brookes contended that the Jews would be partially restored to Palestine *prior* to their conversion, but only after they have allied themselves with the Antichrist.[80] This point was to take many twists along the winding premillennial path. Brookes concluded the chapter with a characteristically premillenarian eulogy of God's chosen people:

> Found among all nations, and yet not mingling with any, they are still a distinct and peculiar people, surviving the sweeping revolutions of the past, and reserved for a sublimer destiny than the genius of the most ambitious statesman has sought to attain for his country. . . .
>
> . . . Hebrew history . . . is a dark enigma indeed unless studied in the light of God's prophetic word. . . . Already they are largely controlling the course of current events by their splendid intellectual endowments, for not only is it

> well known that the continental press of Europe is mainly in their hands, but in the more stately journals of science and philosophy, in the professorial chairs of the Universities, in the council chambers of royalty, in the management of finances that constitute the sinews of war, they are quietly and unconsciously forecasting their approaching greatness, when the vail which even unto this day is upon their hearts shall be lifted at the coming of their Messiah to give them the light of the knowledge of the glory of God in the face of Jesus Christ.[81]

Prophetic magazines blossomed to help spread the scent of the "budding of the fig tree." James H. Brookes published *Truth* from 1875 to 1897.[82] *Prophetic Times* was edited by Joseph A. Seiss, president of the board of the Philadelphia Lutheran Theological Seminary and also editor of the *Lutheran.* One of the points of the creed of *Prophetic Times,* which was published from 1863 to 1881, was "that in the new order of things to come, the house of Israel, or Jewish race, shall again occupy their own land, and hold the first place among the nations."[83]

James H. Brookes was also president of the Niagara Bible Conference, which was the beginning of the extensive prophecy and Bible conference movement which flourished in America through World War I and has survived down to the present. In 1878, Brookes drew up a fourteen-point creed for the conference; the last item of this creed dealt with the Jews:

> We believe that the world will not be converted during the present dispensation, but is fast ripening for judgment, while there will be a fearful apostasy in the professing Christian body; and hence that the Lord Jesus will come in person to introduce the millennial age, when Israel shall be restored to their own land, and the earth shall be full of the knowledge of the Lord; and that this personal and premillennial advent is the blessed hope set before us in the Gospel for which we should be constantly looking: Luke 12:35-40; 17:26-30; 18:8; Acts 15:14-17; 2 Thess. 2:3-8; 2 Tim. 3:1-5; Tit. 2:11-15.[84]

A three-day New York Prophetic Conference in 1878 attracted sufficient interest to warrant a special edition of the *New York Tribune.* Bishop William R. Nicholson of the successionist Reformed Episcopal Church lectured on "The Gathering of Israel." He asserted the certainty of the restoration of the

Jews, arguing that "if so literally have been fulfilled the prophecies which foretold their sufferings and their preservation, equally sure are the predicted grandeurs of their future."[85]

In the same year appeared *The Approaching End of the Age* by H. Grattan Guinness, an English author. It was widely read and cited in the United States. Guinness was a historicist. His calculations placed the last possible culmination of Daniel's prophecies in 1923;[86] and he believed "that the great closing Armageddon conflict is at hand."[87] Expecting that Israel would be restored to Palestine before the end, he saw signs of this in "the elevation in the condition of the land and people of Israel, the removal of Jewish (political) disabilities, the formation of the Universal Israelite Alliance, the exploration and survey of Palestine, the decay of the Turkish Power."[88] The fall of Jerusalem to British and French troops and the issuance of the Balfour Declaration in 1917 appeared to be such pointed fulfillments of Guinness' expectations that his book was reissued in a revised edition in 1918.

An international Prophetic Conference was held in 1886 in Chicago. Conference proceedings were published the next day in Chicago's *Inter Ocean* newspaper and a bound edition appeared within ten days of the closing of the conference.[89] Nathaniel West lectured on "Prophecy and Israel," reflecting a very deterministic philosophy of history which is characteristic of premillenarian attitudes toward Israel.

> History itself is Messianic. Events do not come to pass because predicted, but are predicted because ordained to come to pass. . . .
>
> The fortunes of Israel are, have been, and will be precisely what God intends. . . .
>
> A divine causality pervades all. Israel, already in the front in centuries gone by, shall yet be in the front again.[90]

Another speaker, William G. Moorehead, Professor of New Testament at the United Presbyterian Seminary, Xenia, Ohio, spoke on "The Antichrist," listing "the principles now at work in our modern society which, if left unchecked, will soon make the advent of the Antichrist not only possible, but certain." These Satanic influences were socialism, nihilism, anarchy, naturalism, materialism, humanitarianism, and spiritualism.[91] When this Satanic socialism became wedded to the Russian "Gog" in the 1917

Bolshevik revolution, the premillennialists identified the combination as a double portion of evil.

The prospects of Russia, however, seemed more the concern of the British students of prophecy than the American. Britain was faced in the last quarter of the nineteenth century with Russian expansion into the Balkans.

The following is from an article on Gog and Magog by Walter Scott in the June 1888 issue of *The Prophetic News and Israel's Watch:*

> Great Britain with the United States stands face to face with this Russian power; and these two sides will come into one final, awful struggle. We judge that the tide of Russian conquest will flow on to the frontiers of China. The ascendence of Russia in the East and the revival of the old Roman Empire in the West necessitate the meeting of these two dominating opposing powers; and the great Jewish question must be settled at Jerusalem, the city of the Great King, leading to the millennial triumph of Israel and her headship over the nations of the world. We believe, from the place assigned to Russia in the Word of God, that her legions will sweep over the plains and mountains of Asia and become the dominant power over all the East until she falls forever on the mountains of Judea.[92]

This expectation seemed fulfilled in Russia's interest in the Sino-Japanese War (1894-95). In *The Future of Europe: Religiously and Politically, In the Light of Holy Scripture,* Alfred H. Burton wrote in 1896 that "no European Power is occupying itself today more busily than Russia in the affairs of the Far East." But he assured his readers that "the Word of God speaks of the future and the end of Russia in no uncertain manner" and that the study of Ezekiel 38 and 39 and of Daniel 8 and 11 "will give a clearer insight than anything else into the affairs of Russia and the Far East."[93]

The beginning of a political movement in 1897 to restore the Jews to Palestine appeared to be the fruition of premillenarian as well as Jewish dreams. Anti-Semitism had grown in Europe, especially in Russia, during the latter years of the nineteenth century and Dr. Theodor Herzl, author of *The Jewish State,* responded by calling the first Zionist Congress at Basel in 1897. The aim of the movement was to create a home in Palestine for

Jewish people. The government of England offered in 1903 to provide areas for settlement in Uganda, but the majority of the Zionists rejected any attempt to sidetrack their main objective. In 1910 C. I. Scofield commented on Jeremiah 16:14, 15:

> I must ask you to note that the restoration is from a world-wide dispersion, and the "land" as identified beyond peradventure as "their land that I gave unto their fathers." Not the United States, not England, not any land where the Jews may have temporary peace and prosperity, but Palestine.[94]

James M. Gray, dean of Chicago's Moody Bible Institute explained the anti-Semitism as the hand of God. Israel had failed "to be a faithful witness to Jehovah before the other nations of the earth, and in consequence, is suffering the dispersion and the persecution which, alas! we know about today."[95] Gray, however, on the basis of Isaiah 14, predicted a more aggressive role for Israel in the future. He contended that the text had not yet been fulfilled for "Israel does not possess the people of the earth for servants and for handmaids. She has not yet taken them captives whose captive she was, nor does she yet rule over her oppressors."[96]

In the years prior to 1917, Zionism was hailed as the leading sign of the end of the age. William E. Blackstone, author of the most widely read premillenarian work, *Jesus Is Coming,* taught that Zionism was the sign of the budding fig tree (Luke 21:28-31). Dr. Isaac M. Haldeman, pastor of the First Baptist Church, New York City, in a sermon entitled "The Zionist Movement" called Zionism "the climacteric sign of the restoration." He felt that "a vital and fully equipped nationality" was the Jew's need of the hour and that Zionism provided the proper prerequisite to a Jewish national resurrection which would allow the Jew to be able to "lift up his head and walk in the ordained power that is his."[97] Haldeman's interpretation of Scripture required, however, that the Antichrist should appear *before* the final restoration: "The scriptures teach that this man will be the prime factor in bringing the Jews back, as a body into their own land; that he will be the power that shall make Zionism a success; that through him the nationalism of the Jews shall be accomplished."[98] The sequence here is Antichrist, restoration, conversion.

Zionism and Russian anti-Semitism were both depicted as

fulfillment of prophecy by the founder of the premillenarian Christian Missionary Alliance denomination, A. B. Simpson. In Jeremiah 16:16 Simpson saw the "hunters" as Russia hunting the Jews out of their places of exile and saw the "fishers" as Zionism drawing the Jews back to Palestine.[99] He used elaborate calculations to support the significance of Zionism. He found that Daniel's 1,260 years subtracted from the 1897 of the founding of Zionism brought one to 637, the date that Omar under Mohammed had captured Jerusalem. Therefore, Zionism signified the end of the times of the Gentiles. Simpson was not sure how long it would take God to accomplish the restoration—but he was sure it had begun.[100]

These samplings of prophetic writing demonstrate that the premillennialists approached the World War I era with definite predispositions. They were pro-Zionist and anti-Russian. The culmination of this predestined restoration of Israel and rise of Russia was to be the battle of Armageddon. This, then, was the frame of mind with which the premillenarian confronted the war and its results.

There were also other sources of anti-Russianism and pro-Zionist feeling in American life which, indeed, served to reinforce premillenarian sentiment as well as soften resistance to premillenarian ideas. There was strong sentiment opposing Czarist violation of human rights in Russia's imprisonment and exile of revolutionaries and in her anti-Semitic outbursts. At Easter in 1903 anti-Semitic violence broke out in Kishinev. Russian mistreatment of Russian Jews who as American citizens had returned to visit Russia also produced negative public reactions. These anti-Russian sentiments were encouraged by Jewish propaganda groups, and American businessmen also encouraged antagonism toward Russia as railroad and marketing interests in Manchuria and north China found themselves in competition with Russian interests.[101]

Armageddon—Almost

The time cannot be far off when Russia's millions, augmented by the armies that she will gather from these other nations, will be thrown by their rulers into Palestine in order to destroy the nation of the Jews.

—*Our Hope,* August 1916

We are not yet in the Armageddon struggle proper, but at its commencement.

—*The Weekly Evangel,* April 10, 1917

The most striking sign of the times is the proposal to give Palestine to the Jews once more. . . . November 2, 1917 was a red-letter day in the world's history when the British Foreign Secretary addressed his now famous letter to Lord Rothschild on this subject.

—*Our Hope,* July 1919

World War I stimulated the premillennialists to a tiptoe expectancy and also provided tantalizing fulfillment of some of their longings. The war itself came as no shock to these opponents of postmillennial optimism; they had not only looked toward the culmination of the age in Armageddon, but anticipated "wars and rumors of wars" as signs of the approaching end. R. A. Torrey, dean of the Bible Institute of Los Angeles, wrote in 1913 before the war ever began:

> While we talk peace, we are increasing our navies and our armies. We are squandering untold millions in schemes for destroying the lives of our fellow men and for protection and extension of our own nation. We talk of disarmament, but we all know it is not coming. All our present peace plans will end in the most awful wars and conflicts this old world ever saw![1]

Such predictions, when fulfilled, produced more than just an I-told-you-so attitude; they served believers as demonstrated proof of the validity of their whole literalistic theological system. During the war, Arno C. Gaebelein, editor of *Our Hope,* reprinted his prewar doomsayings. In 1909 he had said, "To believe that the age is improving, that the church and the nations are going to establish universal peace is unscriptural,"[2] and in 1911, "How could some men expect peace in these days when every nation trembles and makes the most colossal preparation for war!"[3] The premillennialist may legitimately be castigated for being a pessimist, yet he sees himself as an optimist looking for the blessed hope of the rapture and the subsequent reign of the Messiah. Any sign of the end is a signal to rejoice: "Look up . . . for your redemption draweth nigh" (Luke 21:28). As Torrey wrote for the Moody Bible Institute publication during the war, "As awful as conditions are across the water today, and as awful as they may become in our own country, the darker the night gets, the lighter my heart gets."[4]

The term *Armageddon* was figuratively applied to the war in the popular, secular press. But some premillenarians saw the war as the beginning of a literal, prophetic Armageddon. *The Weekly Evangel,* the official publication of the recently organized (1914) premillenarian denomination, the Assemblies of God, cited Revelation 16:14-16 as the chronology for the end-time: verse 14 spoke of a world war, verse 15 spoke of a secret rapture, and verse 16 spoke of Armageddon. "We are not yet in the Armageddon struggle proper, but at its commencement, and it may be, if students of prophecy read the signs aright, that Christ will come before the present war closes, and before Armageddon. . . .The war preliminary to Armageddon, it seems, has commenced."[5] C. I. Scofield thought that the war would be the death struggle of the present world system which would be succeeded by the Kingdom of God.[6] Certain particular aspects of the war were also depicted as prophetic. Isaiah 19:23, "In that day shall there be a highway out of Egypt to Assyria," was cited as speaking of the railroads between Cairo and Jerusalem. Funded by the Turks and British, these railroads became known as the "Milk and Honey Express."[7]

Some premillenarian commentators explained the war simply as God's punishment for the nations' treatment of His chosen people. James M. Gray, dean of Moody Bible Institute, was quoted as explaining that "the trouble in the whole gentile world today is attributable to the treatment of the Jew."[8] Another view envisioned God's purpose in the war to be the development of the Jewish nation. Walter Scott in his book, *At Hand,* stated: "The final issue of all European and Asiatic conflicts will be the shining forth of Christ's glory and triumph of the Jew."[9] A speaker at the New York Prophetic Conference held shortly after the armistice observed in retrospect: "It seems then clear that divine providence has used this horrible war to take Palestine from the Turk and make it possible for the Jewish people to return."[10] The common denominator in all these evaluations was God and the Jew; God's hand was in everything, and the purpose of it all was the Jew. While variations on the above themes were quite common among premillenarians, one analysis was apparently unique: an *Evangel* writer said that as an answer to world-wide days of prayer on October 6 and 7, 1912, the war actually began October 7, 1912, when Bulgaria declared war on Turkey.[11]

As the war developed, speculation arose about the outcome in light of prophecy. One inclination of the premillenarian press was to grasp every conceivable morsel of prophetic significance from the secular press. *The King's Business,* published by the Bible Institute of Los Angeles (Biola), cautioned against unwarranted interpretations of prophecy: "Even writers and papers that have hitherto shown no great interest in prophecy are now giving voice to the wildest explanations of current events supposedly from the standpoint of Bible prophecy." Editor R. A. Torrey then cited, for the sake of example, extensive passages from *Our Hope* in which the author categorically affirmed that the war was not the battle of Armageddon nor was it the Great Tribulation, the chief rationale being that the Jews were not yet back in Palestine. The word of caution expressed by *The King's Business* was derived from historical experience: "Had we lived a century ago, when Napoleon was at the zenith of his power, we might well have supposed that the final drama of prophecy had begun."[12]

As Palestine appeared more and more in the news, however, such sobering advice only served to augment the excited expectation of restoration. Only a few months later, Torrey himself cited an article from *Literary Digest,* "A New Kingdom of Israel," which suggested that in the general opinion the best solution for Palestine was the establishment of a Jewish state under the protection of one of the great powers. He also quoted extensively from the *London Daily Chronicle* the "novel suggestion" that the new Jewish state be placed under United States protection. All of this he found to be "exceedingly interesting to students of prophecy, and especially to those who had been looking for the speedy return of the Jews to the Holy Land."[13]

With somewhat less caution, the *Evangel* tended to draw freely from the colorful Jewish press such items as the following with a London, July 22, 1916, dateline: "The British Government has made it known officially that the Powers will strive after the war towards the restoration of Palestine to the Jews." Antedating the Balfour Declaration by more than a year, this report was based solely on an informal correspondence of Sir Edward Grey, the Secretary of Foreign Affairs, to the effect that Jewish interest in Palestine would not be overlooked.[14] A year later an *Evangel* writer justified this persistent apocalyptic attention to the Middle East: "Even the secular daily newspapers and the popular worldly magazines talk glibly about the speedy prospect of the Turk being driven out of Jerusalem and Palestine; and the Holy City and land being given to returning Jews, under the protection of Britain and her allies." The conclusion was then drawn that the premillenarian prophetic scholars had "made no mistake."[15]

Our Hope reported that Jewish restoration was "more than

possible" and that the rumors of their return were an indication of the "rapid preparation" for it.[16] Likewise, Moody Bible Institute's *Christian Workers Magazine* noted the widespread interest in restoration, calling Israel "the key unlocking the mysteries of the future" and saying the return "may be very near."[17] The use of a Jewish flag during the war was seen as momentous: "It heralds more than anything the coming national revival and the final suffering and tribulation of this wonderful people."[18]

At a time when the British war effort in the Middle East was at a low ebb, the *Evangel* confidently asserted, "As God is working with the nations, He will drive the Turk out of Palestine and cause his ancient people to take possession of it."[19] The naive assumption seemed to be that the withdrawal of the Turks would leave the land totally vacant. Later when British forces were having successes, the *Evangel* cited reports in *Prophetic News* of a Jewish lecturer telling how the Jews were returning by the hundreds, while the Turks were leaving by the thousands: "Thus God was providing home for his people the Jews, making way for their return which is very near."[20] There seemed to be a total lack of awareness that withdrawal would not leave the land uninhabited, but would simply remove the Turkish Empire's control over the native Arabs and a small Jewish minority.

Although anti-Semitism during the war continued to be considered a prophetic fulfillment, the premillennialists did not approve it. *Our Hope* applauded the report that the Spanish government had voiced its opposition to the "persecutions, deportations, and lootings" of Jews in the Holy Land, and made the observation that Spain had the truth of God's word, "I will curse them that curse thee."[21] The *Evangel* lamented the increased persecution of Jews in Poland.[22] Another writer attributed Japan's successes against Russia at the beginning of the century to God's "chastisement" on the Russians for their treatment of Jews. "It is a serious thing to meddle with the people of Jehovah's choice."[23]

Anticipation of significant events was also enhanced during the war by the calculations of historicist theologians. One of these was the widely respected W. E. Blackstone whose system was summarized in 1916 in *The Alliance Weekly* and also reprinted in the *Evangel*. Blackstone arrived at his dates by concluding that "the punishment of Luke 21 is the same as that of Lev. 26, and that therefore the *times of the Gentiles* are measured by the *seven times* of Lev. 26; that is, 360 multiplied by 7, which equals 2,520 days." Using the year-day system, he then added 2,520 years to various possible dates that the times of the Gentiles might have begun: 606 B.C., the capture of the Holy Land by Nebuchadnezzar; 595 B.C., the departure of God's glory from Israel (Ezek. 8:4—11:23); and 587 B.C., the destruction of Jerusalem. Thus he arrived at the possible terminal dates of 1915, 1926, and 1934. Relying on some other sources resulted in slightly different dates: 1916, 1927, and 1935. Then he rhapsodized:

> As Israel lost the rule of their land at the beginning of these *Gentile times,* it would seem that the first terminal date would mark some kind of a beginning of the restoration of the land. Does not this give great significance to the Zionist movement on the part of the Jews and to all that is now being said and done by Gentiles, to secure Palestine for the Jews, in the outcome of the present war? . . .
>
> How inspiring is the thought that, if 1915 or 1916 shall prove to be the first terminal date, then the nineteen years more to 1934 or 1935 may cover the end time with its whirl of events, including the reign of the "ten kings," the antichrist, the 7-year covenant, the complete destruction of Gentile government, the repentance, forgiveness, and new birth of Israel,—a nation born at once, restored; and under God's grace and favor to become the center of a world-wide theocracy.

Blackstone did not feel that his date-setting was in any way unscriptural, for he did not know when the rapture of the church would be. "We only know that it must be before He comes with us (I Thess. 1:7-10) when He comes on down to the earth to smite the antichrist (2 Thess. 2:8) and deliver Israel in the day of Armageddon (Rev. 16:13-16; 19:11-21)."[24]

A year later the *Evangel* was asking, "Will Christ come in 1917?" pointing out that the deliverance of Jerusalem seemed imminent. If so, then 1917 was the terminal year of the times of the Gentiles. It was also pointed out, however, that it might be "some years" before a Jewish state was actually set up. There was no question about the system of dating, only the starting point: "To the same extent that the starting point varies, so must there remain a doubt as to the terminal date."[25]

This was then the crescendo of anticipation into which the Balfour Declaration was introduced. The essentials of the text are contained in one sentence, the latter half of which was consistently neglected in the premillennialists' response:

> His Majesty's Government views with favour the establishment in Palestine of a national home for the Jewish people, and will use their best endeavors to facilitate the achievement of this object, it being clearly understood that nothing shall be done which may prejudice the civil and religious rights of existing non-Jewish communities in Palestine, or the rights and political status enjoyed by Jews in any other country.

President Woodrow Wilson had been a party to the preparation of the Balfour Declaration and he enthusiastically endorsed it. Prophetic considerations were evidently influential in his decisions, or at least supported him in those decisions. As one student of Zionism and American foreign policy has analyzed him: "As the son of a Calvinist minister he had been raised on Old Testament tales of Jewish exile and longing for a return to Israel."[26] Indeed, Rabbi Stephen Wise reported him to have said, "To think that I, a son of the manse, should be able to help restore the Holy Land to its people!"[27] Wilson too did not attach much significance to the limitations of the latter part of the declaration, for he told Wise, "Palestine will be yours."[28]

The response of the *Evangel* representing the more emotional wing of premillennialiasm was euphoric:

> Do not we, who are looking for the coming of our Lord, and the "New Jerusalem," feel a thrill go through us as we read of the dry bones coming together (Ezek. 37), and the words of Christ when He said, "Now learn a parable of the fig tree"? . . . Hallelujah, our summer is nigh![29]

Another writer mixed his ecstasy with a patriotic Manifest Destiny:

> Today we are thrilled when we think of the sacred privilege that has been granted to our beloved country in being allowed by God to enter into the Holy City, and to thus deliver it from the thraldom of both the Turk and the Moslem. . . . We are, therefore, likely to see in the near future a Jewish State in Palestine. It may be in a month or two, it may be in a year or two; but the intention is to restore the land to the people and the people to the land.[30]

Clearly some people let their hopes outweigh the terminology in the declaration; in a pamphlet on "The Lessons of 1917," R. A. Torrey referred to "England's declaration that Jerusalem is to be turned over to the Jews"[31]—something more than merely "the establishment in Palestine of a national home." *Our Hope* observed that, of course, the restoration of Israel had to come to pass "some time"—it was "impossible that this should not come to pass." The Jewish movement was referred to as "the sign of all signs."[32]

The considered response of W. W. Fereday in an editorial in *Our Hope* a year and a half later was perhaps the best synthesis of the many implications of the Balfour Declaration for the premillenarian:

> Palestine for the Jews. The most striking sign of the times is the proposal to give Palestine to the Jews once more. They have long desired the land, though as yet unrepentant of the terrible crime which led to their expulsion therefrom. November 2, 1917, was a red-letter day in the world's history when the British Foreign Secretary addressed his now famous letter to Lord Rothschild on this subject. Prophetic Scripture supposes the Jewish people back in the land during the next crises. Thus in Rev. xi. a temple is divinely acknowledged in Jerusalem, and Dan. ix. 27 speaks of a treaty to be made by the head of the Western Empire with the people. Isaiah xviii. 1-6 distinctly speaks of an effort to be made by a maritime Power to restore the Jews to Palestine apart from God. Man is busy, but God is not moving, yet He considers in Heaven his dwellingplace. There is a mass of Prophetic Scripture yet to be accomplished, but no prophecy can be accomplished until Palestine is again in Jewish hands. Prophecy revolves around the despised Jew: and if Jewish restoration is imminent (as it appears to be), how near we must be to the fulfillment of every vision![33]

The premillenarian responses may be contrasted with that of the *Christian Century,* which Hertzel Fishman has suggested embodied the mainstream Protestant reaction of that era. Fishman says, "In the month following the publication of the Balfour Declaration in November, 1917, the *Christian Century* had warned against taking seriously the millennarians who were euphoric with 'Second Coming propaganda.'" The warning was felt to be necessary due to the "wide vogue" of premillenarian doctrine.[34] This leading liberal Protestant weekly has maintained a consistent antipathy toward Zionist aspirations to the present day.

On December 9, 1917, the Turks abandoned Jerusalem to the advancing British forces under General Edmund Allenby without attempting a defense—a fact to be colorfully elaborated by the premillenarian authors over the years. The *Evangel* carried an article, "What It Means. The British in Jerusalem," in which the author recounted an article from the secular press which recorded the responses of various Jewish and Protestant leaders to the question of the meaning of the imminent fall of Jerusalem for the church and for the world. The *Evangel* article lamented the responses which averred that "the Jews would return in unbelief and that the Christian leaders of today have utterly failed to grasp the import of what is likely to be one of the most significant and far-reaching events of this momentous period." Jesus had prophesied in Luke 21:24, "Jerusalem shall be trodden down of the Gentiles, until the times of the Gentiles be fulfilled." Thus if Jerusalem fell, it meant that "automatically the time of the Gentiles closes."[35]

In another article probably written confidently before the fall, A. B. Simpson of the Christian Missionary Alliance was exultant:

> How stupendous the significance of this event must be is impossible for the most intense language to exaggerate. This great event is therefore a note of time, a signal from heaven, and the marking of an epoch of history and prophecy. An age-long period of more than twenty-five centuries is closing, and a new age is about to begin or has already commenced. However gradual its progression may be and however slowly its preliminary unfoldings may appear, the fact remains that we have entered a new zone and we are already in the beginning of the end.[36]

In a subsequent piece, he called the city's fall "the best news in a thousand years," pointing out that the preparation for the event had begun with the advent of Zionism in 1897 exactly 1260 prophetic years after the Turks had captured Jerusalem in 637.[37] Such a historicist view was also represented in the *Evangel* in an article which stated that "all schools of interpretation" were in agreement that history was in the time of fulfillment of the prophetic 2,520 years and that the latest date possible was 1934.

"Surely with the British flag flying today over Jerusalem, we are touching the time when Jerusalem shall be no longer trodden down, but shall be the home of the free."[38]

Another response to the fall of Jerusalem was to call conferences. Over three thousand gathered for the meetings of the Philadelphia Prophetic Conference, May 28-30, 1918. A highlight of the conference was a lecture, "The Capture of Jerusalem," by A. E. Thompson, who had been the pastor of the American Church in Jerusalem at the beginning of the war. He pointed out that this event had been expected by prophetic students for years: "Even before Great Britain took possession of Egypt, there were keen-sighted seers who foresaw the day when God would use the Anglo-Saxon peoples to restore Jerusalem."[39] Another conference convened in New York in Carnegie Hall after the armistice at the call of Arno C. Gaebelein, editor of *Our Hope*. The fall of Jerusalem was interpreted there also: "To us true Christian believers it is the sign that the times of the Gentiles are rapidly nearing their close."[40] Still another convention, the Jewish Prophetic Conference, was held in Chicago the following year. Two thousand people expressed their premillenarian concern for the Jews by passing resolutions:

> Be it resolved that we pledge ourselves daily to pray . . . that the day may speedily come when the dark shadows of 2000 years may flee away, and the long promised day of righteousness and peace may come for Israel's race. . . .
>
> AND FURTHERMORE be it resolved that we express in every other possible way our sympathy to the Jewish people in the present crisis, doing whatsoever we can in their behalf, and that a copy of these resolutions be sent to the President of the United States.[41]

Not only did the political and military machinations of the war seem to fulfill premillenarian predictions, but writers also appealed to physical phenomena to reinforce their system of interpretation. The prophets Joel (2:23) and Zechariah (10:1) had spoken of a "latter rain." In a note at Zechariah 10:1, Scofield in his reference Bible had interpreted this latter rain as both physical and spiritual—but yet in the future. *The King's Business,* however, quoted statistics showing that the average annual rainfall in Palestine had already gradually increased. In the 1860s the average had been 21.87 inches, in the 70s 24.60, in the 80s 27.69, and finally in the 90s 28.86—an increase of seven inches. This was interpreted as a restoration of rainfall in preparation for the restoration of the people, but the article conveniently failed to mention that complete rainfall records had begun to be kept only in 1846 and that the average rainfall in the 1850s had been a greater amount—28.82 inches.[42] According to the *Evangel:* "Now that the latter rain has returned, the country will soon blossom as the rose"—in fulfillment of Isaiah 35:1.[43]

One argument raised by opponents of the restoration of the Jews to Palestine was that there was not enough room for them in the land. The premillenarians countered with Biblical claims of even greater territories that exceeded even the wildest Zionist dreams. In an address at the Mountain Lake Park Bible Conference in Maryland, Joseph W. Kemp spoke on "The Jewish Tragedy" and pointed out that God had promised even more land to Abraham in Genesis 15:18: "Unto thy seed have I given this land, from the river of Egypt unto the great river, the river Euphrates." The speaker confessed that this territory had never been more than partially held by Israel; nevertheless, he asserted that the "promise waits for complete fulfillment, which will assuredly take place in the near future."[44]

Commenting on the suggestion that a new Jewish state would include Mesopotamia, *Our Hope* noted that that was "exactly what God has promised to the natural descendants of Abraham."[45] In responding at another time to the question of the size of the land, the editor affirmed that the "immense territory from the Nile to the fertile plains of Mesopotamia" would belong to Israel in the future. He was not necessarily advocating such a move by the nations, however, for he believed that this would not transpire until the land had been given to the Jews by the returned Messiah.[46]

These discussions took no account whatsoever of the existing inhabitants of these territories. The *Alliance Weekly* approvingly cited an article from the *Boston Evening Transcript* which said that "no one to any extent inhabits and cultivates this fair portion of the earth." The author explained that God had controlled history so that neither the Crusaders nor the Russians had ever been able to take the land: "Everyone knows that Russia, with superstitious devotion, would have populated Palestine, so, when the

Jew was ready to return, it would have been occupied." The restoration of the Jews was now to settle everything. The writer explained all the past by saying, "The Jew and Palestine have been the underlying cause of the whole Eastern question that has agitated Europe for a hundred years." He thus ignored any mundane theory such as imperialism or Russia's need for a warm water port.[47]

The support for restoration and Zionism was almost universal among premillenarians, but there were those who had second thoughts. Protestant missionaries in the Middle East of the old-line denominations were usually resistant to Jewish nationalism. This was especially true of those missionaries who worked among the Arabs. A writer in *The King's Business* recognized the reality of the situation and admitted, "The Zionists are going to oppose us," but he was optimistic that the true Christianity of the premillennialists would "lead and direct them aright" when the Zionists discovered that true Christianity was not a persecuting Christianity.[48] *Our Hope's* doubts, on the other hand, seemed to stem from a reassessment of its earlier enthusiasm:

> What the Jews are doing today is an infidel movement which will land them in the darkest night. We mention these facts for the sake of so many of God's people who begin to see these things, but think that the ever increasing efforts of Zionism to regain the land is the restoration of which the prophets have spoken. It is not. The true restoration and blessing of Israel comes with the Coming of the Lord.[49]

This did not mean that God's hand was not in everything; it just implied that not everything that happened was good or right. The unusual aspect here is that a critical attitude was expressed toward Israel's actions; such antipathy was usually reserved for Russia and her accomplices, in spite of the fact that Russia, too, was part of God's movements according to the premillenarian philosophy of history.

The best representative expression of this attitude toward Russia was embodied in the wartime book, *At Hand,* by the English author, Walter Scott. In it he reiterated views he had expressed nearly forty years before:

> We, of course, rejoice in every check given to Russia in the Near and Far East, but we are perfectly satisfied that by the force and strength of her battalions she will yet crush all opposition. She is the destined master in the East. Her battalions will by sheer strength of numbers sweep all before them.[50]

He predicted, moreover, on the basis of Ezekiel 38:13, which refers to the "merchants of Tarshish," that Britain's wartime alliance with Russia would not last long.[51]

In the early part of the war, Russia seemed to follow premillenarian expectations. In an article in *Our Hope,* "Russia and the Future," Arno C. Gaebelein observed that the statesmen of Europe recognized the ultimate menace of Russia, just as Biblical scholars knew that this great power of the North would play a prominent and to herself fatal part during the predicted end of the age.[52] In another piece he cited an entire article from the London publication, *Scripture Truth,* which explained that "Russia has yet to play a prominent and most malevolent part in these very countries before Israel is established without menace or fear in the land promised to her of old by Jehovah." The author interpreted the "phenomenal successes" of the Russians against the Turks to be in line with scriptural predictions. He contrasted this to the total failure of the British campaign in the Dardanelles:

> But what is so significant is that Russian arms are alone successful. In spite of the gallantry of the British troops in the Dardanelles the campaign there proved to be a complete failure, and the despatches of the generals commanding, describing the failure, leave the impression upon the mind that some unseen force was against them, for nothing seemed to transpire as was intended. But when the decision was made to withdraw the troops everything changed. . . . It seemed as though God's hand was against the armies of Britain while they remained in territory that must come under another Power according to His Word, but was for them from the moment the decision was taken to withdraw.

All of this supposed determinism indicated that "the time cannot be far off" when the hordes from Russia swollen by the masses from her newly conquered territories would come to Palestine to destroy the Jews. Then God Himself in a "fierce judgment of fire" would slaughter these "multitudes of Gog" in fulfillment of Ezekiel 39:12.[53] This great Armageddon seemed all the nearer as England and France reluctantly consented to Russia's war aim of domination over Constantinople after the war. Gaebelein saw this development as "very significant."[54]

Russia's diminishing power toward the end of the war left the premillenarians temporarily frustrated regarding the fulfillment of their prophetic interpretations, but they were able to rapidly recover their confidence after the war as the Bolsheviki quickly assumed the diabolical role. In March, 1917, a provisional revolutionary government was established in Russia and was succeeded by the Bolshevik revolution in November. During this period *Our Hope* was carrying a series on the prophecies of Ezekiel; the commentary on chapter thirty-eight appeared the month of the Bolshevik revolution. Gaebelein there made the common assertion that all students of prophecy agreed that *Rosh* meant Russia, but then found it a bit difficult to grapple with the revolutionary situation:

> We write this at a time when Russia is passing through horrors upon horrors. A revolution changed the autocratic government into a democracy and that promises now to give way to anarchy. . . . From what is written in this chapter we learn that Russia will ultimately return to the old regime and will once more become a monarchy to fulfill her final destiny as made known in this sublime prophecy.

This temporary upheaval was interpreted as punishment upon Russia for being "the most pronounced and bitterest enemy of the Jews." Gaebelein affirmed: "Today the Jews in Russia may have bright hopes of getting their rights and complete emancipation at last," but ultimately Russia will turn against them as Pharaoh did.[55] In an article written just prior to the March revolution, the *Evangel* had expressed hope for religious liberty in Russia,[56] but by the end of 1918 *The King's Business* was able to pontificate from the high throne of hindsight:

> Many in America went quite wild with anticipation of great things when the revolution of 1917 took place, but all of us who knew Russia anticipated the very outcome that we now see. No real good could be hoped for for a nation that had treated the Jew, God's chosen people, for generations as the Russians have treated them.[57]

Later the same theme was continued with accounts of thousands of Jews murdered in the Ukraine, massacres "more horrible than the worst of those committed under the old Czarist regime. . . . It appears that the invading Bolsheviki and the resisting Ukrainian government both claimed that the Jews were hostile—the old story."[58]

By February following the November revolution, Gaebelein was calling the spirit manifested by the Bolsheviks a universal spirit that was growing, a "spirit of lawlessness" predicted by the Word of God.[59] After a couple more years, Gaebelein had completely restored Russia to her on-rolling destiny: "The Soviet movement in Russia is victorious, and will before long spread over all Asia."[60] *The King's Business* took a different tack, however, lamenting that the number of Jews in positions of Bolshevik leadership would cause a general reaction against all Jews when the "inevitable fall of the Bolsheviki" arrived.[61]

Another aspect of the Russian setback was her capitulation to Germany in the Treaty of Brest-Litovsk in March, 1918. Large territories of eastern Europe were to be given to German control. The treaty was interpreted as an ominous portent of a monstrous northern confederation of Gog and Gomer, but there was also an immediate concern for the anti-Semitic problem involved. Gaebelein commented in *Our Hope* about the fate of four or five million Jews in the conquered area: "If Germany should be successful in holding this territory then the Jews may well prepare for the worse. It is the shadow of their coming tribulation."[62] Germany did not succeed in holding the territory, but in retrospect the words still seem prophetic. The Nazi ultimate solution of the Jewish problem in World War II would not seem out of character for Germany in the eyes of men like Gaebelein.

At the Philadelphia Prophetic Conference shortly after Brest-Litovsk, A. E. Thompson in his discussion of the capture of Jerusalem predicted that "with the end of the war, Germany and Russia, with other nations in alliance, will be in a sore plight." On the basis of Ezekiel 38:11, 12, he believed that these destitute nations would attempt to grab up the riches of a restored Israel in Palestine. Although these nations had lost their chance for Jerusalem in 1917, "they will never rest till they besiege it again."[63] The end of the war brought reports of financial chaos in Germany, and *Our Hope* responded with a warning: "The danger of a Russo-German alliance is a real danger." This was not a new twist for Gaebelein; he had speculated in his 1917 commentary on Ezekiel that Germany might "become united to Russia and march under the prince of Rosh into the land of Israel."[64] Gaebelein predicted also a revived Roman Empire which would be opposed to this alliance.

The idea of a revived Roman Empire was not new, but it was to be given new interest and impetus in the 1920s and 1930s by the ascendancy of Mussolini and Italy (and also in the 1950s and 1960s by the development of the European Common Market). Leadership of this great future power was supposedly to fall to a personality known, among other things, as the *Antichrist.* The Antichrist's role was to be important in the relations between Russia and Israel. There developed various versions of the scenario, but the general scheme was that as Russia came down to invade Israel, she was to be met by the forces of the Antichrist. Some versions saw Russia defeated by the Antichrist who was to be, in turn, conquered by God; others depicted the two forces joining together to be vanquished by God. During the war, Dr. Isaac M. Haldeman, pastor of the First Baptist Church, New York City, had developed this theme in a sermon, "The Falling Stone, or the Overthrow of the Last Kaiser." According to Haldeman, Rome would be revived in a tenfold form. The Antichrist would then be invited by the ten kings, possibly "democratic kings," to rule the world as Prince of Rome. He was to be from Babylon, originally a military leader who became king. Foreseeing that Germany and Russia would combine to advance in the east, the Antichrist would set up a Zionist state as a buffer. Making a seven-year treaty with Israel, he would break it after three-and-a-half years and turn upon her, initiating the Great Tribulation. He would then be faced with rebellions in Egypt, but eventually return from there to meet the forces from the north and east at Armageddon.[65] Periodicals such as *The Christian Workers Magazine* and the *Evangel* reflected upon similar schemes during the course of the war.[66] With the rise of fascism during the 1920s, the Antichrist tended to take the center stage of premillenarian interest as Russia was relegated to sideshow status, albeit still a leading attraction.

Immediately after the war, America was caught up in an anti-communist frenzy, the great "Red Scare" of 1919-20. Suspected subversives were jailed or deported and all dissenters from the political status quo were objects of suspicion. Premillenarians, too, were addicted to the national hysteria, but their condition was more than just an overdose of Americanism—they had swallowed multiple megadoses of anti-Russianism, anti-utopianism, anti-Catholicism, and anti-world-statism, together with a wee bit of anti-Semitism. Certainly they shared the prejudices of their fellow Americans, were defensive of "the American way of life," and succumbed to patriotic propaganda; but their developing anti-communism stemmed from a deeper loyalty than mere allegiance to fatherland or nationalism. They found common cause with those who opposed communism (threatened power-elites or shareholders in the American economic system), but their own literature reflected mainly a fear of the threat to their sincere, deep religious commitment—a fear reinforced, of course, by the above prejudices.

Perhaps a psychological case could be made that their fanatical anti-communism was an overreaction to suspicions about their own loyalty during the war, but any demonstration of that from their literature would be dubious. The accusation of being subversive had been embodied in an article in *The Biblical World,* "The Premillennial Menace," by Dr. Shirley Jackson Case, Professor of Early Church History and New Testament Interpretation at the University of Chicago. He spoke of the "detrimental character" and the "serious menace" of the pessimistic doctrines of the premillennialists. "By proclaiming that wars cannot be eliminated until Christ returns and that in the meantime the world must grow constantly worse, this type of teaching strikes at the very root of our present national endeavor to bring about a new day for humanity, when this old earth shall be made a better place in which to live, and a new democracy of nations shall rise to render wars impossible."[67] It must be admitted that few premillenarians had such utopian dreams about democracy, but certainly, even at a minimal level, democracy was considered the least bad form of human government. Of course, there were those such as Walter Scott who still believed in the divine right of kings: "The further we are removed from God's idea of power in the world—an *absolute and universal* monarchy, as was the

Babylonian—we are, of course, a witness to our own departure and failure from the original grant of government conferred upon the Gentiles."[68] Such views were, however, the exception rather than the rule. Dr. Case made further accusations implying traitorous activity on the premillenarians' part: "A premillennialist might well want Germany to win" because that would be a step toward a worse world—a prospect which the pessimistic premillennialist expected immediately prior to the catastrophic end of the world and his hoped-for new kingdom. Case refused to accept the premillenarians' own analysis that they did not oppose the war, since they viewed the war as happening by "divine permission."[69] Such invective did not undermine the work of the premillenarians at all—even their critics came to their defense in this particular circumstance.[70] They probably relished the attention directed to their cause.

The main thrust of premillenarian anti-communism was opposition to communism's endemic atheism—an identification that does not begin with Karl Marx, but can be traced back at least to the French Revolution. This aspect of their opposition, however, was one which they shared with most Christians—certainly all conservative Christians. The form of the opposition was quotation of statistics, reporting of incidents, or direct statements from the mouths of real, live Communists. For example, *The Christian Workers Magazine* cited *Literary Digest's* quotations of a newspaper report of the Senate Judiciary Committee's findings on Bolshevism:

> It has confiscated all church property, real and personal. . . .
> It has suppressed Sunday-schools and has expressly forbidden the teaching of all religious doctrine in public, either in schools or in educational institutions of any kind.[71]

Churches, Sunday schools, and Bible institutes were the main harvest fields of all premillenarians—the threat of such suppression was terrifying. Tertullian's words, "The blood of the martyrs is the seed of the church," was a cliché of current circulation, but none advocated that now was a time to start from scratch and replant. The most devastating type of criticism of communism by the premillenarians took the form of quoting remarks such as the following, which was ascribed to the Russian revolutionary, Michael Bakunin:

> The lie must be stamped out and give way to truth. The first lie is God. The second is right. Might, my friends, forms the sole groundwork of society, and when you have freed your minds from the fear of God, and from that childish respect for the fiction of right, then all the remaining chains which bind you and which are called science, civilization, property, marriage, morality and justice, will snap asunder like threads.[72]

For Arno C. Gaebelein the threat of the Communists and the radicals was "perhaps the most serious in the history of the American republic."[73]

Besides the antipathies which premillennialists shared with other Americans and other Christians, there were many that stemmed from reasons all their own. They were anti-utopian—not that others were not anti-utopian, but the position of the premillennialists was different. They were critical of all utopian systems: communist, socialist, syndicalist, or anarchist; in their view the good life could be attained only through spiritual rebirth now, or through admission to the coming Kingdom of God. Gaebelein had synthesized this view: "Bolshevism is the violence of the wicked aiming at God's order in government, and the overthrow of everything."[74] The premillennialists were also anti-foreign—this attitude grew out of their anti-Catholicism. Anti-Catholicism they shared with the tradition that antedated the Reformation, but theirs differed. Catholicism was for them more than a heresy; it was destined to be revived as an autocratic, end-time power. This general feeling toward Catholicism is well expressed in one of I. M. Haldeman's prewar sermons at the First Baptist Church, New York City, entitled "The Scarlet Woman." Taking his text from Revelation 17:1-6, 18, he emphatically asserted:

> It is the prophecy that the Roman Catholic Church will again be carried and supported by nations of the Roman earth, and will once more rule and reign with temporal power.
>
> It is the divine forecast of the revival of Romanism.
>
> THIS REVIVAL HAS ALREADY BEGUN.[75]

The prewar deluge of Catholic immigrants into the American labor pool was a potential harvest field for radical labor agitators—a foreboding mixture to the apocalyptic mind. For example, Gaebelein's response to crisis times is not surprising.

> The exposure of nationwide plots to establish a Soviet government in our country and to overthrow the government of the United States has been startling. Many of the strikes during the past year, the steel strike, the New York printers strike and the coal miners strike were brought about by radical, anarchistic agitators of foreign birth, aiming at the abolishment of law and order so that an industrial chaos might result. Our government has been slow in acting; it has treated these foreigners, enemies of everything that is right and decent far too leniently. But now action has come and every lawabiding citizen hopes that the utmost force will be used to rid our land of this terrible element.[76]

The specter of a world-wide revolution to usher in the communistic dictatorship of the proletariat also coincided with apocalyptic anticipation of a world-state ruled by the Antichrist. The anti-world-statism of the premillennialist not only reinforced the antagonism toward communism, but buttressed a profound skepticism of all international bodies: the League of Nations, the World Court, the United Nations, or even just "entangling alliances"—it was a broadly conceived isolationism.

It is obvious by now that anti-communism, especially when wedded to anti-Russianism, was more to these people than just a political question; it was potentially a fanatical crusade, with overtones of a martyr complex: "If God be for us, who can be against us?"

One other aspect of anti-communism which premillennialists shared with other elements in American society was a residual anti-Semitism. This tended to crop up periodically in discussions of the number of Jews in the Russian revolutionary movement. Trotsky was always included, but figures as high as 60 per cent of all the leaders were mentioned. The association of radicalism with Jews was not peculiar to premillennialists, but their view does seem to have a unique flavor—some even felt that the Antichrist himself would be a Jew. Gaebelein may be selected as an example again as he grinds out his diatribe:

> The ringleaders of the worst gang in New York City were nearly all Jews. It seems apostate, infidel Jews are everywhere more or less connected with anarchy, especially in Russia.[77]

This was the frame of mind that would give credence in the 1920s to rumors of an international Jewish conspiracy.

Also, at the close of the war, there was little optimism reflected concerning the peace treaties or the League of Nations. *Our Hope* had no hope that the League would prevent war. *The King's Business* expressed a grasp of the problem that other publications did not reflect. It observed that prior to the war the Jewish population in Palestine had risen to 120,000 or one-fifth of the total population, but that their number had been vastly depleted by war, emigration, and disease. Then, without the characteristically premillenarian wild-eyed enthusiasm, a realistic observation was made: "The problem before the Peace Conference, therefore, is to establish in Palestine such political and administrative organization as will enable the Jews from all parts to build up their national home without infringing the rights of other nationalities occupying the country, and in dealing with this task it will have the best wishes of all who desire to see God's ancient people back again in their own land."[78] The recognition that other nationalities had any rights at all was unusual among these restorationists. More true to form was the speaker at the New York Prophetic Conference who had flatly predicted: "Whatever the decisions at the Peace table may be, one thing is sure, Palestine and Jerusalem will pass back into the hands of their original owners[;] they will get it without money, and without price, even as Jehovah declared in the Law of Moses." This was not pure optimism, however, for he reminded his audience that the restoration would bring another invasion (presumably by Russia) and the Great Tribulation to the Jews. Although not fulfilled in the sense that he envisioned, his prognosis is a fascinating understatement: "This war is not the last war which the holy land has seen."[79]

In the immediate postwar period, premillennialism came under concerted attack, particularly in a series of articles in *The Biblical World*. This bombardment gave some general indication of the extent of the premillenarian advance. During the war Shirley Jackson Case had observed that "the danger is not restricted to a single locality; it has become nationwide."[80] In 1919, Dr. T. Valentine Parker of the First Baptist Church, Binghamton, New York, said, "Their influence is permeating our churches."[81] Various comments were made in *The Biblical World:* "The Protestant churches of the United States are facing a crisis in religion."[82] "Its injurious effect can already be seen in hundreds of churches throughout the United States."[83] But the premillenarians gleefully quoted their critics. *Our Hope* cited the lament of the president of Auburn Theological Seminary:

> The spirit of premillennialism is dividing the whole Protestant Church of America. . . . Doctor Chapman and Billy Sunday and nearly all the evangelists hold this doctrine. Here is a school of thought that is captivating the church of today.[84]

The focus of all this criticism was the failure of the premillenarians to join the great cause of the social gospel and to help usher in the great age of the Kingdom of God on earth. The social gospel was, and has continued to be, rejected by premillenarians on a theological basis. Another point of criticism was much more telling, however, and has seemingly grown more goading through the years. This was the censure of the generally nonpolitical bent of the premillenarian and his attitude toward the state and toward social improvement. This prevailing attitude of the premillenarian had been expressed in Nathaniel West's 1889 book, *The Thousand Years:* "What we are pleased to call the Christian State, is simply the Christian-Beast, either the *Horns* of the Beast, or the *Toes* of the Colossus!—a Beast whose power is *in check* for the present, but soon to be *unchecked* and drive Christianity back to the wall."[85] The charge against such a predisposition was irresponsibility:

> Nineteen centuries have passed by, during which, according to adventism, this new age has been imminent. There is nothing in premillennial teaching to compel us to believe that the world may not need to wait nineteen or twice nineteen centuries more, since, according to men like Dr. Scofield and Dr. Pierson, "imminent" with premillennialists means simply "next on the docket," whether near or remote. For an indefinite period, then, adventism has nothing to suggest to us but a passive pessimism over against a pagan and hopelessly evil social order.[86]

Premillenarians may have been irked by the criticism, but they were not chagrined, not at the time anyway. They went merrily on their doomsaying way, interpreting not every falling leaf—as medievalists—but nearly every international event as God-ordained and prophetically significant.

Although World War I had not produced the expected Armageddon—not yet anyway—premillenarians were not disappointed. The Balfour Declaration made the Jewish restoration seem imminent, Allenby's victory at Jerusalem augured the end of the times of the Gentiles, and the Soviet giant seemed a foreboding threat; the stage was set, once again, for the dramatic end.

The Twenties Roar Faintly—Bear, Beast, and Young Lions

Current international events are assuredly finger posts to Armageddon.

Christabel Pankhurst
—*The Lord Cometh,* 1923

Here you have read that Russia is going to war with Palestine. That is coming. . . . There is where we are to-day. Therefore, we may expect very shortly that this conflict will take place.

—*The Pentecostal Evangel,* 1928

If the writer should hazard a prediction he would be inclined to say that the outcome of the present situation will finally confirm the Jewish claim and will eventually speed up developments for setting the stage for the final act of the end of the age.

—*The King's Business,* 1929

The pietistic holiness strain in premillenarian thought prevented participation in the high-living uproar of the 1920s, but there was excited anticipation as the circus menagerie of Biblical symbols faintly roared in the caverns of time's stadium, restlessly awaiting the fatal rush to the arena. The Russian bear recovered providentially from the dual wounds of war and revolution, and premillenarians continued the traditional game of bearbaiting. The identity of the Beast, sometimes called Antichrist, was not quite so clearly recognized, being variously represented as Mussolini, the League of Nations, or—more traditionally—the Catholics. America's growing nationalism and recent rise as a world power necessitated the discovery of a significant prophetic role for this new major power. America was accordingly identified as a young lion of British pedigree, destined to stand with Britain in the final struggle of the age.

As premillenarians reflected on the years of the war, they continued to see the hand of God in it all. "God's greatest purpose in the world war was to shake Palestine free from the grip of the Turk," according to *The King's Business* in its regular feature section, "The Chosen People, the Land and the Book: Notes Concerning the Jews and Prophecy." The writer admitted that there were other purposes, but this was the greatest. The freedom of the Jews to return to Palestine as a result of the war proved that God was still alive and at work on behalf of Israel. Therefore, "all believers ought to rejoice in this fresh evidence of the interest of God in men."[1] This purpose of the war was regarded as the "budding of the fig tree" of Luke 21:29-31 and as an indication that "the kingdom of God is nigh."[2] *The Pentecostal Evangel* linked major turning points of the war directly to the hand of God in Palestine: "It is a remarkable fact that when Turkey surrendered [Britain] had just captured the last portion of the Promised Land."[3] "The most significant feature of the late war was the retaking of this whole [Biblical] territory. . . . When this was accomplished by General Allenby . . . war ceased."[4] Speaking of the Zionist movement, one *Evangel* writer said:

> It looked as though they would not be able in any way whatever to establish themselves as a nation again. Then God began to work and the war came. If you want my explanation of the war, I believe there was one object which God had

> in view, as God always has an object in view, and that object was that He might deal with Israel. I believe that was the real purpose that God had in permitting the war to take place. It was not until the peoples of the world had done something for Israel that God permitted the war to stop.[5]

It is not surprising that believers in the sovereignty of God would refrain from attacking the method that God uses in achieving His purposes, but it seems tragic that such discussions pass without even a slight lament for over eight million dead human beings—God's purposes were costly. This involved not just the physical losses of sons, fathers, husbands, and sweethearts; but, for the most part, the relegation of eternally lost souls to the unending punishment of hell, according to most premillenarians' doctrine. Although God was given the credit for the purposes accomplished by the war, a Congregational minister writing in *Moody Bible Institute Monthly* assigned all blame to the devil:

> While evil abounds, God restrains. In the hours of this age, when hell-born forces seemed about to triumph, God has restrained. In the late World War, He restrained. Bad as it was, it was not as bad as it would have been, if Germany had won. God heard our prayer and had mercy upon us. He, not we, beat back the foe.[6]

This inconsistency of giving God the credit, but not the blame, is, of course, the age-old Christian dilemma of the origin of evil; the discussions of the premillenarians appear particularly simplistic and naive as this dilemma was not even mentioned.

Even beyond the immediate objective of retrieving the Promised Land for Israel, the war was recurringly interpreted as having another end in view: "The recent war was a great rehearsal for the final war at Armageddon."[7]

The saga of the capture of Jerusalem continued to grow, making General Allenby into somewhat of a folk-hero among premillenarians. He was joined to the ranks of the Maccabeans of the pre-Christian era, and was to be joined later by the hero of the 1967 war, Moshe Dayan. A speaker at the 1922 Southern Baptist Convention contrasted the elaborate preparations for the assault on the city with the ease of the capture without the shedding of blood.[8] Sir Henry Galway's account of how Allenby had made up his mind beforehand that he would not damage the holy places was retold. Allenby telegraphed the British government—the government told him to do what he thought best. He then telegraphed the king—the king told him to pray about it. So Allenby assembled his troops and prayed for special guidance; and before the meeting was over, the message arrived that the Turks had withdrawn.[9] One writer exclaimed, "The fiendish Turk was chased out and Jerusalem was taken without a gun having been fired upon or in the city! This was the work of God!" This sequence of events was attributed to the fulfillment of prophecy; the certainty of Israel's return was given anecdotal illustration:

> The Turks during the days of the Crusaders coined a saying: "The Christians will take Jerusalem when the river Nile flows into Palestine." That meant that they would never take Jerusalem. God heard the challenge of the Turks, and the only good thing I have ever known the great oil company of America to do was done in this connection. They placed a great quantity of pipe for a pipe line near the Suez Canal. When the British forces started for Palestine they commandeered the pipe, and began to pump the water from the Nile up to their troops. On and on they went, and finally they were pumping the river Nile into Palestine, and the Turks lost the land. There are some people who have so little sense as to deny the Divine inspiration of the Bible.[10]

Another story that continued to circulate was the return of the "latter rain." In articles in the *Evangel* just over three months apart, one article spoke of the return of the rains after God had withheld them for two thousand years, whereas the other referred to a one thousand-year drought.[11] Neither provided any supporting evidence, and both failed to mention that rainfall records had been kept for only the past eighty years. There is no evidence of significant changes in Palestinian climate during historical times. As a matter of fact, average yearly rainfall in the 1920s was the lowest on record.[12]

Various aspects of the general theme of the restoration of Israel continued to occupy the premillenarian mind. Every development was given prophetic significance; each crate of oranges shipped, every kilowatt of power produced was a sign of God's guiding hand. God's timetable was not absolutely predetermined, however; it could be influenced by the believers themselves. Readers of *The King's Business* were admonished: "Christians should pray for the restoration of the Jews to their land, for thus, as well as by the saving of souls, we may help to hasten the day of the Lord's coming."[13] "All believers in the Divine Word of Promise do well to pray that the Lord will bring another exodus to pass, in gathering from the nations of the earth His people."[14]

There was some question, however, over the method that God would use in accomplishing His purposes. Were the Zionists to be the means or not? *The King's Business* was skeptical of a scheme by the Zionists to raise $125,000,000 for land purchases in Palestine. The journal pointed out that, according to prophecy, it would not be necessary for the Jews to buy the land. The implication was that the Zionists were not in keeping with the will of God. "When God's time comes, they will not have to buy the land."[15] Only a few months later, though, the same columnist offered the Zionist movement as an example of God's working through gradual methods to accomplish His plans for Israel.[16]

One popularizer of interest in Israel, restoration, and prophecy was Christabel Pankhurst, whose colorful background as a leader of Great Britain's militant suffragettes gave her an intriguing appeal among the conservative premillenarians. She spoke throughout the United States, including engagements at Moody Bible Institute and the Bible Institute of Los Angeles. In her 1923 book, *The Lord Cometh!*, she included the Zionist plan for the return of the Jews, along with the rejection of the Turk from the land of Palestine, as one of the "signs that are now heralding the end of the Age."[17] The *New York Times* reported her 1925 lecture series in New York's Ascension Memorial Episcopal Church: "Concerning the return of Christ, Miss Pankhurst said one thing was conclusive—the Jew was back in Palestine and his national home being restored. This was 'the supremely important factor in world affairs today' because it was 'the decisive practical guarantee that the Son of God is soon to appear.' "[18] Not content with the usual vague generalities, she placed her credibility on the line by predicting, "The year 1925 will see a big advance toward the final crisis of the closing age. A last effort to save the world situation by human means will be made. A number of nations will confederate and will accept the headship of a dictator, who will be the Anti-christ of prophecy."[19] This report in the Northern

Baptist's *Watchman Examiner* referred to her presentation as "impassioned" but offered no critical comment. Being a false prophetess, however, did not disqualify her in premillenarian circles; in 1927, the *Moody Bible Institute Monthly* carried her speculative views on the restoration of Israel and the formation of a ten-kingdom confederacy in Europe and Asia.[20]

In Palestine itself, the restoration was strongly resisted by the Arabs, and violence prevailed in Palestine throughout the decade, occasional rioting sometimes breaking out into open warfare. The Arabs had supported the British during the war with full expectation of achieving national independence from the Turks. The success of the British colonel, Lawrence of Arabia, was possible only because of such a belief. At the time of the capture of Jerusalem, General Allenby had announced, "The object of war in the East on the part of Great Britain was the complete and final liberation of all peoples formerly oppressed by the Turks and the establishment of national governments and administrations in those countries deriving authority from the initiative and free will of those people themselves."[21]

Gradually the Arabs became aware of the British betrayal; rioting broke out in the spring of 1920, and in 1921 the Palestine Arab Congress sent a formal protest delegation to London. Britain's uncertain policy of supporting Zionist goals while at the same time appearing to favor Arab independence movements necessitated various shifts in policy statements. This was further complicated by conflicts within the government over what the goals should be, let alone how they should be implemented. The Arabs had looked forward to the implementation of President Woodrow Wilson's Fourteen Points through the peace settlements, including the self-determination of nations. Such a lofty dream soon dissolved into the nightmarish reality of British and French imperialism in the Middle East. This reality had been embodied in the secret Sykes-Picot agreement during the war that carved the former Turkish territories into British and French spheres of influence. Under the League of Nations these became "mandates," a hypocritical name for colonies—with vague benevolent goals in some distant future. President Wilson had sent a commission to the Middle East prior to the Versailles Treaty. This King-Crane Commission had advised the American peace delegation against the policy of Jewish immigration and the Balfour Declaration. Later, the commission's final report recommended that "Jewish immigration should be definitely limited, and that the project for making Palestine distinctly a Jewish commonwealth should be given up."[22] But the British and the French view prevailed. That is not surprising considering Wilson's support of the Balfour Declaration back in 1917.

The Arab protest movement eventually caused Britain to reinterpret the Balfour Declaration in order to avoid an immediate Arab rebellion. A memorandum by the Colonial Secretary, Winston Churchill, on June 3, 1922, stated that "the terms of the Declaration referred to do not contemplate that Palestine as a whole should be converted into a Jewish National Home, but that such a Home should be founded *in Palestine*." This was a blow to Zionist aspirations and was duly reported by *The King's Business* as such. Churchill was clearly the villain in this situation, and the journal commented that "in spite of enemies within Israel and enemies without, the plan of God will be carried through, and finally all Israel will return to their own land."[23] Two months later, the magazine devoted two full pages to a discussion of the issues. It favorably reported that the United States Senate the previous May had unanimously passed a resolution favoring "the establishment in Palestine of the National Home for the Jewish people" and that this had brought "great joy and satisfaction, and fresh courage" to the Zionist movement. This was not to be reflected in American policy, however, as the Department of State throughout the 20s and 30s usually avoided supporting Zionist interests because of American oil interests and general isolationism. In this article, a policy statement by Churchill was interpreted favorably, even though his accurate appraisal was anti-Zionist: "The only cause of unrest in Palestine arises from the Zionist movement and the British promises in regard to it." The article emphasized, rather, the other aspect of his statement: "The task in Palestine is one that England has imposed upon herself and which she is bound to perform unless she is prepared to admit that the word of England no longer counted throughout the Near East." Churchill was referring to Britain's Palestine mandate which had been approved by the League of Nations on July 24, 1922, but this was interpreted by the writer as a commitment to carry out the Balfour Declaration. Moreover, President Warren Harding was quoted as saying, "I have always viewed with an interest which I think is quite as much practical as sentimental, the proposal for the rehabilitation of Palestine, and the restoration of a real Jewish nationality, and I hope the effort now being carried on in this and other countries in this behalf may meet the fullest measure of success."[24] Even his enthusiasm did not quite measure up to the level of the magazine's own excited response to the establishment of the mandate: "No one who has at heart the cause of justice to the Jews, or who awaits the fulfillment of prophecy regarding their return to their own land, can learn without emotion that this return is now legally opened and confirmed by the League of Nations."[25]

The discussion over the right of the British to impose Jewish nationalism upon the Arabs in Palestine eventually produced a widely-cited response in support of the Jews. Thomas M. Chalmers in a pamphlet entitled "Israel in Covenant and History" developed a sixfold defense of the Jewish takeover of the land. He said, "Israel's possession of Canaan as an everlasting inheritance is based on an indefeasible title. The Jewish people have six titles to Canaan based on the six modes of obtaining property in land." The first was by homestead law. God had set aside the land for Israel 251 years before Abraham, the father of the Jews, was even born. The second was by gift or grant; since God had given the land to the Jews He could not have given it to the Canaanites who already lived there when Abraham migrated. The third was by covenant; since Christ had been circumcised, He was heir to Canaan and to all the world (implying He could give it to whom He wished). The fourth was by conquest—Joshua had conquered the land after the Jews' bondage in Egypt. The fifth was by right of tenure. Israel had possessed the land for a total of 1450 years, and "Israel lost no rights by leaving the homestead, or by eviction, or by the Moslem conquest." (Nothing is said of the Arabs' tenure or right by conquest.) The last was by purchase, not the purchase of land by returning Jews, but by the Redeemer Christ Jesus.[26] No multiplication of weak Scriptural argument, however, could mollify the basic moral injustice of the claim that the Jews had more right to Palestine than did the native Arab population. Arguments were to no avail anyway; after 1917, the claim to possession was decided on the basis of military power—the same way it had always been decided. When England would find possession not worth the cost in military power in 1948, possession would shift to the Jews themselves—again through the means of military might.

Britain's mandate was interpreted by *The King's Business* as similar to the action of Cyrus, the King of Persia, in allowing the Jews to return to Jerusalem after their captivity in Babylon as recorded in the Book of Ezra.[27] A writer in the *Evangel,* however, compared the beneficence of Cyrus to the Zionist movement itself, stating that both demonstrated how the hand of God uses instruments that are not necessarily submissive to Him.[28]

The deep emotional level of the premillennialists' response to the expected restoration is illustrated in one parishioner's recollection of A. B. Simpson, founder of the Christian and Missionary Alliance: "I can recall how my pastor in those days, A. B. Simpson, wept aloud in his pulpit as he announced the sensational news that Jerusalem and Palestine were no longer to be 'trodden down' under the heels of the Turk, but that all 56 signatory powers of the League of Nations Covenant besides the United States had approved the Balfour Declaration."[29]

There was concern among premillenarians about the Zionists' setbacks in the late 20s; there seemed to be a loss of momentum in the headlong rush to Armageddon. In 1928, the editor of the *Evangel* regretfully cited figures from the *Literary Digest* which showed that in 1926, 13,081 had immigrated while 7,365 had left Palestine; but in 1927 only 2,713 had immigrated whereas 5,071 had left. The editor reassured his readers by citing the statement of Thomas M. Chalmers in the *Sunday School Times* that the Zionists were recovering from their temporary setback and that there had been a marked growth over the whole ten-year period.[30] By 1929 the *Moody Bible Institute Monthly* could bolster its confidence with statements like the following:

> Within the first hundred years of Cyrus' edict not more than 60,000 exiles found their way back to the homeland, but during the last decade more than 100,000 have done so, while the stream of immigration continues to flow uninterruptedly. Greater things are expected in the future, and especially now that the movement has been taken out of

> the handful of so-called Zionists and become the task of all the people of Israel. Why cry "failure" in the face of such facts?[31]

While the apparent consensus of premillenarians was that the restoration either had already taken place, was just beginning, or was imminent, there appeared a dissenting view that established other prerequisites. *The King's Business* reflected one school of speculation that said the Jews could not return to Palestine until *after* the return of the Messiah, the Second Coming of Christ. Charles C. Cook, founder of the conservative Christian publishing company which bears his name, stated in an article, "The International Jew," that "Palestine's possession by the Jewish people is not an immediate prospect." It could not happen until the times of the Gentiles had ceased, and that era could not cease until the return of Christ. This view was based on an interpretation of Nebuchadnezzar's dream in Daniel 2 in which the stone (the symbol of Christ) destroys the image (the symbol of Gentile power).[32]

A later article by Thomas M. Chalmers concerning the Palestinian mandate observed that there might be "a great inrush" of Jews and a vast development of Palestine, but that "until the Lord comes the hand of the Gentile must be on Palestine." He felt it was necessary for the Gentiles to remain in power to prevent the Arabs from exterminating the Jews, and that the necessary prerequisite for the Jewish return was their conversion to Christianity. "Israel will not jump at once to full control of Palestine. That will never come again while the Jews remain in rebellion against their true Sovereign, the Lord Jesus Christ."[33]

Still another author somewhat later reflected a slight modification of this theme, stating that "the Zion movement is one of the greatest forces, and one of the most futile institutions ever established by a deluded people. If the money of the universe were put into the hands of the Jews, and all the transportation facilities of the world were theirs, they could not be gathered in that land at the present moment." The preliminary event called for by this writer, though, was not the regeneration of the Jews, but the return of Christ, the King of the Jews. They were to be restored to the land by Christ, and this was to occur prior to any wholesale conversion on their part.[34]

The above views did not reflect any particular editorial philosophy of *The King's Business,* but represented the common confusion and conflict in interpreting supposedly clear, but evidently obscure, Scriptural passages. At the same time the magazine also carried the opposite view. It was expressed by J. A. Vaus, who was Superintendent of the Jewish Department of the Bible Institute of Los Angeles (Biola). He admitted that "some Bible students entertain the conviction that the present Zionist movement, for the establishment of a Jewish National Home in Palestine, is doomed to failure because, as they claim, it is a man-made movement, which leaves God out of all considerations." But Vaus saw the current progress in Palestine as the "beginnings of that great return." "The fact that Israel is going back in unbelief and that Palestine is destined to become a center of Jewish culture, that the Temple will be rebuilt with a consequent revival of Judaism, is not proof that the present 'return' is not the one predicted in the prophetic books, for we are, by the prophets, led to expect that the national conversion of Israel would *follow* and not precede the return to Palestine."[35]

The Pentecostal Evangel buttressed its view of restoration prior to the Second Coming by reporting contemporary Jewish prophetic interpretations which paralleled that view. A Zionist leader by the name of Dr. Sokolow was cited as saying that the ancient prophets had forecast centuries before that the Messiah would come after the Jews had returned to their homeland and that this restoration presumably had already been accomplished since Jews of every nation were represented by the immigrants.[36] Also quoted was similar material published in the *London Christian Herald:*

> The secretary of one of the synagogues says, "The Jews have been waiting two thousand years for Britain's help, but the British will not always remain here. A certain rabbi making a prophecy seven hundred years ago, foretold that the British would come into Palestine in 1916, but that they would leave before the expiration of a quarter of a century." This has yet to be fulfilled. "Then," the rabbi said, "there will be a big war here. The last world war will occur in Palestine. The kings of the earth shall fight against the Jews in Palestine, but the Messiah will come and cause the enemy to be defeated. The Messiah will be recognized as the great world

> Leader, the law of the Lord shall flow out of Zion, and nations will learn war no more."[37]

In face of continued Zionist success in subsequent years, this "Restoration Now" view prevailed. Although in this era the dissenting view was considered as a viable interpretation by some premillenarians, after the establishment of the state of Israel in 1948, it virtually disappeared.

Along with this question of immediacy, rumors of the impending destruction of the Mosque of Omar (Dome of the Rock) or the Mosque el-Aksa and the rebuilding of the Temple continued to crop up. The Biola journal reported the publication of a Jewish catechism in London which said that whenever the Jews returned to their land and again constituted a state a temple would be built and the sacrificial laws restored. The reporter commented that the Scriptures clearly teach that the Jews will return in unbelief, but that they will have a new temple and re-establish temple sacrifices.[38] The necessary destruction of the Arab center of worship, the Mosque of Omar, was referred to in a classic understatement as "a delicate problem." It was noted that "the Jews can hardly be expected to take steps to restore the temple on the chosen site until they have a majority in Palestine."[39]

Another apparently serious speculation was that an alliance of the Masons and the Jews might rebuild the Temple since the Masons claim that their order was founded by King Solomon at the building of his Temple.[40] The Jews' expectation of an imminent rebuilding was duly reported:

> Chief Rabbi Kook [Kuk?] of Jerusalem has announced that a new Yeshibah will be founded in the Holy City for the purpose of instructing men of priestly and Levitic parentage in their duties in the Temple. This includes formulas of sacrifices, etc. The rabbi believes this to be an urgent necessity, since he perceives the rebuilding of the Temple as near at hand.[41]

An author in the *Evangel* exulted in the news that repairs on the Mosque had been halted because the Moslems could not produce a title deed to the property. He called it "a wonderful thing" and interpreted the event as a significant indication that "God has wrested Palestine from Islam."[42] Another writer, a lady evangelist, expanded the report: "The Temple is to be rebuilt.... We understand that the Jews are hoping to return to the Levitical sacrifices in the near future." She did not find it surprising that no title deed to the Dome of the Rock had been found. She then recounted how in giving a prophetic message recently in an evangelistic campaign she had held up the Bible and said, *"The promise* to Abraham, Isaac and Jacob is the *land-title* to the temple site."[43] The *Evangel* editor, writing on "Signs of the Approaching End," reported a rabbi as saying, "The Mosque of Omar will be torn down soon, and a wonderful temple, like Solomon's, will be built there."[44] A Jewish writer was quoted on the significance of rebuilding the Temple: "The Jewish National Home cannot be complete without it, and I would go even further and say that Palestine will never be flourishing until the temple building is fully established in all its ancient glory."[45] Another article, "The Sure Word of Prophecy," cited press dispatches from Jerusalem reporting that permission was being sought by zealous Jews to build altars at the Temple site and restore the sacrifices, and that prospective priests were already suspected of practicing ritual sacrifice.[46]

This blatant anti-Mosque attitude was just one example of a generally anti-Arab disposition held by most premillenarians. This antipathy was not derived from any hatred of the Arabs themselves or of their actions, but simply was inherent in the premillenarians' view of Biblical restorationism. They did have perhaps somewhat of a tragic sense about those unfortunates who just happened to be descendants of Israel's twin brother Esau, who had sold his birthright to his younger twin. But God had said, "I hated Esau" (Mal. 1:3), and since Esau's descendants opposed the restoration of God's chosen people, it was predestined that they would just have to suffer the consequences. Another view held that the Arabs were the descendants of Ishmael, Abraham's illegitimate son, who, not being the promised heir of the land God had given Abraham, had been cast out. The development of this anti-Arab antagonism can be observed throughout the 20s and has continued down to the present. In 1922, following Arab protests in Palestine and London concerning the implementation of the Balfour Declaration, the *Evangel* carried a reprint of an article from another journal, *Morning Star,* which contained a letter written to a rabbi. The author of the letter encouraged the rabbi to take comfort from Jeremiah 31:10 ("He that scattered Israel will gather him"), and commented, "He is gathering him, and the *enemies* of the Jews can not hinder it."[47]

The King's Business reflected the view that the Arabs would quiet down once they began to share the "beneficial results of Jewish industrial enterprise." It was stated that the Arabs would not suffer any hardship whatsoever from the restoration of the Jews, because, after all, they still had the whole of Arabia with its million square miles, and, in addition, all the land that had been freed from the Turks. The Arabs were only nomads who had created "neither material nor spiritual values" in the land. In keeping with this view Lord Shaftesbury was quoted: "Give the country without a people to the people without a country."[48] One article, citing a missionary to Palestine writing in the *Jewish Missionary Herald,* even reflected a blanket prejudice:

> The poor Arab—what has he? The Turk has robbed him even of his character! What could the Zionists rob him of? The charge that the Jew is robbing the Arab is absolutely false.[49]

Thus some premillenarians continued to hold the naive view that desertion by the Turks had left Palestine a great vacuum that was sucking the Jews back by some inevitable law of nature. Many never even considered the question of the justice or injustice of the Jews' replacing or overpowering the native—Arab existence was completely ignored.

Arab resentment in Palestine erupted into rioting as a result of an incident at the Wailing Wall on the Day of Atonement in 1929. The Wall was believed to be a fragment of Herod's Temple, and the Jews regularly gathered there for prayers. A minor incident—the attempt of the Jews to build a partition to separate the male and female worshipers—escalated into conflicts in which the Jews counted 133 dead and 339 wounded, and the Arabs suffered 116 dead and 232 wounded. Virtually all the premillenarian popular press took note of this tragedy. The Moody paper quite moderately observed that the Jews were expanding and increasing their power under English and American aid and "the Arab is naturally jealous and alarmed." The proper response for the premillenarian was indicated: "But meanwhile the student of prophecy is on the keen edge of expectancy wondering how much longer it may be 'until the times of the Gentiles be fulfilled.' "[50] The Biola publication took sides without caution, "Regardless of whether the question is settled by arbitration or by the sword, the Jew is, according to the Scriptures, the rightful owner of Palestine. If the writer should hazard a prediction he would be inclined to say that the outcome of the present situation will finally confirm the Jewish claim and will eventually speed up developments for setting the stage for the final act of the end of the age."[51] In *Our Hope,* Arno C. Gaebelein reversed his position of ten years earlier when he had said that Zionism was not part of the prophetic restoration, but he still did not expect blessing for the land until the return of Christ:

> These outbreaks should be a warning to the Zionists that their dream of glorious restoration will not be easy sailing. If they only would believe what their own prophets say they would soon discover that only troubles and disasters await them in their unbelieving attempt. What has so recently happened will happen a thousand times worse during the time of Jacob's trouble, the great tribulation. Yet they will go ahead with their plans and succeed in this remarkable national revival. Even so it must be to make the fulfillment of prophecy as to the end of the ages possible.[52]

The *Evangel* called upon a statement by Albert Einstein to substantiate its own attitude toward the Arabs in the crisis: "During the whole of the work of Jewish colonization not a single Arab has been dispossessed; every acre of land acquired by the Jews has been bought at a price fixed by the buyer and the seller." This was a distorted interpretation of "dispossessed," because the hardest pressed of the Arabs were not the landowning class but the tenant farmers and squatters or bedouins on government lands who were being removed from their traditional livelihood. The writer found it particularly significant that the "Jews have bought—strange purchase!—Armageddon at a cost of nearly $5,000,000."[53]

The *Evangel* also responded with a long answer to the question, "Will the Temple Soon Be Rebuilt?" Concerning the Arabs themselves: "Carnal men will always oppose the will of God." The author reflected his deterministic antipathy by pointing out that the British Prime Minister, Ramsay MacDonald, was a supporter of the Jewish cause and was opposed to the current Arab agitation: "But back of Great Britain and its premier is God, who is hastening to perform His prophetic word. He will not fail in His promise to His friend Abraham." Then was included an anecdote from the crisis. British carrier-based planes had nosedived and corkscrewed to "within an ace of the Dome of the Rock," and "the government made a threat that if the Mufti allowed the Moslems to go out of the Mosque of Omar and cause a breach of the peace, they would send aeroplanes to bomb and blow up the Mosque." The report then morbidly observed, "These very Arab disturbances, where the wrath of man is manifest, are likely to contribute to the praise of God in the accomplishment of His purpose—the getting rid of the Mosque of Omar which could be destroyed in a few minutes by a fleet of British bombing planes." The article closed by citing various Jewish sources indicating a strong desire to build the Temple again.[54] Blessed are the peacemakers?

The Arab plight was thus rationalized as the result of God's just hatred of an unproductive, lazy, belligerent people who had sold out their birthright to the Jews. The infusion of Jews supposedly would be best for the Arabs in the long run anyway. On the other hand their existence was sometimes just ignored.

The British government responded to the rioting by sending a Royal Commission to investigate the causes of the violence. Its report blamed the general Arab antagonism toward a Jewish national home, and it recommended that all land sales to Jews be stopped and that Jewish immigration to Palestine be curtailed. In contrast to the premillenarian response to the riots, the liberal Protestants generally supported the view of the commission. The *Christian Century* hoped the commission report would spell the end of the policy of the Balfour Declaration. It blasted the declaration as "a mischievous and ambiguous promise" that "could not be realized consistently with justice to other elements of the population."[55] Hertzel Fishman has analyzed as "passive" the prevailing attitude among American Protestants during this period toward a Jewish state in Palestine.[56]

Although premillenarians staunchly supported the restoration of Israel, they continued at the same time to be infected by the endemic anti-Semitism in American society. They continued to accept the phenomenon of anti-Semitism itself as prophetic, either due generally to the Jews' sins against God, or due particularly to their rejection of Jesus as the Messiah. Another aspect of the anti-Semitism of the premillenarians, the identification of Jews with radical movements, was reinforced by the controversy in the early 1920s over the legitimacy of *The Protocols of the Elders of Zion*. The *Protocols* was a forgery which purported to be a record of a Jewish conspiracy to rule the world. It included declarations such as the following:

> By the severity of our doctrines, we shall triumph and shall enslave all governments under our supergovernment. . . .
>
> Do not think that our assertions are without foundation: note the successes of Darwinism, Marxism and Nietzscheism *engineered by us. The demoralizing effects of these doctrines* upon the minds of the Gentiles should already be obvious to us. . . .
>
> We will present ourselves in the guise of saviours of the workers from oppression when we suggest that they enter our army of Socialists, Anarchists, Communists, to whom we always extend our hand under the guise of the rule of the brotherhood demanded by the human solidarity of our social masonry.[57]

In America the *Protocols* appeared in various papers in Boston and New York, but was given its widest circulation in a series of articles in Henry Ford's paper, the *Dearborn Independent,* and then issued collectively as *The International Jew.*[58]

Writing in the *Evangel,* one of the better-known premillenarians, D. M. Panton, assumed the *Protocols* to be legitimate.[59] The article, "The International Jew," by Charles C. Cook in *The King's Business* was a response of multiple prejudices. At first he blamed the Catholics:

> It is possible that it is all a clever piece of Roman Catholic propaganda, prompted by jealousy of the Jew for securing settlement in Palestine, with possible possession of its shrines and holy-places—and also a skillful move, on the part of Rome, to divert attention from its own ambitious plans to seize the world! We know that whatever the Jews are proposing in this respect Rome has far outspread them, for it has long been highly organized and functioning, and that its avowed purpose is to sit upon the throne of temporal power and give reality to the purport of the triple crown!

Cook was not sure that the *Protocols* was merely forged propaganda, however: "If they are forgeries, then they are among the cleverest specimens of deception ever devised, for even allowing the latest possible date of their production, there have been historical occurrences since that coincide exactly with the plan laid down in these documents, and the predictions contained therein." But given either verdict, Cook was "led to add the following reflections":

> The Jewish race is morally fully capable of doing all that is charged against it. It is at present rejected of God, and in a state of disobedience and rebellion. . . .
>
> As a race Jews are gifted far beyond all other peoples, and even in their ruin, with the curse of God upon them, are in the front rank of achievement; but accompanying traits are pride, overbearing arrogance, inordinate love for material things, trickery, rudeness and an egotism that taxes the superlatives of any language. Oppressed are they? Indeed, and subject to injustice more than any other race, and yet never learning the lesson of true humility. . . .
>
> These cheap adulations [of editors, ministers, and politicians] are usually based on no better foundations than self-interest, for the unregenerate Jew usually has a very unattractive personality. There is a reason for his being persona non grata at resorts and in the best society; who can deny it?[60]

Such a catalog of anti-Semitic attitudes was not the general rule, but the editorial policy that permitted it can neither be excused, nor reported without revulsion. The same journal earlier had explained the wave of anti-Semitism as a sign of the times, saying that Scripture showed "that a gathering of the Jews to Jerusalem must take place in a compulsory way, that God's wrath upon them will cause them to emigrate from the various countries to Jerusalem."[61] At another time, another explanation: "The self-malediction—'His blood be on us, and on our children' (Matt. 27:25)—has loosened unceasing judgment on the Jew down all the Gospel ages."[62] And still another view, this one citing the *Evangelical Witness:*

> The Christian is not swayed by these cross currents of racial animosity, but from his Guide Book he sees that in the final woes of this age judgment not only falls upon the Christ-rejecting Gentile nations, but in the convulsion of the peoples

> the Jew is made to drink a final draught from the cup of bitterness, when two-thirds of the nations will be wiped out in the time of Jacob's trouble. This chastisement of the Jew is the result of his own sins and national selfishness, as surely as the final judgment of the Gentiles is well merited by their godless career.[63]

Later, an even more curious situation—in view of the fact that Russia was predestined to invade Palestine, and try to recover it from the Jews—was explained:

> There are twenty-four Jews today trying to control Russia, and out of that has come the miserable mess that presents itself to the world. Why? Because no people, no individual and no nation can reject Christ and lay the foundations of a permanent government. It cannot be done.[64]

Thus the premillenarians justified the injustice to the Jews as ordained by the just judgment of God. Either "they asked for it!" or "they had it coming!" or "it was for their own good!" Not one stopped to consider Jesus' prayer on the cross: "Father, forgive them: for they know not what they do."

Whereas pervasive anti-Semitism was modified by love for the Jewish people as God's chosen people, the antipathy for Russia was not modified at all. There was particular confusion during this period, for Russia was identified with all forms of evil. It has been shown above that Russia was identified as being run by the Jews, while at the same time it was accused of anti-Semitism; the country was also identified as Antichrist, the leader of the revived Roman Empire, but simultaneously as Gog, the leader of the great northern confederation which was supposedly to fight *against* the Antichrist. In "The Red Terror," an article in the Biola publication, an evangelist pointed out the significance of identifying the color red with Russia and with the Antichrist. The two beasts in Revelation were supposedly Lenin and Trotsky, but Lenin was "simply the awful shadow of the great Red king that is surely coming to reign over a great Red world." This beast was to be ridden and controlled by a Red harlot. "This Red harlot symbolizes the coming world federation of religion. It will be a Red religion, a religion that will flaunt the Red flag of communism."[65] The more traditional interpretations had identified this harlot as the Catholics or as the liberal Protestants. Another article, "Christ and Antichrist in Russia," in the *Moody Monthly* cited a statement by "one of the best known of modern Russian philosophers," Soloviev, predicting that "Russia would develop into the kingdom of the Antichrist and with this development would come a personal Antichrist as ruler." The author believed this paralleled the Biblical picture of coming events.[66] Awareness of all this confusion about Russia's roles prompted one writer in *The King's Business* to confess, "There is such a diversity of opinion concerning Russian affairs, that one wonders whether anyone knows anything very definite about this mysterious country from the North," but there was no doubt in his mind that it was "destined to play [a large] part in the final assault upon Palestine when the battle of Armageddon is on."[67]

On the issue of whether the United States should diplomatically recognize Russia or not, the Moody paper printed a criticism of those who favored recognition and who claimed that the Russians were not carrying out a propaganda campaign in the United States and an atheistic campaign in Russia. The author cited Zinoviev, chairman of the Third International, as quoted by Izvestia: "Our propaganda necessarily includes the propagation of atheism which must now form one of the branches of our party activities." For the premillenarians, such a policy naturally precluded any possibility of recognition.[68] The *Evangel* likewise reported to its readers the anti-God campaigns in the Soviet Union.[69]

Developments in the Far East were depicted by the *Evangel* as "increasing indications of the end." The United States' Immigration Bill of 1924, which excluded Japanese immigration to America, was referred to as a "rebuff given by our Congress" which would drive the Japanese into an alliance with Russia. A similar result was expected from the coalition of the Chinese Nationalists with the Communists and their reliance on Soviet advisors. "Thus the way is being paved for the future alliance foreshadowed in the prophets, an alliance that leads to the invasion of a regenerated Palestine." All this signified the approaching end of the times of the Gentiles and the gathering of the armies of the earth to "fight together against the Son of God and perish at Armageddon."[70]

By 1927, the editor of the *Evangel* considered Armageddon as an increasingly imminent event; the cause was to be Russia's long-standing need for a warm water port in the Mediterranean: "We do not think the time is far off when the Russian bear will make another attempt to get water, and this time it will be to secure the sea coast of Palestine. The returning Jews have spent such vast sums in this land, that it is presenting a vast prize to greedy nations." He cited C. I. Scofield and James M. Gray as authorities for the identification of *Rosh* in Ezekiel 38 with Russia.[71] Another writer a year later also spoke of the nearness of Armageddon. Referring to Ezekiel 38, he said,

> Here you have read that Russia is going to war with Palestine. That is coming. . . . There is where we are to-day. Therefore, we may expect very shortly that this conflict will take place.[72]

Another explanation that was given for Russia's supposed interest in Palestine was the increasing awareness of the value of the mineral products in the Dead Sea.[73] God had supposedly reserved this wealth for the use of His restored people in the twentieth century.[74]

Premillenarian discussion of the great northern confederacy of Germany and Russia gained momentum in the 1920s, but would not peak until the Nazi-Soviet Pact of 1939. Speculation was stimulated by the Genoa Conference of 1922 which produced the Rapallo Treaty of 1922 between Russia and Germany, renewing diplomatic relations between the former belligerents and providing for economic and political co-operation. In its special section on "Notes Concerning Prophecy: And Signs of the Times," *The King's Business* at the time ran a subheading, "Russia-Germany Combine," which began with the assertion: "Prophetic students have long seen the probable formation in the near future of the great northern power spoken of in Scripture." It was assumed that the union was already a fact. "As to the union of Germanised Russia, and what it signifies, do we wonder, in the light of recent events and what is suspected, what the outcome will be?" What was "suspected" was that a military alliance existed between Russia and Germany, that German military officers were reorganizing the Russian army, and that the Krupp munition workers had been transferred to Russia to manufacture arms.[75] The *Evangel* explained that the reason for this "Russo-Teutonic" alliance was a future invasion of Palestine to exploit the "great financial structure" the foundations of which the returning Jews were already laying.[76]

This great confederacy was probably to be augmented by the hordes from the Far East, the "Red Peril" combining with the "Yellow Peril." Readers of the *Evangel* were told, "The fear of Teutonic vengeance disturbs the sleep of statesmen and the specter of a Russo-Germanic-Mongolian alliance lurks ever in the background of European politics."[77] On the authority of Arno C. Gaebelein's study of the Talmud the "Gomer" who accompanies "Gog" (Ezek. 38) was assuredly identified as Germany.[78] This idea was amplified by Leonard Sale-Harrison, whose popular writings included the book, *The Coming Great Northern Confederacy: or The Future of Russia and Germany,* which by 1928 was in its fourteenth edition. This work pointed out that the son of Gomer was Ashkenaz (Gen. 10:3) and that "it is very remarkable that the German-speaking Jews, one of the classes into which the Jews of the dispersion are divided, are called the 'Ashkenazim,' a masculine plural Hebrew word, which denotes the family or people of Ashkenaz, amongst whom they have been dispersed." Sale-Harrison also claimed that old German maps bore the name *Ashkenaz* or *Gomer* and that the modern name Germany had its origin as *Gomerland.* In reflecting upon the Rapallo Treaty he explained that "all the efforts that the Democratic Nations made to block the future Russo-German alliance were futile. This was prophesied to come to pass, and God's Word cannot fail." The actual attack upon Palestine was to come when the Jews had been gathered to their homeland; and since this was already happening, Sale-Harrison could conclude that "the day is not far distant when the actual conditions will be ripe for the fulfillment of this wonderful prophecy of Ezekiel 38."[79]

By the end of the decade, then, premillenarians believed that the Russo-German confederation was virtually an accomplished fact and that Armageddon was "not far off," "not far distant," or expected "very shortly." Such pessimistic fatalism had practical implications for the church which were quite explicitly drawn: "For the Church the issue is clear. She should not exhaust her powers fighting the battles of democracy at the polls or engaging in crusades in the vain hope of bringing world peace."[80] Such attitudes can be partially explained as a conservative reaction against the social gospel's emphasis upon the salvation of human *communities* rather than upon the rebirth of *individuals.* Nevertheless, the following assertion (which was made at the time of the Washington Disarmament Conference in 1922) can be understood only as a logical extension of theological pessimism: "It is true, many prayers were offered on Armistice Day for the divine guidance of the Disarmament Conference, but may we at this time consistently pray for world peace when the answer we seek would be in contradiction to God's program revealed in His Word?"[81] One wonders what had become of the psalmist's advice, "Pray for the peace of Jerusalem" (Ps. 122:6).

In the rush to Armageddon, a question arose in the 20s concerning who would fulfill the role of the Antichrist, the opponent of Russia. The contenders for the part (in this era) were the League of Nations and Mussolini. It must be kept in mind that the term *Antichrist* is used very loosely and broadly. John, the only writer to use the term, had said, "As ye have heard that antichrist shall come, even now are there many antichrists" (I John 2:18). Hence, the premillenarians could speak of communism or liberalism as embodying the spirit of Antichrist which was already at work in the world, while at the same time they expected a personal Antichrist who would somehow coincide with the other apocalyptic symbols, particularly in the Books of Daniel and Revelation. The formation of the League of Nations produced immediate speculation. The following appeared in the *Prophetic News* and the *Evangel,* and was reprinted in a collection which went through at least five editions:

> The World War thus originated by demon teachings has produced the result predicted in Revelation 16:14. It has gathered together all the kings of the earth and of the whole world. It has gathered them into a league of nations which will become the preparation of the nations for Armageddon. The gathering or leaguing of the nations together is the signal that the end is in sight. The Peace Conference at Paris had unconsciously set the stage for Antichrist and Armageddon.[82]

The King's Business devoted an entire article to the League in which it was depicted as the continuation of the Roman Empire that is supposedly symbolized in the image of Nebuchadnezzar's dream (Dan. 2). The feet of the image are composed of iron and clay. "The toes of the feet indicate the federation of ten kingdoms of nations which now occupy the territory which composed the ancient Roman Empire. . . . The League of Nations is composed of iron and clay." This symbol was in turn tied in with the Beast of the Apocalypse: "The man who will finally dominate the World League of Nations will be the Politico-Beast described in Daniel, and in the Book of Revelation. He is the Anti-Christ!"[83] This revived Roman Empire was specifically elaborated upon in an article in the *Evangel* which detailed how the European countries were shuffling territories which had, or had not, been part of the ancient empire; England had lost Ireland, which had not been part of the empire; Germany had lost Alsace-Lorraine and was losing the Ruhr, which had been part of the empire; Austria and Hungary had lost the territory south of the Danube, which had been; and, of course, "God was behind all." There was even a reason given for the rapid withdrawal of American troops after the war: "They have no right there according to prophecy, as America was never part of the Roman Empire."[84]

The dynamic rise of the flamboyant Mussolini, however, soon focused premillenarian interest upon Rome itself as the center of the revived empire. Christabel Pankhurst listed the "reappearance on the map of the lines of ancient Rome" as one of the signs of the end of the age. She assessed the significance of this development: "Current international events are assuredly finger posts to Armageddon, the last great conflict before Jesus, the Prince of Peace, banishes war from the earth."[85] By 1925, the *Evangel* was enthusiastic: "Bible students have long watched for the first signs of the revival of the old Roman Empire." Mussolini was referred to as "the strongest character in world politics today" and the restoration of the empire meant that "the climax is near."[86] One writer even conceived of the converging of both contenders for the role of Antichrist:

> Why, therefore, should it be thought incredible that a revived Roman Empire may be in process of formation as another link in the wonderful chain of events of the last days? May

> it not be that Mussolini's dream will affect the future of the present League of Nations? Who can tell? The one thing that would give power to the League would be the presence of a strong personality who would force himself by circumstances to its leadership; or a new Roman combine of nations may draw to itself those destined to form part of that confederacy which will for a time dominate Europe and wield the despotic power of the Anti-Christ.[87]

This combination was not ruled out in an article that appeared somewhat later in *The King's Business,* "Christ and Antichrist." Both the League of Nations and the revival of Rome were depicted as part of the plan of Antichrist.[88]

Oswald J. Smith, the influential pastor of People's Church, Toronto, expected the appearance of the Antichrist within a couple years. Writing in the *Evangel* in 1926, he told of a prophecy made by a Rabbi Michael in 1868 which had predicted a great war in about 1913—close enough for World War I. The rabbi had also predicted the emancipation of the Russian Jews, which Smith saw in the overthrow of the Czar. But the most significant prophecy was the complete redemption of Israel by 1928, which coincided with the speculation of other prophetic students.[89] Smith himself drew no specific conclusion, but the implication was clear—only two years were left. In 1927, the *Evangel* readers were informed that Mussolini had announced the revival of the Roman Empire: "Thus the dream of the revival of the ancient Roman Empire is a dream no longer."[90] But only nine months later, at least one *Evangel* writer did not share this confidence. In an article entitled "Mussolini: Is the World Preparing for Antichrist?" the conclusion was drawn that Mussolini was probably not the Antichrist, even though he was certainly preparing the way for Antichrist.[91] Such speculation continued to be popular even through the next decade.

With Armageddon so close at hand, Americans naturally wondered if the United States would be involved in the great conflagration. Since America had not been able to avoid involvement in World War I and had now taken an increasing role in international affairs, it did seem likely that such a momentous event would entangle the United States. Many who believed in the literalistic fulfillment of prophecy discovered symbols they could ascribe to the United States. The *Evangel* reprinted a piece from the *Jewish*

Missionary Magazine entitled, "The Shadow of Armageddon: Will America Take Part in the Conflict?" It proclaimed: "That the United States will be involved is plain from Ezek. 38:13, where Britain is referred to under the figure of 'the merchants of Tarshish with *all* the young lions thereof.' In that word *all* we see the place of our land in prophecy, for no one can deny that Britain is the modern land of the lion symbol or that our nation is a young lion of Britain."[92] A very high recommendation was given to a book by Reginald T. Naish, *The Midnight Hour and After!* Between 1920 and 1928 it went through seven editions totaling 50,000 copies. Naish's chapter on "Armageddon" explained that the merchants of Tarshish clearly stood for "a great trading nation." Therefore, "when we learn that this trading or shopkeeping nation has 'young lions' belonging to her, we can hardly doubt but that Great Britain and her colonies are intended to be described."[93] Such leaps in reasoning—from Tarshish to Britain and from lions to colonies—were perhaps in keeping with a long tradition of apocalyptic speculation, but hardly in line with a commitment to literalism.

A similar theme appeared in a sermon delivered at a Keswick conference and reprinted in various publications including *Christ Life, The King's Business,* and *Moody Monthly.* The question, "Does the United States Appear in Prophecy?" is answered, "Probably." The key passage is Isaiah 18, particularly the first two verses: "Woe to the land shadowing with wings, which is beyond the rivers of Ethiopia: that sendeth ambassadors by the sea, even in vessels of bulrushes upon the waters, saying, Go, ye swift messengers, to a nation scattered and peeled, to a people terrible from their beginning hitherto; a nation meted out and trodden down, whose land the rivers have spoiled!" Discarding the standard view that the reference is to Egypt, the author says that the wings denote the spread eagle; and since the United States is the only country which has an eagle with spread wings as its insignia, it must be the land in question. Besides, only very important countries send ambassadors by the sea; this would rule out Egypt. The author corroborates his thesis by pointing to the reference to "young lions" in Ezekiel 38:13.[94]

And so it was that ten years after the peace treaty and ten years before another war would burst forth, the premillenarians faced a clear and present danger of war from which America could not escape. The lion and eagle were destined to stand with God and fight Beasts and bear on behalf of God's chosen children. One 1929 article, "The Spiritual Values of Armageddon," quite aptly summarized premillenarian concern over the momentous spiritual forces struggling in the universe.

> In an article in *The Sunday School Times* of May 7, 1927, the writer pointed out how the political situation in Palestine is shaping itself for that very struggle; Great Britain and the signatories of the League of Nations pledged to defend Palestine in case of invasion, while Russia and the newborn Asiatic League of Nations hang like a threatening war cloud on her northern horizon and turn envious eyes on the vast potential and actual wealth of that little land which trusts in the protection of the hated merchants of Tarshish or capitalistic nations. Ezek. 38:9-13. . . .
>
> Now suppose Russia should invade Palestine. This would be not merely a challenge to the order of things existing among the nations, but a challenge to God's purpose and order. It would provide a clean-cut test of Russia's national morality. Jehovah has promised Palestine to the seed of Abraham forever, Gen. 13:15; 15:18. The title lies in openly preserved documents for any one to read. If Russia tried with eyes open to amend the covenant, would not this be a declaration of war against Jehovah, the most immoral act of which a nation could be guilty? And all the nations who abetted her would share in her guilt.[95]

Balfour Betrayed

And in this hour, authoritative voices in every land are telling us in no uncertain tones that it is not a matter of years, but of months, when the battle flags of the nations will again unfurl, and the scourge of the earth will be on the march— to Armageddon!

—Louis S. Bauman, *The King's Business,* 1934

The present return of the Jews to their own land is but the beginning of that prophesied. . . . It will gather momentum as the months go by, but this is certainly the regathering prophesied as the final one, which is a remarkable and unmistakable sign that we are in the latter days.

—Leonard Sale-Harrison
Moody Bible Institute Monthly, 1936

The menace of the 1930s arms race was the concern of the whole world, but for the premillenarians it was the preparation for Armageddon. Moreover, Armageddon itself was hailed as a "wonderful" and "glorious" fulfillment of prophecy. The apogee of rising expectations was reached with the Nazi-Soviet Pact of

1939, an event which was a perfect rendezvous with prior premillenarian forecasts. Premillenarian hopes, however, would soon be aborted in 1941 when Hitler invaded Russia, temporarily ditching their prospects of a great northern confederation of Gomer and the Russian bear "clawing at the gates of Jerusalem." The rising storm of Nazi anti-Semitism had brought waves of new immigration to Palestine in the mid-thirties, vindicating premillenarian faith in the inexorable restoration of Israel, but by the end of the decade there were cries against Britain's betrayal of the Balfour Declaration—she was attempting to limit the number of immigrants.

"Has Britain betrayed the Jew?" was a question asked even in 1931. Keith Brooks, editor of the nondenominational monthly, *Prophecy,* showed concern about the report of the commission which had been appointed as a result of the 1929 riots at the Wailing Wall. He did not believe that the Jews had been betrayed intentionally, but that England's attempt at conciliation had been fraught with miserable blunders. "The decision of the wailing wall commission is evidence of this folly."[1] An article in *The King's Business,* "Palestine Is for the Jew," also discussed the commission's recommendations that Jews be made to understand that the Wailing Wall belonged to the Moslems, that Jews might worship there under certain restrictions, and that no benches or screens were to be used. Observing that the Arab-Jewish question was "by no means settled," the author asserted:

> But the end is determined. Palestine is for the Jew. The land is Israel's—not by reason of Great Britain's pledge, but by divine decree. The Abrahamic covenant, not the Balfour Declaration, is the Jewish Magna Charta to the land of Palestine.[2]

Charles G. Trumbull, editor of *The Sunday School Times,* cited the much more positive response of *The Advent Witness* to the situation. In a curious interpretation, it was noted that the Wailing Wall is mentioned in Scripture: "Their heart cried unto the Lord, O wall of the daughter of Zion, let tears run down like a river day and night: give thyself no rest; let not the apple of thine eye cease" (Lam. 2:18). The question was then posed: "Why has God for the first time allowed man to impose silence on His ancient people and thus interfere with the inspired word of His servant

Jeremiah, 'Let tears run down like a river day and night'?" The response was a rhetorical question, reflecting the silver lining which the premillenarians discovered in even the darkest clouds: "Are we not justified in believing that something remarkable will happen soon concerning the Jew, the Temple area site, and that ancient Wailing (Western) Wall?"[3] Perhaps an even more appropriate figure than the silver lining would be the one which the premillenarians themselves frequently used, "The darkest part of the night is just before the dawn."

The various periodicals continued to lament the plight of the Jews in their conflict with the Arabs and in their dealings with the British. The *Evangel* reported that there were strong protests against the anti-Jewish attitude of the Royal Commission that had investigated the 1929 riots, and then approvingly cited the policy recommendations of Hamilton Fish of the House Committee on Foreign Relations: "The re-establishment of a Jewish National Home is a moral obligation assured by the governments of the world with Great Britain as the executor of that obligation. She must administer that obligation in the sense accepted by other people or she must confess her inability to do so, so that proper action may be taken."[4] Aaron Judah Kligerman, writing in the *Moody Monthly,* admitted that the historical position of the church for centuries had been that the Jews had lost their chance and that there was to be no restoration of a national Israel, but only a spiritual Israel—the church. He proceeded to establish the "true" teaching of Scripture—that the restoration was yet in the future. Kligerman then asserted that the restoration had already begun with the Balfour Declaration:

> There may be much politics connected with that declaration. England may not be sincere. The Arab may be stirred again and much more blood may yet be shed. Be as these may, I believe that "he that scattered Israel will gather him, and keep him, as a shepherd doth his flock" (Jer. 31:10).[5]

The *Christian* speculated that the "awful blow" of the Jewish setbacks might cause them to turn to God.[6] The extreme literalism of the *Evangel* interpreted the attempt to limit immigration as the fulfillment of Isaiah 27:12, "Ye shall be gathered *one by one,* O ye children of Israel."[7] *The King's Business* expressed a very moderate opinion (for premillenarians), apportioning partial blame for the situation to the Jews themselves.

> As in most unfortunate incidents, there has been fault on both sides. It is quite evident that the Jew has not come to Palestine to live with the Arab, but quite apart from him. The Jew in Palestine is frequently bigoted, and often carries "a chip on his shoulder." It is well known that the Jews themselves were partly to blame for the riots of 1929. But this does not justify the Arab for his falsehoods which helped to incite the trouble, nor for the murder of men, and even women and children, of which he is guilty. It was an Arab massacre, in which Jews sought to defend themselves.

The author then argued for a Jewish national home on a pragmatic basis—to prevent them from turning to Bolshevism, but he recognized that the Arabs had to be provided for too. Even such moderation in the premillenarian camp did not prevent the conclusion that the end was predetermined and the confident assertion that "the Jewish nation is to have a future in Palestine."[8]

Various elements of the restoration continued to be interpreted as prophetic signs of the times. The revival of the Hebrew language was seen as a fulfillment of prophecy. Writing in *The King's Business,* Louis S. Bauman said:

> The renaissance of the Hebrew language is one of the most striking present fulfillments of the prophetic Word. Hear the prophecy:
>
> "Therefore wait ye upon me, saith the Lord . . . my determination is to gather the nations, that I may assemble the kingdoms, to pour upon them mine indignation."
>
> That means Armageddon's battlefield. But, when the nations are marshalling their hosts for their last awful conflict, the Almighty says: "Then will I turn to the people a pure language, that they may call upon the name of the Lord." See Zeph. 3:8, 9.[9]

Bauman was pastor of the Open Bible Church in Los Angeles and was on the faculty of the Bible Institute of Los Angeles. His articles and books were in turn cited in various other premillenarian publications.

Other particular events, such as the first oil line from Iraq to Haifa and the revival of a militaristic spirit among the Jews, were also considered significant. In 1935 appeared a booklet by

George T. B. Davis entitled *Rebuilding Palestine According to Prophecy*. It was a virtual catalog of the economic developments in Palestine together with appropriate Scriptural forecasts.

Determinism according to prophecy was the consistent response to every conflict. In 1933 and 1934 the Arabs rioted against both the British and the Jews. *Our Hope* observed that it was a mistake for the Arabs to think that they could dislodge the Jews: "Zionism is no longer an experiment. The Jews will not only remain in Palestine, but they will expand and the population will increase."[10] The *Evangel* commented on British attempts to restrict immigration: "One may as well attempt to destroy the solar system as attempt to hinder God's plan for his people. Jer. 31: 35-37."[11] "We need not guess, or be ignorant concerning Israel's future, for it is the one nation whose history has been written in advance."[12] This same theme was the subject of a collection of articles, *The Jew and His Destiny,* by Edward Hilary Mosely. He stated that "the Jew furnishes the key with which we may unlock the meaning of all history."[13] D. M. Panton quoted the German philosopher Hegel: "The history of the Jew is a dark, troublesome enigma to me. I am not able to understand it. It does not fit in with any of our categories. It is a riddle." To this Panton added: "Moreover, it is the key, and the only key, to all history."[14] Such determinism was based upon literalism; the *Evangel* reported a story that the directors of Lloyd's Bank of London had been skeptical about granting a $2,500,000 loan to the Jewish Agency, but when the president of the bank read to them Ezekiel 37, they voted unanimously to grant the loan. The implied message: even wise businessmen interpret the Scriptures literally.[15]

In February, 1934, the *Evangel* reminded its readers that H. Grattan Guinness had calculated that the fulfillment of Daniel's prophecies would occur in 1917, 1923, or 1934, and asked the question, "What Will 1934 Bring?"[16] The lesson was drawn that if the end was near for Israel, it was even nearer for the church, so people should work and pray. In the first issue of 1935 it was observed that many had thought that the Lord would return in 1934. Then was provided the enlightening information that in 1909 Guinness had written another book, *On the Rock,* in which he had calculated that the end would occur in 1945 instead of 1934. The advice of Jesus (frequently forgotten by the premillenarians) was recited: "Be ye therefore ready also, for the Son of man cometh at an hour when ye think not."[17] The question quite naturally arises: Why had no one mentioned Guinness' more recent book before? Apparently this would not have served the purpose of premillenarian writers; one cannot terrorize people into the Kingdom of God with predictions of retribution some ten years hence.

Because of pressures in Europe, particularly in Nazi Germany, Jewish immigration in 1935 (under relaxed immigration rules) reached a record of 61,834.[18] For the Arabs, too, this was a foreboding sign of the times—and they protested by a general strike in April, 1936. The premillenarian attitude towards the situation was predictable. In that same year the Southern Baptists published two books by the Jewish Christian, Jacob Gartenhaus—*What of the Jews?* and *The Rebirth of a Nation: Zionism in History and Prophecy.* The response of Gartenhaus to the Palestine problems is representative of premillenarian fatalism: "The Jew will have Palestine with or without the help of Britain or any other nation on the earth! When and how this will come about, we do not know; but come about it will!"[19] He asserted what the proper attitude toward the Zionist movement should be: "To oppose it is to oppose God's plan."[20] Gartenhaus blindly supported the Zionist movement. The main problem in adopting this attitude is that even if the end (the restoration of Israel) is accepted as a legitimate objective, the end does not justify the means. Such an attitude was hardly in keeping with traditional Christian ethical systems.

The extreme self-confidence of Gartenhaus was reflected in Leonard Sale-Harrison's article that same year in *Moody Monthly,* "The Approaching Combination of Nations As It Affects Palestine." It was inconceivable to these premillenarians that history might go on for a while. Sale-Harrison asserted: "The present return of the Jews to their own land is but the beginning of that prophesied in this passage [Ezekiel 37]. It will gather momentum as the months go by, but this is *certainly* the regathering prophesied as the *final one,* which is a remarkable and unmistakable sign that we are in the latter days."[21] Even what was apparently meant by the *Evangel* to be an understatement of this premillenarian attitude has proved to be mistaken. In 1933 it reported the thirty-three-year lease of 17,500 acres for colonization by the Jews with an option to renew the lease for two additional periods of thirty-three years. The writer then blithely editorialized: "We believe that, long before the first thirty-three years expire, the Divine Ruler will come who will give them the land *forever.* Ezek. 37:25-28."[22]

Fulfillment of prophecy was not the only basis of premillenarian support for the restoration; there were also selfish motivations. As the *Evangel* bluntly put it, "Some may ask, 'What is the practical value to us of all these things happening to the Jews?' There is much value: for great blessing comes to the Gentiles in the restoration of the Jews."[23] Zechariah 8:23 was cited as supporting evidence: "In those days shall it come to pass, that ten men . . . shall take hold of the skirt of him that is a Jew, saying, We will go with you: for we have heard that God is with you." But according to the usual premillenarian interpretation of this passage—certainly according to *The Scofield Reference Bible*—this refers to a time after the church has been taken out of the world. Hence whatever happens to the Jews at that time will be of value to "the Gentiles," but certainly too late to be of any "practical value" to the church.

Another argument was an appeal to American nationalism: "Every nation on the face of the earth that has persecuted and mistreated the Jew has had to pay for it. . . . That is the reason America is enjoying more prosperity than the rest of the world." It was also explained that the real reason the Czar had been shot by the Bolsheviks was his terrible treatment of the Jews.[24] In a 1938 comment on President Roosevelt's decision to allow Jewish refugees from Germany to come to America, the *Evangel* stated: "Nations, like individuals, reap as they sow. And we are confident that the nation which grants refuge to the wandering sheep of the house of Israel shall in nowise lose its reward." This expectation of reward was based on Genesis 12:3: "I will bless them that bless thee, and curse him that curseth thee."[25]

This same argument was used in opposing Britain's decision to limit Jewish immigration to Palestine. *Moody Monthly* prophesied doom: "Pharaoh issued a similar edict in Egypt some millenniums ago, but it worked more disastrously for the Egyptians than the Hebrews, and we predict that history will repeat itself." This editorial was the occasion for an interesting exchange with a reader. The editor had observed that the Jewish minority in Palestine would never quietly submit to the will of the Arab majority there.[26] One reader took issue in a letter to the editor, saying it was not easy to see why the majority should not rule in Palestine just as they did in democracies in the United States and the United Kingdom. The editor's terse rebuttal was a straightforward statement of the premillenarian mind which believes that the normal rules of international law do not apply to the Jews.

> The British limitation of the Jewish population in Palestine is doubtless good human statesmanship for the time being, but when Great Britain or any other nation begins to deal with the Jew in Palestine it enters on supernatural territory, and the ordinary rules of statesmanship do not work.
>
> Our friend thinks that the Jews in their God-given land should govern themselves, or be governed by the principles that maintain in a democracy like the United States; but with all his intelligence and piety he has read the Scriptures to small purpose when he thus thinks. The Jews were, are, and always shall remain a peculiar people, and the reason why a "reversion" should be "sanctioned" in their case, and why it certainly will come to pass, is because Jehovah has so ordained it.[27]

This idea, that God blesses those who help the Jews and curses those who oppose them, regardless of circumstances, was also a major theme of Louis S. Bauman's 1934 book, *Shirts and Sheets*.[28]

There is some irony in these suggestions of the proper direction for governmental policy, for the premillenarians along with other conservative Christian groups opposed church involvement in politics and social action as advocated by the liberal churches—the so-called social gospel. But this kind of issue involved premillenarians at a very deep emotional level. They had likewise involved themselves in the political issue of national prohibition during the 1920s and early 30s and to a lesser extent (in the periodical literature, at least) in opposing the Catholic presidential candidate, Al Smith, in the 1928 election. By and large, however, they were reluctant to let their approval or disapproval of policies grow to the level of political action.[29]

The persecution of Jews in Nazi Germany stimulated discussion of anti-Semitism in the mid-thirties and thereafter. Premillenarian views continued to be ambivalent. On the one hand, there remained an undercurrent of anti-Semitism as in American culture in general, but on the other, there existed a theological reaction against it. Arthur D. Morse in his 1967 book, *While Six Million Died,* has lamented the lack of any moral outcry by Christianity against these Nazi horrors.[30] But among the premillenarians there was seen no need for moral indignation against the persecution, since they had been expecting it. The *Evangel* responded to German anti-Jewish propaganda by referring readers to God's warning to Israel in Deuteronomy 28:15, 37: "But it shall come to pass, if thou wilt not hearken unto the voice of the Lord thy God, to observe to do all his commandments and his statutes which I command thee this day; that all these curses shall come upon thee, and overtake thee. . . . And thou shalt become an astonishment, a proverb, and a byword, among all nations whither the Lord shall lead thee." German anti-Semitism was accordingly seen as a fulfillment of prophecy: "Israel is out of place, and is therefore a source of irritation to the Gentile nations, instead of being a blessing, as God intended that they should be."[31]

Another comment regarding the general European anti-Semitism depicted these developments as part of the on-going plan of God for the nation; they were "Foregleams of Israel's Tribulation." Premillennialists were anticipating the Great Tribulation, "the time of Jacob's trouble." Therefore, they predicted, "The next scene in Israel's history may be summed up in three words: purification through tribulation."[32] It was clear that although this purification was part of the curse, God did not intend that Christians should participate in it. Clear, also, was the implication that He did intend for the Germans to participate in it (in spite of the fact that it would bring them punishment)—and that any moral outcry against Germany would have been in opposition to God's will. In such a fatalistic system, to oppose Hitler was to oppose God.[33]

Wilbur M. Smith writing in *Moody Monthly* predicted that "all Europe will yet be fevered with this poison of anti-Semitism." In his view this poison would force the Jews to immigrate to Palestine where the final great surge of anti-Semitism would be the invasion by "the king of the North"; and in desperation the Jews would then turn to Jehovah for deliverance.[34] For the premillenarian, the massacre of Jewry expedited his blessed hope. Certainly he did not rejoice over the Nazi holocaust, he just fatalistically observed it as a "sign of the times." Even the moderation toward the restoration expressed by the editor of *The Alliance Weekly* produced the same result—"wait and see."

> Are we looking today upon the beginning of the last sifting process? In the light of world movements it seems as if that were likely. Anti-Semitism was never so rampant or so widespread, even in the darkest times of the middle ages. But we cannot be dogmatic in the matter. Palestine is being prepared, but is not yet ready for the final reception. We shall wait and see.[35]

In 1934 Biola's Louis S. Bauman offered an extended discussion of anti-Semitism in *Shirts and Sheets: or Anti-Semitism, a Present-day Sign of the First Magnitude.* This book was a fair representation of the ambiguity of the premillenarian attitude toward the Jews. Bauman's basic theme was opposition to persecution of the Jews, yet he believed God had permitted persecution because of the Jews' self-condemnation at Jesus' crucifixion: "His blood be on us, and on our children" (Matt. 27:25). He placed part of the blame for anti-Semitism on the Jews: "The Jew is the world's archtroubler. Most of the Revolutions of Continental Europe were fostered by Jews."[36] The Jews—especially the German Jews—were responsible for the great depression. Even worse days of terrible judgment were to come, yet God would judge the nations that persecuted them. It was all a glorious sign of the first magnitude.

> Foolishly, the nations are becoming anti-Semitic, providing the cause for Armageddon. Frantically, the nations are running their munitions factories day and night, preparing the weapons for Armageddon. Fearfully, the nations are shuddering as they meditate upon the imminency and the sure horrors of Armageddon. Hopefully, however, the *saints* look forward to the day *after* Armageddon when the ages-long night shall give place to the glorious sunrise of the new age.[37]

These many crosscurrents were summarized in "Hands Off," a poem by R. H. McCartney which Bauman included in his treatise.[38]

Hands off, ye fools! Beware of what you do—
To man or nation, 'tis most surely true
A curse on those who persecute the Jew!
Ye have not marked him—surely 'tis his God—
He standeth now beneath chastising rod—
Yet greatest rebel on the earthly sod!
Jehovah set apart, and not in vain
With a more fatal mark than once on Cain
For centuries the butt of grief and pain.
They had been sinners—surely sinners great;
Jehovah chose them for a high estate
That they to earth His glory should relate:
To stand His witnesses to near and far—
Who to earth's night should be a glorious star
To give hope to a world that sin did mar!
When all the world a whoring from Him went—
Debauchery and wickedness man's sole intent;
'Twas then Jehovah in His sovereign grace,
Took by the hand, to have one chosen race,
To set the Jew before the wide world's face!
They were to be His monuments of grace,
His priests, His witnesses to human race—
Head of all nations during time and space. . . .

Hands off, O Gentile! or be grief your dower—
They still are girdled by Jehovah's power;
Who else could keep them for a gracious hour?
Tho' curse be on them yet—and they must go
To ghastly depths of suffering and woe—
Yet woe to hand who shall that woe bestow!
Hands off, I say, for lo, Jehovah still
Hath a high place, now wretched Jews shall fill—
And none can hinder that—what is His will! . . .

A renovated world—a new-born earth—
No curse of sickness, nor a case of dearth,
A world of happiness, and song, and mirth!
Lo, then the Jew once more takes highest place;
The priests, the leaders of the human race—
But, then, blood-washed in Christ's atoning grace,
Of former evil in the Jew—no trace!
A heaven on earth shall be in every space—
And earth behold—
THE GLORY OF CHRIST'S FACE!

The irony of the "Hands Off" attitude was that it resulted in closing the eyes or looking the other way as the German "final solution" of Jewish extermination developed. Pleas from Europe for assistance for Jewish refugees fell on deaf ears, and "Hands Off" meant no helping hand. So in spite of being theologically more pro-Jewish than any other Christian group, the premillenarians also were apathetic—because of a residual anti-Semitism, because persecution was prophetically expected, because it would encourage immigration to Palestine, because it seemed the beginning of the Great Tribulation, and because it was a wonderful sign of the imminent blessed hope.

The Nazi persecution also stimulated new interest in *The Protocols of the Elders of Zion.* Arno C. Gaebelein in his book, *The Conflict of the Ages: The Mystery of Lawlessness: Its Origin, Historic Development and Coming Defeat,* seemed to provide legitimacy for the Nazi attitude. He ridiculed claims that the *Protocols* had been proved a forgery and emphasized that the whole program of conspiracy was actually being carried out by the Russian Communists. He claimed that "a painstaking and deeper study of the Protocols compared with present day world conditions, must lead, and does lead, to the conviction, that the plan of the Protocols, whoever concocted it, is not a *crude forgery.* Behind it are hidden, unseen actors, powerful and cunning, who follow the plan still, bent on the overthrow of our civilization."[39] Thomas M. Chalmers writing in *The King's Business* also saw Satan's hand in the *Protocols;* however, he assured his readers that Satan was using it, not to destroy "our civilization," but to stir up hatred of the Jews themselves, trying to exterminate God's chosen people. This was not a moral wrong to be resisted, however: "Since Satan has advanced so far in his murderous campaign, we may expect all nations to join in this warfare."[40]

In *Shirts and Sheets,* Louis S. Bauman spoke of the *Protocols* as a divisive issue among premillenarians; but he refused to take sides as to whether it was a forgery or not, saying that it did not make any difference anyway, for even if it were legitimate, it represented the views of only a small group of Jews and was no stigma upon the whole race.[41] *Time* magazine carried a report that the *Protocols* was being distributed by Moody Bible Institute.[42] Although this was denied by the institute, apparently *Time's* editor believed it to be a credible possibility. The *Evangel* consistently condemned the document as a forgery, but even in 1935 (as if the *Protocols* were authentic) reported the reading of a paper criticizing the document before the Prophecy Investigation Society —it still remained a viable issue.[43] Even by the end of the decade, a leading light of the premillenarians, William Bell Riley, could still accept the *Protocols* as genuine.[44] It is impossible, of course, to assess the extent to which the *Protocols* deceived and thus influenced the attitudes of the premillenarians, but the firmness with which a paper like the *Evangel* opposed the prejudices aroused by the document indicates this was a serious problem.

Just as the *Protocols* seemed to be a perennial concern, rumors of the impending rebuilding of the Temple also flourished. In 1931, it was reported that the Jews had applied to the League of Nations for an allotment of land in the heart of Jerusalem to rebuild the *Temple*.[45] The probable basis of this story was the plan for a synagogue—hardly a new Temple.[46] The next year a similar discussion of the possibility of rebuilding included the recounting of an earlier attempt by the Roman Emperor Julian to rebuild the Temple in A.D. 368. The Roman historian Ammianus Marcellinus had reported that those efforts were frustrated by the appearance of mysterious balls of fire which prevented the workmen from building.[47] Julian was warned by Christians that the Temple could not be rebuilt until the Antichrist appeared. In commenting on this story the *Evangel* said, "The two sanctuaries—the Church and the Temple—cannot coexist (it would seem) in the gospel era, although they over-lapped in its opening decades."[48] It was implied that since the Temple was about to be rebuilt, the Antichrist must be even more imminent. Arno C. Gaebelein reiterated the tale that young men of the tribe of Levi were being trained in preparation for reinstitution of the ancient temple rituals.[49] In 1936, *Dawn* magazine spread the report that Rabbi L. J. Schwefel, lecturing in Denver for the Jewish National Fund of America, had predicted, "Eventually the Temple of Solomon will be built in Palestine."[50] A similar story was cited from *The British Weekly,* which quoted Lord Melchett as saying, "The day in which the Temple will be rebuilt is nigh, and I will work for the rest of my life to rebuild Solomon's Temple in the place of the Mosque of Aksa."[51] Evangelist Charles S. Price greeted such a prospect with relish: "When the Jew under the protection of some great power—(for they could not do it alone) tears down the Moslem Mosque of Omar and builds his temple, then the Moslem world will gnash its teeth in rage."[52] He continued:

> Even if the Jews were driven out they would soon come back. Their temple has to be built. The House of the Lord has to be established. As long as the many Arabs or Moslems remain in Palestine such a thing would be impossible. But remember that in spite of what dictators, nations, empires or confederacies might do to prevent it, this has to be brought about because the Word of the Lord has proclaimed it.

Preacher Price then broke forth into an ecstatic song of Israel's hope:

> Back to the land where we lived long ago,
> Where Jordan rolled south to the plain,
> Out of our exile to Abraham's home
> Our God is to bring us again.
> With marble and cedar and silver and gold
> Our temple will once again raise
> Its glorious head, while we worship within
> And the God of deliverance praise.[53]

Although the prospect of a rebuilt Temple was not one of the major concerns of the premillenarian mind, it foreshadowed the premillenarian interest in the outcome of the battles over the Holy City in 1948 and 1967—a Jewish Jerusalem was a necessary prerequisite to a rebuilt Temple.

The Allenby legend also persisted during the 30s and was further embellished. *Prophecy* picked up a story from the *London Daily Telegraph* that General Allenby had been disappointed with his transfer from the western front to Egypt, saying, "The last man failed, and I do not see why I should succeed." He had been reassured, however, by General Beauvoir de Lisle, who referred him to the prophecy in H. Grattan Guinness' book, *Light for the Last Days,* which pointed to 1917 as the year of the deliverance of Jerusalem. "Allenby was much impressed by a prophecy which was to prove so remarkably accurate," according to *Prophecy*.[54] The editor of *The Sunday School Times* recounted that C. I. Scofield had written on the occasion of Allenby's capture of Jerusalem, "Now for the first time we have a real prophetic sign."[55] William Bell Riley claimed that even Allenby's strategy had been prophesied. The Turks had surrendered the city out of fear of the airplanes flying overhead. This fulfilled the prophecy of Isaiah 31:5: "As birds flying, so will the Lord of hosts defend Jerusalem; defending also he will deliver it; and passing over he will preserve it."[56] Encouraged by the large number of what they considered fulfilled prophecies, the premillenarians anticipated further fulfillments.

In response to the Arab strike and terrorist activities of 1936, the British sent a Royal Commission to Palestine to investigate. Headed by Earl Peel, the commission reported on July 7, 1937, that the differences between Arabs and Jews were irreconcilable and recommended the partition of Palestine into two independent states. The cities of Jerusalem, Bethlehem and Nazareth were to be in a separate mandated area under British control. The Arab Higher Committee rejected the proposal and eventually the British government also concluded it to be impractical. The premillenarian response was varied. The *Evangel* initially cited one writer who interpreted the partition as an obstruction of the prophetic scheme because God had promised the land to Israel (not Ishmael) and had promised to make the Jews one nation (not two states).[57] Ten weeks later the *Evangel* quoted from the *Advent Herald,* which found the partition to be a fulfillment of Zechariah 13:8: "And it shall come to pass that in all the land, saith the Lord, *two parts* therein shall be cut off and die (the land—two thirds—will languish under Arab control) but *the third* shall be left therein."[58] Partition was also depicted as the fulfillment of Joel 3:1, 2: "For, behold, in those days, and in that time, when I shall bring again the captivity of Judah and Jerusalem, I will also gather all nations, and will bring them down into the valley of Jehoshaphat, and will plead with them there for My people and for My heritage Israel, whom they have scattered among the nations, and *parted* my land."[59] At one point Britain seemed to be extolled for establishing the independent state of Israel; at another she was castigated for fulfilling this passage and playing the role of Antichrist.[60] Here is another illustration of the dilemma of the premillenarians—whether to apply the test of ethics or the test of determinism. With Britain they were not consistent, whereas with Russia they regularly applied the rule of ethics while with Israel they always measured by the rule of determinism.

During the 1930s, liberal American Protestants found the idea of a Jewish state repugnant. Opposition to the suggested partition was one manifestation of this attitude. Hertzel Fishman noted that from the theological position of liberal Protestants "the notion of a sovereign Jewish state was simply too unpalatable to digest. The idea of a resurrected 'old Israel' was too radical to accept."[61] The *Christian Century* spoke out on the ethical injustice of the partition plan which would transfer 225,000 Arabs out of their ancestral homeland.[62] Evidently the premillenarians did not even consider such a problem.

Throughout the decade, premillenarians continued to be almost uniformly anti-Arab. The basic postulate of their position was that the Holy Land belonged to God and that He had given it to the Jews. The following argument appeared just after the 1929 riots under the heading: "Who Has the Strongest Title?"

> At a recent meeting of Arabs at Haifa, Captain R. G. Canning stated: "The soil of Palestine belongs to the Arabs, and it has been so since 630 or even before. Is not that a good enough title?"
>
> In the year 1857 B.C., Abraham said unto Eliezer his servant: "The Lord God of heaven sware unto me saying, unto thy seed will I give this land." And Eliezer testified to Laban and Bethuel, "Sarah, my master's wife, bare a son to my master when she was old: and *unto him hath he given all that he hath.*"
>
> Jacob testified to Joseph also: "God Almighty appeared unto me at Luz in the land of Canaan, and blessed me, and said unto me, Behold I will make thee faithful and multiply thee . . . and will give this land, after thee *for an everlasting possession.*"
>
> Who has the prior right to the land, the Arabs or the seed of Jacob?[63]

The point was that the land was given to Isaac—not Ishmael, and to Jacob (Israel)—not Esau. No matter which ancestry was ascribed to the Arabs (Ishmael or Esau), they had been left out. In *The King's Business,* one writer called the conflict "the age-old jealousy of Ishmael toward Isaac," but in an article appearing eight months later, another writer spoke of "the ages-lasting quarrel between Jacob and Esau." Both arrived at the same conclusion, however, one speaking of Arab hostility as a "foe that must go down," and the other claiming that all arguments over the land were merely "useless quibbling"—for "Palestine . . . belongs to Jacob."[64] When it was reported that the Arabs were forming organizations to preserve Palestine for the Arabs, the *Evangel* simply commented, "They forget, however, that Jehovah is the Landlord of Palestine."[65]

It was difficult for premillenarians even to conceive the possible justice of the Arab cause. The *Evangel* blamed the 1929 riots on the "insidious propaganda" of the Communists; in the late 30s, the rebellion was credited to German propaganda and influence.[66] The Germans' propaganda was certainly a factor and possibly the Communists' was, too, but completely overlooked was the enduring common denominator of the situation—Arab nationalism and anti-imperialism—certainly understandable, whether one approved or not.

Furthermore, the Arabs were cast in a demonic role in the fulfillment of the end-time prophecies. In analyzing the 1929 outbreaks, the *Jewish Missionary Magazine* predicted, "At the next big outbreak probably Pan-Islam will rise in arms against the British empire, causing another world war and ending in the final battle of Armageddon."[67] Similarly, *The King's Business* spoke of the "present death-struggle": "Knowing the tremendous forces that back the lawless Arab, not only the Moslem *certainly,* but the world's lawless communistic forces *most probably* . . . it is not hard to see that the spark that may soon set the world aflame for its last bloody struggle may find its tinder in Palestine."[68] The editor of *Prophecy,* Keith L. Brooks, went even further: "The Arab and Moslem world is not only anti-Semitic, but is out and out anti-Christ."[69] On the occasion of the murder of the British District Commissioner for Galilee by Arabs in 1937, Brooks categorized the event as fulfillment of prophecy: "It was written concerning Ishmael, 'His hand shall be against every man.' Gen. 16:12."[70]

A series of articles on the Arab-Jewish problem appeared in *The King's Business* in 1930. Arthur W. Payne played upon the paper's name as he said, "They that did the King's business helped the Jews, we are told in the Book of Esther. Whose business are they doing who not only deliberately hinder, but plunder and murder them ruthlessly time after time as the Arabs have done in the years 1920, 1921, and now in 1929?"[71] A response to this assignment of a diabolic role to the Arab was written by W. F. Smalley of Jerusalem. This was one of the few defenses of the Arab position published in the 30s in the premillenarian literature. Smalley argued against a simplistic view: "We cannot say that simply because the Jews were here first they have the right to return. Both Jew and Arab obtained the land through conquest."[72] In a section titled "Two Conflicting Promises" Smalley recalled that prior to the Balfour Declaration the British had promised independence to the Arabs in the territory including Palestine. The British High Commissioner had made a commitment to Sherif Hussein of Hejaz: "Great Britain is prepared to recognize and support the independence of the Arabs within the territories included in the limits and boundaries proposed by the Sherif of Mecca."[73] The conflicting commitment of the Balfour Declaration was considered by the Arabs as a great betrayal. Smalley undercut the traditional premillenarian image of the Jew by saying, "Most of the spokesmen among the Jews are the militant type, who wave the red flag and cry out their willingness to brandish the sword."[74] If the Arabs were irrational, it was understandable: "They have seen their absentee landlords sell to newcomers the land that they have been cultivating for centuries." Smalley concluded his case under the subtitle, "Shall the Minority Rule?"

> If we are willing to put aside all the ideals about which men talked during and immediately after the war, to the effect that the world was being made safe for small and weak peoples, and to revert to the doctrine that when a nation conquers an area it may rule it as it desires, we may agree that England has a right to give Palestine to the Jews, the Esquimos or the Hottentots. But if we say that people should have the right to be ruled as they desire, an easy solution becomes impossible. . . . It is easy to forget that Palestine has, after these years of freedom for Jewish immigration, some 163,000 Jews as over against about 635,000 so-called Arabs. Shall the minority rule? . . .
>
> What would happen if some power were to conquer our own country and say that since there are forty-seven other states all the inhabitants of California, for instance, should

> be expatriated to another state and that the American Indian who formerly inhabited the country should be reinstated? . . . It is altogether likely that the inhabitants of California would do as much as the Arabs do today.
>
> "But," you say, "whether it appears to us just or otherwise, God has said that the Jews are to return to Palestine, and we are not to put our puny ideas of justice over against His omnipotence." Granted! But has God stated that the Jews will have a *human* government again in Palestine? God has not put His seal of inspiration on the Balfour Declaration. . . .
>
> I want to see the Jew given every right that the Arab has, but I do not like to see three-quarters of the population threatened with being ruled by the other one-fourth.[75]

Such cogent moral appeals had little influence, however, as the weight of opinion continued to rest on the other side. In contrast, *Prophecy* magazine predicted on the basis of Isaiah 14:1, 2 a future role for the Arabs as Jewish slaves: "Disturbance will increase until the Prince of Peace Himself comes—then 'will the strangers be joined with them.' At that time they will be 'servants and handmaids' of the Jews (v. 2) and they [the Jews] shall rule over their oppressors."[76] Also, the Arabs were accused of padding their unemployment figures, and it was asserted that all together not more than 889 refugees had been displaced by Jews.[77] After the Arab revolts of 1936-37 the same type of reaction occurred. Britain now was depicted not as a betrayer, but as a "modern Darius" whose "command must go forth today to inform the Moslem element in Palestine that Israel must be free to build her land."[78] The Jews were identified as peacemakers and extolled for their "policies of friendliness and co-operation towards the Arabs" in attempting to explain to the Arabs what their "true aims and aspirations" were in Palestine.[79] The whole trouble was that the Arabs already knew what the true aims and aspirations were—the expropriation of Palestine—and they rejected them. Premillenarians continued to insist that the prediction of restoration somehow gave it moral validity, and treated the Arab cause with a studied arrogance as follows: "According to the *Courier,* Arabs do not like the Bible, and discourage the purchase of this book as they say it promises to give the land of Palestine to the Jews. Despite the fact that they are not buying the Bible, its promises will be fulfilled to the letter."[80]

Not satisfied with confronting the Arab position with the injury of a Jewish restoration to the Holy Land based upon prophecy, the premillenarians added the insult of supporting Jewish claims to even Arabia, Syria, and Mesopotamia.[81] George T. B. Davis in his booklet, *Rebuilding Palestine According to Prophecy,* concluded by asking a question which he said was in the minds of many, "How will the little land of Palestine be able to accommodate the increasing number of Jews that are returning to the homeland at the present time; and the still greater numbers that will be going back in the years to come?" He answered that, on one hand, there would be intensive development, and that, on the other hand, Abraham had been promised the land "from the river of Egypt unto the great river, the river Euphrates." Thus the land would be able to accommodate several times 15,000,000—the current total of Jews throughout the world.[82] The *Evangel* generously estimated that by extending the Promised Land to 200,000 square miles it could support 200,000,000 Jews.[83] Or, as Oswald J. Smith expressed it, "This royal grant is sufficient to hold all the Jews on earth and yet give each one abundance of room (Gen. xv.18)."[84] Moreover, this was not thought of merely in terms of feasibility, but in terms of certainty: "It may be that by purchase and by Government policy a Jewish State of very small dimensions may be set up in Palestine, but *we know* that in God's own time the land that was promised to Abraham and his seed will eventually be settled by the chosen people."[85] This belief in the extended expansion of Jewish power in and beyond Palestine became an enduring plank in the regular platform of premillenarian attitudes toward developments in the Middle East. Welded with the common xenophobia of Americans which feared the Arab representatives of a culture so foreign to that of the European and American Jews (with whom they could more readily identify), these singularly premillenarian ideas created an impassable bar to any appreciable toleration toward the Arabs.

Britain had hoped to reach an agreement on the Palestinian problem with all the parties involved; but failing this, she issued a unilateral solution on May 17, 1939. This White Paper in effect ruled out the existence of a Jewish national state. A maximum of 75,000 Jews were to be admitted to Palestine at a rate of not more than 10,000 annually for five years in addition to 25,000 from Nazi Germany. After that, none were to be admitted without Arab consent—which was an unlikely possibility. The *Evangel* confidently responded that White Paper or no White Paper "in the world of tomorrow the Jewish national homeland in Palestine will be a reality."[86] *Our Hope* suggested two possible explanations for the British action. One was that she hoped for the good will of the Moslems in India; the other was that she was attempting to woo the Arabs away from the flirtations of Germany and Italy. Although *Our Hope* continued to allow the Zionists only a *possible* role in the restoration of Israel, the journal remained *certain* of that return: "They *shall* go back to their own land. . . . How and when the White Paper will be repudiated we do not know, but that in the end it *shall* be non-effective is a certainty."[87] In stark contrast was the consolation offered by liberal Protestantism in the *Christian Century:*

> What today looks to many Zionists like black defeat, will in the light of history, turn out to be glorious victory. . . . The ambition to make Palestine a Jewish state must be dropped but there is no reason why under the new British proposal it cannot still become a cultural and spiritual center for world Jewry. . . . If Jewish devotion can . . . make of Zionism a demonstration of the universal values in Judaism, social as well as religious, the great blow which has fallen on Jewish hopes with the publication of the British White Paper may turn out to be a blessing in disguise.[88]

Mobilizing for Armageddon

> *There is nothing to hinder now the hordes of Russia sweeping down through both Turkey and Persia to the very gates of Jerusalem. There is the valley of Armageddon.*
>
> —Charles S. Price
> *The Battle of Armageddon*

The same consistency which was reflected in premillenarian attitudes toward Israel was also manifested in an unremitting antipathy toward Russia. Part of that antipathy was derived from the ideological conflict with communism, generating discussions of atheism and atrocities; but most of it centered, as before, upon the prophetic character of Russia herself, focusing upon the arms race and Armageddon.

Premillenarians maintained that the best proof of Russia's atheism came from the mouths of the Communists themselves. Zinoviev was quoted by *Prophecy* as having said, "Our next move will be to climb into heaven and drag God from His throne." To this the *Prophecy* writer replied, "Shaking their fists in the very face of the Eternal God, they say: 'I am against thee, O God

Almighty!' And the answer of the Omnipotent is: 'I am against thee, O Gog, prince of Russia, Moscow and Tobolsk.' "[1] *The Life of Faith* reported on a "Five Year Plan of Atheism" which had been given approval by Stalin. This plan stated, "On May 1, 1937, there must not remain on the territory of the U.S.S.R. a single house of prayer to God, and the very conception 'God' will be banished from the boundaries of the Soviet Union, as a survival of the Middle Ages which has served as an instrument for the oppression of the working masses."[2] The argument was brought closer to home as *Prophecy* cited a declaration of the head of the American Communist Party, Earl Browder: "We stand without any reservation for education that will remove the religious prejudices which stand in the way of organizing the masses for socialism, that will withdraw the special privileges of religious institutions."[3] The atheism was not just an aspect of premillenarian criticism—it was central. The *Evangel* commented on reports of the purge trials of the late 30s: "Out of the same door with faith in God goes respect for human rights, human liberty, and human life."[4]

This criticism extended beyond communism to socialism in general. Louis S. Bauman named socialism, communism, and fascism as the "three unclean spirits like frogs" of Revelation 16:13.[5] N. J. Poysti, writing in the *Evangel,* quoted Dostoevski in *The Brothers Karamazov:* "Socialism is not only the working man's matter, but first of all the atheist's way of building a Tower of Babel: to build without God, not to achieve heaven from earth, but to bring down heaven, without God, upon the earth." Poysti's article, "What Is Bolshevism?" epitomized the premillenarian attitude toward communism—not fear of a political or economic system, but fear of a threat to religion.

> We are probably not interested in it from an economic point of view, but since it has a very definite religious aspect which affects Christian people everywhere, we are interested in just the nature of the relation of Bolshevism to religion, and where to place the blame in the Russian Bolsheviki system.

Poysti does suggest that a possible solution to the problems of capitalism might be the Old Testament system of the year of Jubilee, when property reverted to the original owners every fiftieth year.[6] Another *Evangel* writer gave a singularly premillenarian analysis: "Communism is only Satan's counterfeit of the millennial reign of the Lord Jesus Christ."[7] It is somewhat ironic that the very Marxists who accused the churches of being economic institutions were here being accused by churchmen of creating a messianic counterreligion.

Stories of atrocity and persecution were another expression of common Christian antipathies which were shared by premillenarians. Ernest Gordon in *The Sunday School Times* spread the report of Christians in Russia being fired from government jobs and exiled.[8] The *Evangel* cried in despair, "Some of our best missionaries have been apprehended, and God only knows what will be their fate."[9] Christians were reportedly not being given bread cards and thus prevented from buying food or renting homes. The slaughtering of diseased children, the extermination of the elderly, and the torture of Christians were used as constant reminders of the evil nature of communism. There were statistics in the *Evangelical Christian* that 1,767,600 Christians had been murdered in Russia by 1933.[10] For the premillenarian, however, these were not just expressions of evil in a sinful world, but the direct activity of Satan in preparation for the great struggles at the end of the age. It is interesting to observe that in face of the communist persecution, the premillenarians identified Russian Orthodox believers as Christians; in less perilous situations they would most certainly have been characterized along with the Roman Catholics as apostates rather than as brothers.

This analysis of Russia's activity as demonic found various modes of expression. Communism was referred to as the Antichrist:

> As the days of the great tribulation approach the spirit of Antichrist will seek to possess men as that lying spirit possessed those four hundred prophets, and just as they persuaded Ahab to go up to Ramoth-Gilead to meet his destruction, so will these lying spirits eventually seek to lead the kings and rulers of earth and their armies to go up to Armageddon to meet a similar doom. Back of Bolshevism, as we see it in Russia and other lands; or Fascism, as we see it in Italy; of the Nazi movement in Germany; and of the militant nationalism seen in almost every land, are evil spirits who are bent on the destruction of the souls they dupe.[11]

Keith L. Brooks in *Prophecy* referred to "the demon horde of Russia" and explained, "For centuries it has been difficult to see Russia as the fulfillment of this. . . . But suddenly all is changed. . . . Only those who are wilfully blind to the Scriptures, can fail now to see that Russia will finally play the part in world events that was foreseen by the prophets."[12] In the third of a series of articles on Bolshevism, the *Evangel* analyzed the sinister forces at work: "Satan is mobilizing for the last battle of this age. He has indeed established his headquarters in Moscow and from there is sending forth his emissaries into every corner of this old world to poison the minds of the people."[13]

The spread of this poison in America was a real fear. The *Evangel* quoted the inflated statistics of the *Presbyterian* which was alarmed about a supposed three million Communists in America.[14] A Presbyterian pastor, writing on "The Spread of Communism in Our Land" in *Moody Monthly,* said, "Those of our citizens who have been laughing and saying there is nothing to the communistic menace are due for a rude awakening." He went so far as to say that the Ku Klux Klan might have "a distinct sphere of usefulness" in the near future in combating the Red Menace.[15] This response was an extreme expression, but was truly indicative of the desperate dread of militant, satanic atheism.

The growth of the world-wide arms race was a foreboding dark cloud to most observers, but for the premillenarians it produced the exciting prospect of a silver lining, the blessed hope. A 1936 *Evangel* article entitled "The Trend Toward Armageddon" dramatically observed, "Three international volcanoes on the surface of this trembling old world are showing alarming symptoms of imminent eruption, thus spewing their lava of destruction and death over mankind. . . . How this should thrill the heart of the Christian, who obeys Christ's exhortation and studies 'The Signs of the Times.' (Matt. 16:1-3)." The three volcanoes were the Far East, the Near East, and Europe. "Any one of these three mentioned danger spots could be used by the prince of this world, Satan, as the spark, which could start the Armageddon conflagration."[16]

The Russian army was of particular interest. "The Soviet's Plan for War," an article in the June 1932 issue of *Current*

History, described the size and organization of the Russian army and drew this response:

> For what is this great army preparing? We believe the answer is—a great conflict in Palestine as described in Ezekiel 38 and 39. The Jew will be the center of the picture. Russia may repudiate the Lord . . . but it will have to reckon with Him when this great conflict takes place.[17]

Furthermore, all this was an immediate prospect. In a segment headed "Russia to Lick World by 1934," *Prophecy* carried a report by a Dr. Jenkins who had been sent by the Federated Council of Churches to review conditions in Russia. In an interview, Stalin had told him, "Don't you know that the world powers are uniting to crush Russsia? . . . If we can keep them back till 1934, we will be ready for them."[18] At the end of 1934, in an article entitled "'Prepare *War!*'" Louis S. Bauman was saying, "Authoritative voices in every land are telling us in no uncertain tones that it is not a matter of years, but of months, when the battle flags of the nations will again unfurl, and the scourge of the earth will be on the march—*to Armageddon!*"[19] One of the "authoritative voices" cited was Secretary of the Treasury Henry Morgenthau, who had said, "War in Europe in 1934 seems to me inevitable." Bauman's message was based on Joel 3:9, 10: "Proclaim ye this among the Gentiles; Prepare war. . . . Beat your plowshares into swords, and your pruning hooks into spears." He referred this prophecy to Armageddon. His theme was that there was no hope for mankind to avoid war and that, therefore, the puny efforts of the peace movements were futile, wasted efforts. "We dare affirm that the mission of every true messenger of the most high God is *not* to preach the gospel of peace to the unregenerate nations *as such,* but to preach the gospel of peace by the blood of Christ to the unregenerate individual"—Bauman would have none of the social gospel.[20]

A more belligerent attitude was voiced by the World's Christian Fundamentals Association in its 1937 statement on "World Peace":

> We believe that war is contrary to divine will, and that it is indeed a world menace. We lament the selfishness which sets men at one another's throats. We deplore the destruction of life and property incident to civil, national, or world

> chaos. But we refuse the shibboleth of those proponents of peace whose philosophy, if logically carried out, would leave every city destitute of protection to be plundered by the mercy of the Moscow propagandists.[21]

A 1937 report by the League of Nations that as a result of the arms race 8,200,000 men were permanently under arms was carried in the *Evangel* under the caption, "Preparing for Armageddon."[22] While the premillenarians dreaded the impending war, at the same time they welcomed the prospect as a vindication of their belief in the fulfillment of prophecy and as a sign of the impending rapture of the true believer. They were actively neither isolationist nor internationalist, but passively expected "Armageddon Now!"

The particular role of Russia in the end-time drama and at the battle of Armageddon received a growing emphasis during the 30s as Russian power and potential attracted world attention. The thirty-eighth and thirty-ninth chapters of Ezekiel were fleshed out by an expanding exegesis that continued to identify the various figures. In a sermon at the Assembly of God Church, Springfield, Missouri, Thomas M. Chalmers listed the allies of Russia in Ezekiel 38:6 as Rumania (Riphath, son of Gomer), Armenia and Turkey (Togarmah), and Germany (Ashkenaz, son of Gomer). These would assist in the invasion of Palestine which Chalmers also described:

> The manner of this invasion is given in *verse 9*, "Thou shalt ascend, and come like a storm, thou shalt be *like a cloud* to cover the land, thou, and all thy bands, and many people with thee." And down in verse 16 we have "Thou shalt come up against my people of Israel, *as a cloud* to cover the land."... In half a dozen or a dozen years more (I don't think it will be a dozen years), some fine morning the inhabitants of Jerusalem will see a great cloud—in a few minutes the cloud will develop a *great cloud* of *airplanes* landing tens of thousands of men on the soil of Palestine. Note the expression "they shall ascend." How that describes the rising of a fleet of planes.[23]

Here a leading premillenarian spokesman could not tolerate a figurative cloud, but had to have a literal cloud of something—

nor could he resist the urge to set a date.[24] Others, such as Louis S. Bauman, came near to succumbing to the date-setting temptation. Commenting on the belief of many premillenarians that 1936 or 1937 was the latest possible year for the end of the times of the Gentiles, he stated, "They may *not* be right. We are inclined to believe they are *not far* from right."[25]

Bauman, however, readily admitted that there was conflict in the premillenarian ranks over prophetic identifications: "There has been considerable confusion as to just what peoples will make up this great northeastern federation of nations whose allied hosts shall swoop down 'upon the people that are gathered out of the nations' at the time of the end. It is certain, however, that Russia will be the heart and soul of that great godless federation."[26] A few examples of this confusion will suffice. In contrast to the majority of premillenarians who identified Gomer with Germany, evangelist Charles S. Price in his book, *The Battle of Armageddon,* identified the descendants of Gomer as living in the Crimea.[27] Oswald J. Smith, disagreeing with C. I. Scofield, Louis S. Bauman, and many others, believed that the coming defeat of Russia and the northern confederation was not to be the battle of Armageddon—Armageddon was to come later, after the debris from the battle with Gog had been used for firewood for seven years. There were even discrepancies in the works of individual scholars, such as Louis T. Talbot, after whom Talbot Theological Seminary, the graduate school of Biola College, was named. In one radio address, "Russia: Her Invasion of Palestine in the Last Days and Her Final Destruction at the Return of Christ," Talbot commented on Ezekiel 38:8, "We note in verse 8 that God will lead these people [Russia] down and on to the battle of Armageddon." But in another broadcast, "The Judgment of God upon the Russian Confederacy," he said, "The Roman prince, and not Gog of Russia, is the leader of the enemies of God at Armageddon." He then suggested that the seven years between the defeat of Gog and the battle of Armageddon would be the period of the Great Tribulation.[28] Confusion also arose over the role of the "king of the south" (Dan. 11:40). Louis S. Bauman identified the king of the south as England *allied to* Italy as part of the revived Roman Empire; Alva J. McClain, the president of Grace

Theological Seminary, also identified this king as England, but as an ally of Russia *against* Italy.[29]

But there was no question about the identification of Russia. Bauman was even able to discover Joseph Stalin in Biblical prophecy. In 1937, Bauman published a booklet, *God and Gog: or The Coming Meet Between Judah's Lion and Russia's Bear,* in which he included this curious interpretation:

> While we understand that it was not asked with this event in mind, yet Jeremiah's query is appropriate here: "Shall iron break the northern iron and the steel?" (Jer. 15:12). "Shall iron [Rome] break the northern iron [Russia] and the steel [Stalin]?" It is not without interest to note once more that the bloody-jawed dictator of all Soviets, Josef Dzchugashwill, in his youth changes his name to Josef Stalin, i.e., "Josef Steel."

This is followed by an amazingly unabashed admission of loose exegesis: "It matters not what the Spirit of God may have had in mind when He inspired Jeremiah to write these words, nor whether or not the translators correctly translated, as a matter of fact; the 'iron' of Rome *is* due to grind to powder the 'northern iron' and to pulverize the infidel 'Steel.' "[30] The premillenarian role for Russia had become the measuring stick for Scripture, rather than Scripture being the measuring stick for the interpretation. Not only were the premillenarians confident of their identification of Gog with Russia, but there was nothing preventing the advent of Armageddon *now.* In the words of Charles S. Price in 1938: "There is nothing to hinder now the hordes of Russia sweeping down through both Turkey and Persia to the very gates of Jerusalem. There is the valley of Armageddon."[31]

This prospect was reinforced by events in the late 30s which buttressed the premillenarians' confidence in the validity of their identification of Gomer with Germany. Their prophetic expectation foresaw the formation of a great northern confederation of Germany and Russia which would march to Armageddon, and they believed the Nazi-Soviet Pact of August 23, 1939, to be its fulfillment.

Even early in the decade as Russian-German relations had cooled subsequent to the neutrality treaty of April, 1926, and any alliance seemed impossibly remote, the premillenarians had dogmatically asserted its inevitability. Commenting on the rise of fascism in recent German elections, the *Evangel* in 1930 referred to "the possible prospect of Germany and Russia joining hands and attempting to conquer the world by force of arms in 1934."[32] This comment was made in spite of the fascists' blatant anti-communism. A speaker at the General Council of the Assemblies of God in the summer of 1931 spoke of the "recent alliance" between Germany, Russia, and other countries, saying, "What the Bible calls the great northern confederacy is actually *in the process* of formation."[33] *Moody Monthly* called attention to the words of the former German Kaiser in 1931: "Like the Russians, we cling with all our roots to the East. . . . Germany's next kin is Russia." The editor commented, "If not linked with the West, it stands to reason in the light of current events, that [Germany] will march under the banner of the rising nation of the East, and that is Russia."[34] *Our Hope's* editor, Arno C. Gaebelein, in his 1933 publication, *The Conflict of the Ages,* likewise predicted the ultimate alliance of satanic Russia with Gomer, which he said was probably Germany.[35] Realizing the unlikelihood of an alliance with Russia while Hitler was in power, Thomas M. Chalmers found it necessary to hypothesize that "Hitler and his gang may soon be brushed aside and Russia and Germany will come together in alliance."[36]

Apparently the prospect of such an alliance was generally welcomed by the premillennialists, but there were certain inconsistencies expressed. In a series of articles on Bolshevism the *Evangel* negated its prior enthusiasm for such an alliance: "In Germany, upon which country the Bolshevists place their fondest hopes, there are nearly three million Atheists, solidly controlled by evil men who are subject to Moscow, and *if God does not intervene,* the country will be drawn into a league of wickedness against the whole civilized world."[37] One wonders why God would intervene if He Himself were the very one putting hooks in the jaws of Gog to lead this confederation to Armageddon in fulfillment of His own divine prophecies.

In September, 1936, Leonard Sale-Harrison was reaffirming to readers of *Moody Monthly* the identification of Gog and Gomer as Russia and Germany in spite of the realities of current events.

The proof which he offered for Gomer was "the migration of Ashkenaz, son of Gomer, who peopled the land of Germany."[38] But by the middle of 1937 such dogmatizing turned to speculation about the actual probability of such an alliance. The *Evangel* asked, "A Soviet-German Alliance?"

> For years students of prophecy have seen the prediction of a Russo-German alliance in Ezekiel, chapters 38, 39. Recent antagonism between the two countries has not favored this interpretation. But a change seems to be taking place. According to one newspaper correspondent, "prospects are at last beginning to emerge, in the opinion of informed observers here (in London). With the whole of Europe's diplomatic alignments evidently undergoing one of their periodic overhauls, it is felt that the possibility of Germany and Russia gravitating towards one another again cannot be excluded."[39]

Advent Witness was cited by the *Evangel* for the analysis that the purpose of Stalin's current anti-Semitism was to curry favor with Hitler and attract German technical advisors.[40] According to *Prophetic News,* Germany's General von Ludendorff was strongly advising Hitler to come to terms with Russia and use Russian resources.[41] *Revelation* grasped at straws, speculating that the recent marriage of Prince Louis Ferdinand of Prussia, the grandson of the former Kaiser, to Grand Duchess Kira of Russia, daughter of the Czarist pretender, might be the basis of a revived monarchy that would ally the two countries.[42] *Advent Herald* claimed that a secret plot had been discovered that had advocated overthrowing Hitler and collaborating with the Russians.[43]

Such hopes were supported by similar speculation from the secular press. In 1939, the *Evangel* cited a Paris correspondent: "When you come down to brass tacks, there is no obstacle now to Russo-German friendship, which Bismarck advocated so strongly, save Hitler's fanatic fury against what he calls 'Judeo-Bolshevism.' But Hitler is not immortal and dictators can change their minds and Stalin has shot more Jews in two years of the purge than were ever killed in Germany."[44] Louis S. Bauman in *Moody Monthly* quoted Princess Catherine Radziwill's article in *Liberty:* "The Joseph Stalin of today is no Bolshevik. . . . Nor do I think I shall be much astonished when, one day not far hence, 'enemies' Joseph Stalin and Adolf Hitler decide, publicly, to shake hands."

Bauman then commented, "Those who know the 'sure word of prophecy' expect nothing less than that some day in the not far distant future, the seeming enemy nations, Russia and Germany, will shake hands, whether Stalin and Hitler do or not."[45] *Moody Monthly's* editor quoted a recent book, *Plot and Counterplot in Central Europe,* by Marcel W. Fodor: "Many augurs, with the safe instinct of illogical people, see the spectre of this German-Russian friendship looming on the horizon." Fodor found it difficult to believe that Hitler himself could make such a drastic reversal, but he said, "It would be a mistake to dismiss it as impossible."[46]

This crescendo of expectation grew as the fateful year of 1939 arrived. Yet in the January issue of *The King's Business,* commentator Dan Gilbert criticized the *New Republic* editorial that said Hitler was now in a position to "make friends with Soviet Russia, and participate in a new and probably bloodless partitioning of Poland." Gilbert said, "This development does not mean, though, that a Nazi-Soviet accord is in prospect, or even in sight. It is not—not by a long shot." Nevertheless, Gilbert did believe the long-term direction was unity. He concluded by saying:

> This very trend of events has been predicted plainly by Biblical scholars writing in *The King's Business* during past months, and even years. Louis S. Bauman, for one, showed conclusively and convincingly how Germany and Soviet Russia were due eventually to "get together." This is a striking indication that Bible prophecy is, indeed, "history written in advance." Gaining his light from God's Word, Dr. Bauman was able to see far ahead—into the future—which was closed to the most brilliant minds which relied solely on their own penetrating, but wholly human and therefore limited, insight and foresight.[47]

Such an "I told you so" attitude characterized the exultant response of the premillennialists to the surprise announcement of the Nazi-Soviet pact. The *Evangel* observed: "Students of prophecy have long awaited the day when this alliance would come to pass," and pointed out that in *Mein Kampf* Hitler had set forth his personal philosophy that an alliance with Russia would be fatal to Germany—"But man's plans cannot thwart God's decreed purposes."[48] Louis S. Bauman in *The Sunday School Times* showed that as early as November 7, 1917, in *Christian Herald,* James M. Gray had predicted that it was "likely that one of these days the relationship of Russia and Germany shall become close."[49] Arno C. Gaebelein in *Our Hope* topped that, referring readers to his book, *The Harmony of the Prophetic Word,* which had been written thirty-five years before. He also noted, "In our book, 'As It Was—So Shall It Be,' published over two years ago we predicted that Hitler was rapidly approaching a closer alliance with the Reds." Gaebelein found the event momentous enough to warrant publishing the complete text of the pact.[50]

So the premillenarians found themselves without a doubt that the world was on the way to Armageddon. The blitzkrieg war, begun by Hitler's invasion of Poland on September 1, 1939, produced no rejoicing as might possibly be expected, but it did renew hopes for the rapture of the church. Events appeared to be moving inexorably toward the end. Under the caption, "Armageddon Looms," the *Evangel* remarked, "How near must we be to the last great battle, we wonder, as we read in *Time* about reports of joint action in the Near East being contemplated by Russia and Turkey to overwhelm Syria, Palestine, and Iran."[51] And again advice was given for the proper response of the premillenarian mind: "With the nations rushing on so swiftly to Armageddon the appearance of the Lord should be our constant expectation, for surely His coming draweth nigh."[52]

During the 30s there was much speculation about what nations other than Germany might be possible allies for Russia. Revelation 16:12 was the key text: "And the sixth angel poured out his vial upon the great river Euphrates; and the water thereof was dried up, that the way of the kings of the east might be prepared." The growth of Japanese power and the spread of communism in China brought about the interpretation that these nations were represented by the "kings of the east." The standard views in the nineteenth century had been that the Turks or the lost tribes of Israel were the nations in question. In 1931, *Prophecy* expressed fears that Russia would make China the center of a world-wide revolution: "A Bolshevized China would be the world's greatest peril." On the basis of a domino theory, *Prophecy* advocated direct intervention by England to "restore order and peace in China and thus check the spread of Bolshevik madness in other countries."[53] After Japan's 1931 invasion of Manchuria, the *Evangel* made occasional reference to the *possibility* of the "Yellow Peril" being the "kings of the east," but Louis T. Talbot in *The King's Business* was not so cautious: "In that day, there shall be a coalition not only of the nations which comprised the old Roman Empire, not only of the other nations of Europe with Russia, but a combination of all the dark-skinned peoples—the nations of India, of China, of Japan, of the Mongolian hordes—all of whom will line up under one leadership."[54] After Japan's invasion of China proper in 1937, the *Evangel* too was less cautious: "We read in Rev. 16:12 that 'the kings of the east' will have a part in the battle of Armageddon. Is there not a foreshadowing of this dread event in Japan's brutal rape of China?"[55] A major article by H. A. Ironside, pastor of Chicago's Moody Memorial Church appeared in the January 1938 issue of *The King's Business.* Ironside asked:

> Who are these kings? It is not necessary to guess. The word for "East" is simply "sun-rising." The kings of the sun-rising! Japan has been known as the empire of the rising sun for a millennium. . . .
>
> The puppet king of Manchukuo, possibly Japanese-controlled rulers in other northeastern Chinese territories, perhaps at last an alignment with China itself, and there you have the kings of the sun-rising—all in readiness for the great day of God Almighty—the Armageddon conflict.

Ironside then advocated a proper premillenarian attitude of high hopes: "The tocsin of doom is sounding. The yellow peril becomes more and more ominous. The preparation of the day of the Lord goes on apace. Christian, lift up your head. Your redemption draweth nigh."[56]

Louis S. Bauman had no doubts, either, as he picturesquely explained: "Verily, the Chinese dragon is aroused today; and it became the folly of Japan to prod with the bayonet and to let fall the bomb that has stirred him to frenzy. And when the guns of Armageddon roar, the five-clawed dragon will be there."[57] Just as in the nineteenth century, premillenarians were able to discover in each international crisis a prophetic forewarning so as to give a sense of immediacy to their "tocsin of doom," never learning the lesson of failure, never even admitting embarrassment over their gullibility—as their credibility declined with each succeeding generation.

As in the 20s, prophetic students continued to plug Mussolini as the leading candidate for Russia's antagonist—the Antichrist. Most were not dogmatic about Mussolini, but they were sure about Rome. As *Prophecy* expressed it:

> The Word of God takes account of two definite combinations of nations, which play an important part in the closing hours of this age. The most important is the confederacy of the Roman states, led *no doubt* by Italy. The other is led by Russia.[58]

According to a fascinating account in *The Sunday School Times,* Mussolini himself was interviewed by two Belgian premillenarians, Mr. and Mrs. Ralph C. Norton. Mussolini was asked:

> "Do you intend to reconstitute the Roman Empire?" He answered, "One cannot revive a dead empire, nor recall it into being. We can only revive its spirit, and be governed by the same discipline."
>
> Mr. Norton began to speak to the Premier of the teaching of the Bible regarding the reforming of the Roman Empire, telling him it was predicted of God, and speaking of the alliance of northern nations that would likewise take place.
>
> Mussolini leaned back in his chair and listened fascinated, and asked, "Is that really described in the Bible? Where is it found?"[59]

Louis S. Bauman responded to critics of his position on Mussolini by asserting, "We candidly admit our *opinion* that if the Lord were to call His people away . . . today, Mussolini would appear as the outstanding candidate for the job of the Antichrist."[60] Alva J. McClain later expressed what was probably an even more widely-held view: "While I am not even suggesting that Mussolini is the Willful King in person, surely it ought to be clear that in his Fascist methods and policies we have a remarkable correspondence with the things mentioned in Daniel 11:39."[61] Arno C. Gaebelein did not risk an identification of the Antichrist, but he did believe that the Antichrist was probably already in the world.[62] The *Elim Evangel* expressed the opinion that the Spanish Civil War might provide a pattern for Mussolini's intervention in the Middle East (which would lead to Armageddon), pointing out that:

> In his recent triumphal tour of Libya it was declared that he henceforth is to be known as the "Defender of the Moslems." From 2,000 Arab notables he received the sword of Islam, and was proclaimed the "glorious and invincible leader." Brandishing the sword, Mussolini promised the Arabs that in a short time Rome would show how near to her the Arabs are.[63]

Although Mussolini and Italy were to prove disappointments to such wild-eyed dreams, the foundations were already being laid in the 1930s for a successor to that myth. The role of the revived Roman Empire was to be taken over by the European Common Market in the post-World War II era. Even in the mid-thirties Premier Aristide Briand of France was preparing a plan for a "United States of Europe," which drew speculation from the premillenarians. Arno C. Gaebelein commented, somewhat obscurely, on the idea:

> That such a union will ultimately come is known to every student of prophecy. There will be two great federations in the future. The one is the Western European union, corresponding to the Roman Empire. The other is the Northeastern confederacy, headed by Russia. Mussolini will probably fall more fully in line with Briand's suggestion. We shall follow this movement with keen interest and tell our readers of its progress.[64]

Gaebelein, however, gave no clue as to what particular role he envisioned for Mussolini. The *Evangel* quoted *Revelation's* comments on the idea of European unity: "We know from the Word of God that this plan will not succeed but we know that Europe will be divided into two camps, with western Europe under the dictator who shall later arise in Rome, while eastern Europe will be under the control of the great union between Germany and Russia."[65] Apparently, the point being made was that there could not be a union of the *whole* of Europe.

Perhaps it was due to the isolationist sentiment developing in the 1930s that in spite of an imminent Armageddon, there seemed to be less concern than before about the role of the United States in all these events. Harry J. Steil in the *Evangel* did not equivocate, however:

> Will the United States be involved? Scripture says, "The spirits of demons, working miracles, shall go forth unto the

> kings of the earth and *of the whole world* to gather them to the battle of the great day of God Almighty." Rev. 16:14. "I will gather *all nations* against Jerusalem to battle." Zech. 14:2. Yes, the United States will not escape.[66]

Other writers, though identifying the "king of the south" with England and predicting her defeat by the Roman forces, failed to speculate on the possibility that the United States might be an ally of England in that overwhelming defeat. Louis S. Bauman predicted Britain's defeat together with "any allies" she might happen to have, but did not mention the United States in particular.[67] Likewise, Alva J. McClain discussed the "mutual protection" of the democracies, but chose not to refer to the United States in conjunction with England's expected defeat.[68] The church did not expect to be around for the battles anyway, so there was no great concern. Apparently, forecasting the end of one's mother country did not make good copy—it was less noxious to preach the end of the world.

The Century's Greatest Event

There isn't the slightest doubt that the emergence of the Nation Israel among the family of nations is the greatest piece of prophetic news that we have had in the 20th century.

—William W. Orr
The New Nation of Israel and the Word of God!, 1948

1948, like 1917, was a singular year in which momentous events relating to Russia and Israel again coincided. The independent state of Israel was born and East-West relations solidified into the Cold War. These revolutionary developments churning in the wake of history's most devastating war brought premillenarian anticipation of the end to its highest peak ever. Although the Six-Day War of 1967 would bring Israel's occupation of Jerusalem, and the Korean War or Cuban missile crisis might produce a greater Soviet threat, the juxtaposition of events in 1948 brought in the succeeding months a sense of expectation that would not be equaled again.

Premillenarians in general had faced the advent of World War II with the assurance that the war was part of God's prearranged plan of history. Various explanations, however, were offered in attempts to second-guess God's ultimate purpose in this new rehearsal for Armageddon. After Pearl Harbor, with America involved in the war, the *Evangel* advised its readers, "If you would learn God's purpose in the present World War, watch Palestine," and suggested that the war might lead to the final conflict of Armageddon.[1] As the end of the war approached, the *Evangel* cited the *Prophetic News* of London that just as the purpose of World War I had been the conquest of Palestine and the promise of the Balfour Declaration, the chief outcome of World War II might be the "emergence into prominence in politics and war of 'Gog.'" The *Evangel* commented, "It is amazing how Russia has been transformed, in a few short years, from a backward nation into one of the first rank. There is no doubt that Russia could become a formidable threat to Palestine and any combination of states which might array themselves on Palestine's side."[2] In 1950, in an article entitled "Israel, God's Last-Day Miracle," the author focused on the Jews as the central purpose of the war: "Just as it had taken World War I to prepare the promised land for the Jewish people, it took World War II to prepare the people for the promised land."[3] The Nazi persecution had been the impetus to drive them back to Palestine. On the other hand, a *Moody Monthly* article analyzed the war as a judgment on the nations themselves for their "sordid and inhuman" treatment of the Jews, including Great Britain in particular: "None can ever deny the debacle of dishonor, the British White Paper of May, 1939, in which a great power sought to appease the Nazis, and yet, four months later, found herself involved in the deadliest war of her history."[4] In spite of such a variety of ideas, the premillennialists nevertheless agreed that whatever the purpose, it was all predetermined by God.

When it came to the continuing question of the restoration, however, the proper sequence of predetermined events remained a matter of debate. The question was whether the restoration was to take place before or after the return of Christ—or whether it was to take place before or after the Jews' acceptance of Jesus as Messiah. The issue was not whether the Jews would be restored to Palestine (that was a foregone conclusion), but whether the current Zionist restoration was the final one as prophesied. *The Sunday School Times* avidly supported the current restoration movement, buttressing its claims by amassing authorities. A 1940 article said:

> Three years ago The Sunday School Times met the challenge of those who were saying that the return of the Jews to Palestine in present-day Zionism was not a fulfillment of Bible prophecy, because the Jews are returning to their land in unbelief. In a valuable symposium published in the Times of May 1, 1937, the convictions of half a dozen sound Bible teachers were published, showing conclusively that Scripture predicts that the Jews will return to the land in unbelief, before the Lord's return.[5]

Likewise the *Evangel* carried the statement: "God swore that Israel should be re-gathered in her own land, unconverted, in the latter days. Ezek. 36:24-38."[6] *Our Hope* expressed the belief that "the hunger for land and for labor on the land" was indeed God's keeping His appointment to meet with Israel again, but, nevertheless, it was only a *partial* restoration. The complete restoration would come only after the return of the Messiah and after Jewish national regeneration (Zech. 2:10-12). The invasion of Gog and Magog would come only after Israel was able to "dwell safely" and "dwell securely" in the land (Ezek. 38:8-12)—a situation not in immediate prospect.[7]

Apparently the issue was not conclusively decided, as *The Sunday School Times* allowed expression of the "later restoration" view by Harry A. Ironside even after the establishment of the state of Israel.[8] Sometimes the later restoration idea was somewhat modified to refer to the *complete* restoration of *all* Jews or to a return to an extended Palestine. Such a view did not diminish the enthusiasm for the contemporary movement for it was depicted as a necessary prerequisite to the restoration. In 1941 the *Evangel* explained:

> We all have been thrilled to watch the rebuilding of Palestine and the return of many Jews to that land through the efforts of Zionism. But let us remember that Zionism alone is doomed to ultimate failure. God's Word teaches that "Jerusalem shall be trodden down of the Gentiles, until the times of the Gentiles be fulfilled." Luke 21:24. Not until Christ returns will the Jewish nation go to Palestine as a

> whole, nor will the Jews get full sovereignty over that land. Jewry needs to know this.[9]

This evidently reflected the view of the *Evangel's* editor. But by 1948 the *Evangel* was again able to see God in the movement: "They think it is the skill of their political schemings that has gotten them a Jewish state; but behind the scenes it must be that God is opening the way for the Jews to return to Palestine in greater numbers."[10] However, only two months before independence day, the *Evangel* was still predicting, "The Zionists will never get the Promised Land by their own political schemings and their own armed might. They will get it when they welcome Jesus of Nazareth back to earth as their Messiah!"[11]

Louis T. Talbot in *The King's Business* saw in secular Zionism the coming together of Ezekiel's "Dry Bones" which would *later* be completely regenerated by spiritual breath from God.[12] There was little or no decline in premillenarian support of Israel as a result of these conflicting interpretations of Scripture. Enthusiasm might vary from a high of ecstatic euphoria to a mere thrill of observation, but even the least enthusiastic, *Our Hope,* would after the fact be able to say in 1949: "Even if the nation of Israel should be temporarily dispossessed of the portion of the land over which they now hold sway, this would not invalidate for one moment the fact that Palestine is to be eventually turned over to them in its entirety."[13]

During the 1940s the premillenarian response to Israel tended to center upon three focal points: the British White Paper of 1939, the United Nations partition of 1947, and Israel's independence in 1948. During the war, interest in Palestine declined, but occasional comments did indicate a continued commitment to a Jewish national home in Palestine. The *Evangel* was concerned about unemployment in Palestine, blaming it on the British limitation of immigration—but failed to explain how that could cause unemployment. Readers were advised that "there is need for us to pray for God's purpose to be fulfilled in Palestine."[14] Later the *Evangel* also expressed hope that the British would yet fulfill the pledge of the Balfour Declaration.[15]

In the midst of Nazi anti-Semitism during the war, *The Sunday School Times* in "The Indestructible Jew" still spoke confidently that the Jews were assured of a national home in Palestine.[16] At the beginning of 1943 the *Evangel* quoted Agnes Scott Kent, who had said, "There has been among Christian leaders a steadily growing conviction that the many reverses suffered by the United Nations in the war have had direct connection with our failure to get in step with God in His clear purpose that Palestine is for the Jews. Thus it is of highest moment that the abrogation of the infelicitous White Paper is now under official consideration."[17] When Winston Churchill reaffirmed in 1943 the policy of the White Paper limiting immigration, the news was not welcomed.[18] As George T. B. Davis had written in *The Sunday School Times:* "Immigration of the Jewish people to Palestine might be stopped for a time, but . . . neither Great Britain nor any other government could stop the return of the Jews to Palestine, any more than they could stop the beating of the waves upon the seashore."[19] When the policy was again reaffirmed in 1944, the *Evangel* forecasted: "God will reopen the doors in His own time, never fear, His prophetic plan for Palestine will be fulfilled in spite of all."[20] Such determinism was also put into practice:

> Many friends of Israel, including earnest Christians, have petitioned our government to intervene in the affairs of the British government regarding the "White Paper," on the basis of which the British have restricted Jewish immigration to Palestine. *The Voice*, however, mentions two points that should be kept in mind: (1) When it is God's time to restore His people to the land, none will be able to prevent them. (2) The restoration in which we might help would demonstrate little kindness in view of the awful affliction awaiting them there.[21]

The implication was that nonactive support was the wise policy. Here again, premillenarians shied away from political involvement due to their anti-social gospel bias. Only after the 1944 election was over did the *Evangel* and *The Sunday School Times* happily report that both presidential candidates were supporting a national home for Jews.[22]

During the war the Jews in Palestine had continued to develop their military forces, both the official Hagana (defense) organization and the guerrilla forces, the Stern Gang and the Irgun Zvei Leumi. After the war, the British found themselves unable without undue costs to keep order between the Jewish and Arab bands, and they eventually turned the problem over to the newly-formed United Nations. The United Nations Special Committee on Palestine (UNSCOP) ultimately recommended on August 31, 1947, the partition of Palestine into separate Jewish and Arab states.

Prospects of partition produced the same confused reaction they had before. In 1940 the *Evangel* had greeted prospects of a partition plan under the British White Paper with dire forecasts of doom: "How little do these responsible for this White Paper realize they are placing Great Britain in the pathway of the wrath of God. In Joel 3:2 God said, 'I will also gather all nations and will plead with them (in judgment) for my people, whom they have scattered among the nations, *and parted My Land.*' "[23] But in 1946, another British plan for partition drew a totally different response: "The partition appears to be reasonable."[24] The United Nations' 1947 plan of partition was hailed as "an historic one." It left prophetic students "tense with expectation, believing that the coming of the Lord has suddenly become a long step nearer."[25] But in the very next issue it was pointed out that the punishment predicted in Joel 3:2 for the division of the land was that *all nations* would be brought down into the valley of Jehoshaphat (or Armageddon). "If armed intervention is needed to make the partition plan effective, each nation probably will be asked to send forces to Palestine. How simple, then, will it be for the Lord thus to gather all nations to Armageddon for that great battle!"[26] *The King's Business* likewise foresaw the possibility that end-time events were near.[27]

William L. Pettingill in *The Sunday School Times* predicted that the partition would not endure because the whole land had been promised to the sons of Isaac, not the sons of Ishmael.[28] In spite of its enthusiasm for partition, the *Evangel* said, "No hope for a peaceful solution is seen apart from a co-operative program in which Jews and Arabs work together and rule the country in a coalition government." The writer also believed that the ultimate solution would not be found until the return of Christ.[29] At about the same time, Arno C. Gaebelein in *Our Hope* was favoring Jewish representation in a United Arab Republic as a possible solution.[30] But when the partition plan was presented, he was overwhelmed by the imminent possibility of a restoration and made the following concession to the supporters of Zionism:

> That the Jewish people will be restored to their land in the end is inevitable, since God has so decreed in His Word (Jer. 23:7, 8). That restoration will be a restoration in faith. Now the Jews are seeking to go to Palestine in unbelief. Is there Scripture that leads us to suppose that their efforts will succeed? Yes, although we do not know when it will be.[31]

In *Moody Monthly,* T. DeCourcy Rayner commented on the partition plan by predicting that "the Jews will eventually be given not a partitioned Palestine, but the whole of the land, and ultimately the whole of Trans-Jordan as well."[32]

The Arabs reacted to the partition plan with a general strike, objecting to the terms by which the Jews would get 56 per cent of Palestine and the Arabs (though nearly equal in number to the Jews in the Jewish area) would be treated as a minority there.[33] The chaos that ensued caused Britain to withdraw early and made it impossible for the United Nations to implement the partition plan. The United States, having lobbied hard for United Nations adoption of the partition idea, finally dropped its support in March, and the United Nations decided to abandon hopes of partitioning the country. *Moody Monthly* lamented that decision as a "backtrack" from what had seemed to be "another step toward the fulfillment of biblical prophecy of the regathering of the Jews to Palestine." The situation was analyzed, probably accurately, as follows: "The new move was dictated by political necessity. The United States cannot permit the risk of Russian troops in Palestine as part of a UN police force." Whereas the *Evangel* had believed that partition would lead to Armageddon, *Moody Monthly* now speculated that abandoning partition might lead to Armageddon.[34] On the other hand, the *Evangel* now quoted Agnes Scott Kent, writing in *Evangelical Christian,* as expressing "great joy" over this reversal of policy: "We believe there has been, very clearly, divine intervention in the U.N. vote to part the land between the Jews and Arabs—the land of Abrahamic covenant, which God's Word declares repeatedly and unequivocally is for the Jews. *The son of the bondwoman shall not be heir with the son of the freewoman.*"[35] Thus the premillenarian mind found itself confused as to whether it was supposed to rejoice or cry at particular events, but whichever voice it might listen to, it was either "Armageddon Now!"—or soon, and it was Palestine for the Jews—sooner or later.

During the mid-forties, however, there did begin to appear occasional spokesmen who were willing to admit the weakness of the Jews' claims in Palestine. Arno C. Gaebelein, never overly enthusiastic about Zionism, saw fit to present in *Our Hope* both the Arab and Jewish positions. This did not prevent him from drawing his ultimate conclusion, though, that "the Jews will return to the Holy Land and will abide there in the end."[36] Even more surprising was an admission appearing in the strongly Zionist *The Sunday School Times* in an article by T. A. Lambie, "Palestine Focus of World Attention."

> Of course the inhabitants of the land do not want them. Neither did the Canaanites of old want them, nor the Jebusites, nor any of the inhabitants of the ancient land, and yet they came and they are coming again. God has decreed it. It must be so.
>
> *Of course their right to the land can not be maintained* apart from God. And the nations as a whole reject God. The Arab people in the land do have rights *from almost every human viewpoint*. These rights can never be ruthlessly trampled under foot, and it is difficult to imagine their having a change of heart and becoming willing to admit the Jews.
>
> An irresistible force seems to be meeting an immovable body and how God's purpose for Israel will work out in its inflexible course we can only wonder. It will be worked out, and all that most of us can do about it is to watch, to pray, and to believe.[37]

But in reality, speaking out against trampling the rights of the Arabs under foot was (in Lambie's view) to have little consequence—God had decreed the return of the Jews. "It must be so."

Similar views, written by a "Hebrew Christian," Morris Zeidman, appeared in the *Evangel* just two weeks prior to Israel's independence.

> To be sure Israel will return to the land of Israel. This cannot be prevented, either by the Arabs or any other nations, for the Word of God is sure, and He never breaks a promise given. . . .

> It is clear that aside from the religious point of view and the Bible, *the Jewish people have little or nothing in their favor for claiming Palestine* as their land. In that case, one would think that they would turn to the Bible for enlightenment and guidance regarding constitution and policy of the new State. The Hebrew leaders would then find that Palestine in the Bible was never intended to be a democracy, but rather a theocracy and a kingdom. A theocracy is a State where the supreme sovereign is God, and the will of God is the law of the country. A kingdom usually has a King. This is God's plan for the Commonwealth of Israel.[38]

The peculiarity of these concessions may be contrasted with the more standard premillenarian view that was presented a month later by Aaron J. Kligerman in *The Southern Presbyterian Journal.* He began with a quotation by the British Ambassador to the United States, Lord Halifax: "Palestine has been an Arab country for much longer than the United States has been your country. . . . I know of no argument in justice or democratic thought whereby the Arabs can be denied the right to have any say in its future." After ridiculing the "ignorance" or "unbelief" of the statement, Kligerman presented a sixfold justification of Jewish claims in Palestine. Like most such arguments, however, it was dependent on his opening premise: "It is unique among countries of the world, having been specially chosen by God for the development of His purpose in the earth."[39] Here, again, was the premillenarian preference for determinism over normal justice, a predilection that was inherent even in the admissions by Lambie and Zeidman above.

With the withdrawal of the British from Palestine at midnight on May 14, 1948, the state of Israel was proclaimed. Palestine was immediately invaded by forces from the surrounding Arab states to assist the native Palestinians in their struggle against the Jews, but the advantage quickly swung to the co-ordinated, efficient Jewish forces. After a couple of rounds of fighting with interludes of cease-fire, an armistice was finally established in November, 1948; and in May, 1949, Israel was admitted to the United Nations. The war left about 700,000 Arab refugees homeless—they had fled the Jewish-occupied territories.

Premillenarians were overwhelmed by this fulfillment of their prophecies. Dr. Louis T. Talbot and Dr. William W. Orr, president and vice-president of the Bible Institute of Los Angeles respectively, discussed the news over the Bible Institute Hour radio broadcast; and Orr exclaimed, "There isn't the slightest doubt but that the emergence of the Nation Israel among the family of nations is the greatest piece of prophetic news that we have had in the 20th century."[40] Talbot echoed Orr's viewpoint both on that broadcast and later in *The King's Business:* "I consider it the greatest event, from a prophetic standpoint, that has taken place within the last one hundred years, perhaps even since 70 A.D., when Jerusalem was destroyed."[41]

The elation also left the *Evangel* editor numb with excitement:

> We well may wonder whether we are awake or lost in sleep merely having a very exciting dream. . . .
>
> The events to which we have looked forward for so many years have come upon us. . . .
>
> Beloved, it *can't* be long until our blessed Lord takes us home to be forever with Him. . . . Oh, joy unspeakable![42]

A few weeks later on July 3, the *Evangel* urged support of Israel as a religious duty: "As Americans we rejoice at this season over the birth of our nation; but a few weeks ago another new nation was born—the nation of Israel. And the prophet of the Lord exhorts us to rejoice over that event, for it is one of great importance. . . . Isa. 66:10, 12."[43]

The magnitude of this "greatest event" even brought Arno C. Gaebelein to concede that this might be the beginning of the final restoration of Israel.[44] The *Evangel* commented on the fact that the Jews were being allowed to return in unbelief: "God is permitting them to return to the land He promised them, there to plead with them, to deal with them firmly, and *eventually* to turn them to Himself."[45] *The King's Business* expounded its view: "The nation is to be born, the people are to return to their land in unbelief, great prosperity will come and, climaxing these conditions, will be the personal appearance of the greatest Jew of all time, the Lord Jesus Christ."[46] Some writers did continue, however, to express doubts about the current movement; as one said in July, 1949: "We do not believe that the happenings in Palestine this past year and a half are the fulfillment of the promises made to Abraham, Isaac and Jacob, as respects the Promised Land and their glorious future, but we must believe that God is using this Zionist movement and the two world wars to get the Jewish people in the land."[47]

The United States was the first government to recognize the new state of Israel; President Truman made the announcement only eleven minutes after the proclamation of independence went into effect. Prior to this time, his policy had vacillated between that of Congress (an Israeli state) and that of his State Department advisors who wished to avoid Arab antipathy. A resolution was introduced at the annual Southern Baptist Convention to congratulate Truman on his recognition of Israel, but it failed to pass.[48] The record does not show whether it lost due to lack of support for the state of Israel or whether the delegates did not feel it appropriate to involve the convention politically. Since the general reaction of the secular press around the United States was favorable to Truman's action, it is more likely that the latter is true.[49]

The territory that Israel was able to grab in the 1948 war exceeded that which she would have been granted under the partition plan. Her expansion was rationalized by the argument that the original plan had been negated by the Arab invasion, and that she was justified according to the Balfour Declaration in taking all of Palestine. The *Evangel* apparently reported this with approval, observing, "The day may not be far off when Jerusalem no longer is trodden down of the Gentiles, but the times of the Gentiles is fulfilled (Luke 21:24)."[50] Very soon after the initial fighting, however, there began to appear among premillenarians the first signs of disapproval of Israel's foreign policy. This was the beginning of what has been, ever since, a growing minority that feels the moral test must be applied to Israel's action rather than the mere acceptance of the *fait accompli* as being the determined will of God. The *Evangel* cited comments in *The Bible and the News* concerning Israel's demands for more land as a result of her military victories:

> This assertion that might makes right seriously weakens the moral position of Israel. If Israel considers that additional lands may be added by conquest, they are going contrary to the Scriptures. True, the land grant of Jehovah in Gen.

> 15:18 gives Israel all of this Land, and the edict of God to Joshua was that he should walk upon it and claim it.[51]

But no solution to this Scriptural dilemma was offered. Morris Zeidman, writing in the *Evangel,* expressed the personal struggle shared by these moralists:

> My sympathies are with the Jews, and I believe that Palestine has been promised by both God and men to the Jewish people; but the methods that are being used today to make Palestine a Jewish state cannot be considered Christian and therefore I believe are not of God. . . .
>
> It is most difficult for the Christian to take part or take sides in the politics of the world. The Christian cannot approve of the tactics used in Palestine today.[52]

As time passed, the general trend, though, was approval of Israel's accomplishment. T. A. Lambie in *The Sunday School Times* of July 16, 1949, asserted, "As I read my Bible, the events that are taking place are the beginning of the fulfillment of prophecy for the final days."[53] Even the most moderate *Alliance Weekly* called the new state of Israel of the "utmost importance," and did risk stating the premillenarian consensus that "the time is drawing near for the fulfillment of the ancient predictions." But a word of caution was quickly added: "But to us, as to the Apostles, the same word comes: 'It is not for you to know times or seasons'—they rest still in the authority of the Father."[54]

The city of Jerusalem was especially important to the premillenarian mind; the *Evangel* noted particularly a special decree by the Israeli cabinet announcing that Jerusalem would be considered part of Israel.[55] The old part of the city would not be taken until 1967, but the government soon announced that the new part (which was in Israel's control) would be the capital of the new state in spite of opposition by the United Nations to such a provocative decision. The *Evangel's* response to this action reflected the premillenarian attitude for the next nineteen years—anticipation of Israel's annexation of Jerusalem: "When the Jews gain control of Jerusalem, the times of the Gentiles will be ended."[56] And *The King's Business* added, "We feel that this is another important step in the great chain of events."[57]

Other steps would eventually lead, according to premillenarian thought, to expansion all the way from the river of Egypt to the

Euphrates. This idea has been particularly significant since 1948 and even more so since 1967. The following excerpts from the *Evangel* during the year following Israel's independence are fairly representative of this attitude:

> A hint of Israel's ambitions is given by *Time*. A reporter asked the Premier, David Ben-Gurion, whether he expected Israel's population to grow. He replied: "There are eleven million Jews in the world. I don't say that all of them will come here, but I expect several million, and with natural increase I can quite imagine a Jewish state of ten million." The reporter asked, "Can that many be accommodated within the U.N. partition boundaries of Israel?" The Premier replied: "I doubt it."
>
> The Jews will not be satisfied until they have all the land God promised Abram—from the Nile to the Euphrates (Genesis 15:18).[58]

> And you know the story from May 15 on, how the Jews have been able to withstand the Arabs, and defeat them. In fact, the Jews are taking all Palestine, and I believe that before the trouble is over they will have Trans-Jordan too.[59]

> That young nation has already fought for and won desired lands and will continually wage successful gains until God's original promise is fulfilled completely.[60]

Other journals reflected the same viewpoint. A letter to the editor of *Our Hope* inquired if the Jews had ever before possessed all the land promised to them. The answer was negative, but the correspondent was assured that they would in the future.[61] The readers of *The Sunday School Times* were taught that "the present trouble in Palestine was brought about by the decision to partition, or divide the land," and that "in God's time the land, not part but all, is to be restored to Israel." The area specifically identified was all the land from Lebanon to the Sinai peninsula.[62]

The motivation for premillenarian support of the Israeli policy of expansion was, of course, the belief that it was the determined will of God; but one can also detect a certain fear of God, a dread that if a person (or nation) did not support the chosen people of God, he would be punished for his sin. Christians were regularly admonished to pray for the peace of Jerusalem or for God's purposes to be accomplished there, and were reminded from the Psalms that "they shall prosper that love thee" (Israel). Again the question arises: If all was predetermined prophetically, what was the purpose of prayer anyway? No one seemed to recall Hebrews 12:6, "Whom the Lord loveth he chasteneth." Perhaps those who loved Israel might have chastened the upstart nation for its own good.

Early in World War II the *Evangel* cited *Prophecy Monthly's* approbation of what was supposedly Britain's first policy statement on the Jewish question since the start of hostilities. Cabinet minister Arthur Greenwood had vaguely assured the American Jewish community that after the war "wrongs suffered by the Jewish people in so many countries should be righted." The leading American Zionist, Rabbi Stephen S. Wise, wishfully regarded this as having even greater implications than the Balfour Declaration. The *Evangel* was certain that this purportedly innovative policy would bring the blessing of God upon Britain.[63] When Winston Churchill, who was thought to be pro-Zionist, became Prime Minister, the following was cited from *Christian Victory* in speculating about the significance of the war for Palestine:

> Now that Churchill is prime minister "the future for the Zionist Movement in Palestine looks brighter." There has been a corresponding change in the tide of the war. When Chamberlain was Premier, Britain suffered one defeat after another, but since Churchill took his place the outlook for Britain has become brighter and brighter. There may be a definite relation between British war successes and the Government's more favorable attitude toward Zionist plans to make Palestine a Jewish national home.[64]

Yet only a year and a half later premillenarian critics were saying, "There has been among Christian leaders a steadily growing conviction that the many reverses suffered by the United Nations in the war have had direct connection with our failure to get in step with God in His clear purpose that Palestine is for the Jews."[65]

After the war, the editor of *The King's Business* attempted to account for the dire economic situation in Britain. Refusing to blame it entirely on the war or economic factors, he ascribed it partly to the spiritual condition of the English people. "More than that, there is that blot upon England's character in their shameful renunciation of the Balfour Declaration which promised to the Jewish peoples of the world a national homeland and a national state. Coupled with this, there is the almost daily news of British cruelty in regard to Jewish immigrants."[66] A parallel assessment was made of American economic strength as evidenced by the European Recovery Program (the Marshall Plan). Commenting on Numbers 24:9 ("Blessed is he that blesseth thee, and cursed is he that curseth thee"), W. E. Vine observed, "At the present time, is it not significant that America, which is especially adopting an attitude of favor towards the Jews, is being so abundantly prospered that it can finance impoverished nations in Europe?"[67] The lesson to be drawn from all this was that America should always encourage the Jews toward their ultimate destiny, and it was assumed that criticism of Israeli policies was tantamount to the Biblical sin of cursing—that is, it brought a reciprocal curse.

There was very little expression of anti-Semitism among premillenarians during and after World War II. The *Evangel* did express a tolerant attitude toward the phenomenon, saying that its purpose was to unsettle the Jews and drive them back to Palestine, and *The King's Business* explained that anti-Semitism was due to the fact that Jews are more "clever and aggressive" than Gentiles. (These terms were not used as the equivalent of "sly and belligerent," but as the opposite of "dull and lazy.")[68] Most discussions of anti-Semitism centered around either the Russians or the Germans. At the very outset of the war, *The Sunday School Times* carried Louis S. Bauman's analysis of the invasion of Poland as God's punishment for Polish anti-Semitism.[69] The magazine later carried "A Manifesto to the Jews by American Fundamentalists," which stated opposition to anti-Semitic propaganda in the United States and deplored the use of Scripture as a basis for such an attitude. The conclusion of the statement might be considered by Jews as anti-Jewish, but that was not its intent. "We look forward to that blessed day foretold by the prophets, when through a converted Israel the whole world will learn of salvation through the Lord Jesus Christ."[70]

The Nazi "final solution" of Jewish extermination brought a deterministic response from the *Evangel:* because the Bible says that the Jews will never be wiped out and because God's Word has to be fulfilled, the Nazis would eventually be defeated.[71] Finally, after the war was over, the General Council of the Assemblies of God passed a resolution declaring its opposition to anti-Semitism.[72] With regard to Russia, the *Evangel* in 1949 ignored the past history of anti-Semitism in that country and interpreted the refusal to let Soviet Jews migrate to Israel as an attempt to curry favor with the Arabs. This was regarded as a demonstration of Russia's own interest in Palestine.[73] More realistic had been Bauman's analysis during the war:

> It matters not, it seems, whether Monarchist or Communist wears the crown in Moscow, the pathway of the Jew in that vast territory is a pathway of danger, of sorrow, and of death. The present world stress has made the grizzly old Bear a bit more wary of British and American opinion. But if Soviet power again arrives, as it will, at the place where it can snap its jaws without regard to outside opinion, then the God-conscious Jew will once more know the meaning of the three-thousand-year-old cry: "Woe is me, that I sojourn in Meschech." (Ps. 120:5)[74]

All in all, the premillenarians in general manifested the revulsion toward the Nazi horrors that many Americans shared after the war. But also like most Americans, there was no clamor for the opening of America to these displaced chosen people, only a reassertion that God's plan for them was in the Holy Land.

The anti-Arab disposition that premillenarians had developed in the 1930s was carried over into the war years and was exacerbated as Arab resistance to Israeli expansion developed in the postwar era. Harry Rimmer's 1940 book, *Palestine the Coming Storm Center,* categorized the Arabs as "usurpers" and blamed disturbances, not on the native population, but on immigrant Arabs who had no more rights there than immigrant Jews.[75] The *Alliance Weekly* blamed Mussolini for the Arabs' anti-Jewish disposition, and the *Evangel* condemned German agents for inflaming the "renegade" Arabs against "defenseless" Jews.[76] Despite the general belief in a perpetual hatred between Arab and Jew, these samples of premillenarian attitudes would lead one to believe that if Arabs and Jews were left to themselves, they would somehow "live happily ever after."

Such was not the case, nor did a more carefully considered premillenarian position believe it to be so. After the war as the Palestine conflict developed, the blame was imputed to the

Arabs' jealousy of Jewish economic success. The consistent refrain was that the land was promised to Isaac, not Ishmael.[77] The premillenarian attitude was epitomized in the *Evangel's* analysis of the situation following the first round of the war for independence.

> Even though there may be a temporary truce between the Moslems and Israel because of the pressure of the United Nations, this truce will in no wise change the attitude of "perpetual hatred" (Ezek. 35:5) that the Moslem nations have toward the people of Israel. . . .
>
> We are bidden, "Pray for the peace of Jerusalem: they shall prosper that love thee." Psalm 122:6. But the Holy Spirit prays: "Let them all be confounded and turned back that hate Zion." Psalm 129:5[78]

A revealing contrast exists between the revulsion at the tragic news that the Arabs had destroyed all twenty-seven synagogues in Jerusalem during the 1948 war and the cavalier nonchalance which greeted the prospect of the Jews' destruction of the Mosque of Omar: "It would be no surprise to prophetic students if this were to take place."[79]

When the Security Council voted to admit Israel to the United Nations, Egypt was the only member on the council to vote no. Egypt's vote was called a reflection of the deep-rooted hostility which Zechariah 14:16-19 foresees occurring in the millennium.[80] This was sheer prejudice for the prophecy merely threatens drought on any nation which does not go up to Jerusalem to worship. The only reason Egypt is singled out in Zechariah is that it does not rain there. So she is threatened with plague instead of drought if she does not go up to Jerusalem to worship. The prophecy does *not* imply that Egypt's animosity toward the Jew is greater than that of any other nation. Such was the premillenarian disposition to find little, if any, good in the Arabs.

As a condition for membership in the United Nations, Israel agreed to abide by United Nations resolutions and to internationalize the city of Jerusalem.[81] Resolution 194 (III) of December 11, 1948, called for allowing the return of all refugees who wished to live at peace. But Israel has permitted neither internationalization nor repatriation. Unlike the liberal Protestant press which continually charged the Israelis with responsibility for creating the refugee problem, the premillenarians evidently had little to say.[82] The *Evangel* revealed an anti-refugee stance, but did carry both sides of the issue:

> Many have sympathized with the Arab refugees in Palestine, who have suffered greatly since they fled from their homes before the advance of the Jewish troops. But the *Hebrew Christian Alliance Quarterly* quotes "The conservative *Economist* of London" to the effect that "it was the Jews of Palestine who implored the Arabs to stay in the Jewish State of Partitioned Palestine, and guaranteed them safe keeping and safe lodging, as is now experienced by the 80,000 who remained in Israel.[83]

(Such guarantees had hardly been reassuring, however, when only the month before, the Jewish Irgun and Stern Gang had murdered two hundred fifty Arab villagers at Deir Yassin near Jerusalem.) On the other hand, the *Evangel* quoted John L. Meredith's criticism of Israel: "If they continue to treat Arab refugees as Europe treated the Jewish refugees, Israel will be laying the groundwork for hatreds that may well produce the 'time of Jacob's trouble' foretold in Jeremiah 30:7."[84] Also cited was editor Donald G. Barnhouse's comment in *Revelation* on Israel's refusal to allow refugee repatriation: "Israel must remember that there are promises to Ishmael as well as to Isaac, and they will drink a bitter cup if they continue in their cruel and heartless way. The land has been sworn to Jacob, yes, but Jacob is to rule it one day in righteousness and not in cruelty."[85] These were merely hopeful flashes of insight, however—not the dawning of a new day in premillenarian ranks of judging Israel on the basis of morality.

The liberal Protestant press had not welcomed the establishment of the new state of Israel. *Christian Century* quoted the analysis of the executive secretary of the Southern Baptist Conference who as a conservative Christian did believe in a special relationship of Jews to God, but nonetheless felt criticism of Israel was warranted. "The new nation Israel is a miracle. In honesty, I must add that it is an 'immoral miracle.'" The liberal journal claimed that the words *immoral miracle* summed up what the editors had been saying about the new nation.[86]

However, the majority of American popular opinion was in a general way favorable toward Israel. Nadav Safran in *The United*

States and Israel lists the reasons that most Americans supported Israel rather than the Arabs: (1) nationalistic self-determination gave the Jews a right to exist; (2) the Jews were underdogs due to persecution; (3) Jewish propaganda overwhelmed Arab views; (4) democracy was preferred over totalitarianism; (5) Americans felt akin to the Jewish pioneering spirit; and (6) the drive for achievement was admired.[87] It may be added that anti-Semites preferred that Jews have their own state rather than immigrate to the United States. And even apart from premillenarianism, Safran points out that Americans gave priority in Palestine to Jews because of their direct association with the Bible, rather than to Arabs, about whom they knew very little.[88] An example of this is the strong nonmillenarian stance expressed by Representative Helen Gahagan Douglas: "Jews in Palestine today are making the Bible's prophecies come true."[89]

So the premillenarians did not have a monopoly on Christian support for Israel; what was unique was their deterministic, nonmoral approach and their eagerness. This eagerness was not expressed in direct political action on Israel's behalf, but rather this "greatest event" was heralded in press and pulpit as a sure sign of the end—to goad Christians into action and sinners into the Kingdom. D. Malcomb Leith in his study of Christian support for the state of Israel claims that although premillenarians took no political action, their arguments provided a rationale for support of the humanitarian appeal that was characteristic of Christian action groups such as the American Palestine Committee and the Christian Committee on Palestine.[90]

Various sidelights of the premillenarian preoccupation with Israel continued to be manifest, such as the latter rain, the Allenby legend, the development of Palestine, and the rebuilding of the Temple. Louis T. Talbot recounted that for years the early rains had been "insufficient" and the latter rains had been of "little value," but a few years ago the latter rains had been increased so that the land in some places was able to produce three crops a year.[91] The *Evangel* tied the origin of this "miraculous change in climate" to the first meeting of the Zionist congress in 1897.[92]

In the style of a true storyteller, Louis S. Bauman passed along the emerging legend of General Allenby and the fall of Jerusalem in 1917.

> It was 1917. Out of Egypt marched a long line of British Tommies. At the head of that line marched the British General Allenby. "Allah-Bey! Prophet-of-God!" cried the Turkish soldiers in Jerusalem; "when a leader by that name comes, Jerusalem must go back to the Jews!" For such had been a tradition of the Moslem priesthood for centuries. The Turks decided not to waste their ammunition! Without firing a shot they took to their heels, headed for Constantinople![93]

The miraculous blossoming of the desert like a rose was recounted as a sure sign of the times. The discovery of oil was hailed as God's provision for His chosen people; it would give them prestige among the industrial nations of the world. The purchase of land for agricultural development was depicted as a fulfillment of Jeremiah 32:44: "Men shall buy fields for money . . . for I will cause their captivity to return, saith the Lord."[94] Actually the land had been confiscated without consent from Arab refugees who had not been permitted to return home.

The rumor of the impending reconstruction of the Temple continued to be echoed. During the war *Dawn* reported that all parts of the building had been completed in accordance with a plan by architect G. S. Schick, whose model temple had been exhibited at the Chicago World's Fair in 1934, and were being stored in various cities in America and Europe, waiting shipment to Jerusalem.[95] Starting on July 1, 1947, every Jew was reportedly asked to contribute one shekel toward the reconstruction.[96] As British withdrawal from Jerusalem approached, it was anticipated that some "irresponsible Jews" might destroy the Mosque of Omar.[97] The *Evangelical Christian* reported that a Talmudic seminary in Jerusalem secretly studied animal sacrifice and that the Temple was soon to be rebuilt.[98] The leader of the Irgun was quoted as saying, "The Third Temple as outlined by Ezekiel will assuredly be rebuilt in our own generation."[99] On Israel's first anniversary, the editor of *Alliance Weekly* predicted, "The temple is not yet rebuilt, but it will soon appear in magnificence largely subscribed for by American Jewry."[100]

The record has amply demonstrated the premillenarian philosophy of history to be deterministic. Mechanistic figures of speech were used, such as cogs in a machine or stars in their courses.[101] Figures of natural law such as the certainty of waves upon the seashore were also used, but the metaphor of "invisible hands" did not imply natural law at work as it did to economist Adam Smith in 1776. It meant the direct, manipulative action of a personal God in history.[102] It entailed more than just the intervention of God in the course of history; it depicted God's plan as embodied in the whole of history. This is perhaps understandable in the case of those premillenarians who came out of the Calvinistic, deterministic tradition such as expressed in *The King's Business,* but the Assemblies of God, publishers of the *Evangel,* tended to reflect an Arminian, free-will background. So even those who rejected predestination as a theological principle when applied to individual salvation used it as a philosophy of history when applied to nations.

Although it is difficult to prove from direct statements, when one analyzes the premillenarians' response to Israel, the inescapable conclusion is that their philosophy of history in many cases is equivalent to the antinomian heresy. Antinomian means "against law"; if every action is preordained, then there is no need to measure one's actions by moral law, since the decision to obey or disobey the standard has already been made. If Israel is the elect, and Jewish history is predetermined by God and foretold by prophecy, then ordinary rules of international law (morality) do not apply to God's chosen people; and there is no absolute standard by which they can be judged. This is not implicit in the premillenarian view of prophecy, but it is what has worked out in practice in the response to Israel. Prophecy says that in the last days "evil men and seducers shall wax worse and worse" (II Tim. 3:13), yet premillenarians do not cheer rising crime rates—even though they do interpret them as signs of the times. Neither should they cheer crimes against international law and against humanity, even if they believe them to be prophetic. As John Cumming reminded premillenarians in 1855: "God predicts in His word what He does not applaud in His law."[103]

From Sinful Alliance to Christian Realism

The Red leadership is acting upon the assumption that it can never get into final position to launch the assault on Palestine until "American opposition is neutralized."

The answer to the question, "Will Russia Fight America?" is yes.

—Dan Gilbert, *Will Russia Fight America?*, 1948

That we are nearing the great battle of Armageddon there can be very little doubt.

—D. P. Holloway, *The Pentecostal Evangel,* 1949

Russia moved rapidly during the 1940s through various different relationships on the international scene, from German ally, to British and American ally, to Cold War antagonist; and the premillenarians managed appropriate adjustments at every turn. Russia's invasion and occupation of Poland was called by Louis S. Bauman in *The Sunday School Times* part of a prophetic "battle against God," even though at the same time he said it was God's will to punish Poland for her anti-Semitism.[1] At this point, while Russia was overrunning small countries, of which premillenarians knew little or nothing, the response to Russia tended to be deterministic. The *Evangel* coolly observed, "God is allowing Russia to expand and gain many people, in fulfillment of Ezekiel 38."[2] Such was not to be the case, however, in the postwar era as the United States felt threatened by Russia and premillenarians envisioned the United States fighting hand-in-hand with God, resisting the great forces of evil. Instead of allowing God to fight His own battles, it was deemed necessary to assist Him in the great moral fight against evil—even though the outcome was predetermined. Russia's Baltic and Polish expansion brought renewed assertions from Arno C. Gaebelein's *Our Hope* of her identification with Gog, prince of *Rosh* (Ezek. 38).[3] Louis S. Bauman in *The Sunday School Times* identified Russia as the foremost of Israel's latter-day enemies. But evidently identifying Mussolini as the Antichrist and the current crisis as the end, Bauman believed that Mussolini would eventually stop Russia.[4]

In the early stages of the war, the Nazi-Soviet Pact continued to be a major subject for discussion as most premillenarians saw at least the foreshadowing, if not the final realization, of the great northern confederation of Gog and Gomer in Ezekiel 38. Both the *Evangel* and *The Sunday School Times* foresaw an even closer alliance of Russia and Germany in the future; Bauman, however, confidently predicted that Hitler would not rule the world, nor would Stalin, because that task was prophetically reserved for the Beast or Antichrist.[5] Although it was difficult to see any basis for permanency in this alliance of mutual cynicism, the *Evangel* discovered the common denominator in their joint anti-Semitism.[6] *The King's Business* carried an article in which John Hess McComb, pastor of New York's Broadway Presbyterian Church, warned of the two nations' imminent attack on Palestine: "The attack is all too probable to be ignored any longer as a possibility." He was quite willing, though, to passively accept this impending disaster. "We are convinced that battling for democracy will not save the situation; our duty, as Christians, is clear: We are to snatch from the wreck of this age those for whom Christ died."[7]

By October of 1940, eight months before Hitler attacked Russia, the *Evangel* was speaking of rumors of war in eastern Europe, saying that "many Bible students look for a conflict in which Russia will be victorious over Germany," but adding that whether their interpretation was correct or not, it would all work out according to God's prearranged program.[8] Two months later it was stated that the prediction of Scripture seemed to be that Russian domination would reach the Rhine.[9] Although it did not work out as he expected, Dr. Harry Rimmer's 1940 book, *The Coming War and the Rise of Russia,* made some uncanny predictions. Rimmer identified Gomer as the Balkans rather than Germany and declared, "The final peace in the present conflict will see Russia as the head of a Balkan alliance, in which case the beginning of the league Ezekiel forecasts will be visible."[10] He did not foresee Hitler's attack on Russia, but the formation of the Warsaw Pact in 1955 corresponded to his prognosis. *Our Hope* presented a totally different analysis—Palestine would be invaded after the current war by "the king of the north." This was to be Assyria, not Gog—a mistake made by many interpreters.[11]

Those who had preached that the Nazi-Soviet Pact was the great northern confederacy were dumbfounded by the German attack on Russia in June, 1941. The absence of comment about it seemed to be just one big awkward silence, like a little child caught in a lie. The *Evangel* did manage one meek statement about those whose prophetic system had been smashed by the new twist of events: "There are some prophets who are suffering no casualties. They are inspired writers of Bible prophecy. Their words shall be fulfilled. We may err when we forecast just how and when they will be fulfilled, but in God's own time the entire prophetic plan shall be complete."[12]

Arno C. Gaebelein in *Our Hope* compared Hitler and Stalin to "one demon trying to cast out another" and claimed that he had pointed out that the two nations' destinies were linked.[13] He chose not to recall for his readers that two years earlier he had reminded them of his prediction of a closer alliance of the two.[14] He was quite perturbed about the mutual-aid pact between Britain and Russia, recalling from Biblical history that whenever Israel had allied with ungodly nations she had gone down to defeat. After reiterating Russia's "hell inspired program" he asked, "Can the Church count on God's intervention and righteous help if they make common cause with the worst enemy throughout the entire history of the Church?"[15] He later referred to this alliance as a "sin." The *Evangel* similarly questioned the pact: "Can God answer a nation's prayers for a just peace when they stoop to an unholy alliance to attain that end?"[16]

Russia was still considered the enemy of the church. The *Prophetic Word* was cited by the *Evangel* for the news that after the German invasion Russian churches and synagogues had been filled with worshipers praying for Russian victory, that ten thousand had filled the Russian Orthodox cathedral in Moscow. This was ridiculed as obvious propaganda and readers were told of other more significant news out of Moscow, a manifesto which said: "We mean to bring all the churches of the globe crashing in a gigantic sea of flames."[17] Pointing to the recent exile of two Christians in White Russia, the *Evangel* said that the friendly front Russia was putting on did not make her less anti-Christian.[18] Further proof was later offered by Louis S. Bauman, who pointed out that all churches and synagogues had been closed in Poland, and by *The Sunday School Times,* which quoted Stalin's words to atheists in the newly annexed Baltic states: "The duty of the Godless is to act without mercy against the Church which is, and will remain, the enemy of the Soviet Union."[19] This then was the disposition of premillenarians when Japan attacked Pearl Harbor and they found their own United States an ally of the Soviet Union.

With the exception of Louis S. Bauman's 1942 book, *Russian Events in the Light of Bible Prophecy,* there seems to have been little said concerning Russia in the early stages of this alliance. The argument from silence does not reveal whether this was due to premillenarians' patriotism, discretion, or fear of suppression. Possibly it was none of these, for in early 1943 the *Evangel* gave a hint that other concerns were crowding Russia out:

> In many cases, prophetic students have been so preoccupied with "the revival of the Roman Empire" that they have failed to accord proper importance to the role of Russia. Now that Tripoli has fallen and Mussolini's empire has all but passed away, *interest is switching to Russia.* For it now seems plain that the Red Army will have the decisive role in the defeat of Nazi Germany, and Russia may be the dominant factor in Continental European affairs once the war is over.[20]

The only previous observation the *Evangel* had made was on the occasion of Hitler's setbacks in the winter of 1940-41, arousing new hopes of Russian victory that would in turn lead to a northern confederacy.[21] Bauman's book, however, had been consistently critical of Russia, rehearsing the evil of the Communists since the revolution. One of his themes is reflected in the title of chapter ten, "Any American or British Alliance with Gog Is Abnormal." He cautiously blasted American foreign policy, arguing from a moral stance that martyrdom was preferable to compromise: "The author does not want to be critical of the United States and Great Britain for accepting assistance from a beast in order to destroy a beast. Nevertheless, it is his conviction that it would be better for America to go down fighting a glorious fight to preserve the political and spiritual faiths of our fathers than to live and be so conscienceless as to wink at the crimes of Russia."[22] He predicted that the result of the war would be that atheistic Russia in victory would pose an enormous threat to religion in Europe, causing ten nations to unify in a great revival of the Roman Empire to resist the great northern confederacy.[23] Thus was the world shaping up for the great battles of the end. So ran Bauman's thesis, and his work was glowingly recommended to readers of *The Sunday School Times*.[24]

During the last couple of years of the war in Europe, the *Evangel,* too, became openly critical of the Russian ally. In May, 1943, the observation was made: "There are many who believe that the final struggle of this age will find Germany and Russia arrayed together against the United States, Britain, and the Mediterranean powers. . . . It may not be a popular thing to say at the present time, but it is not hard to envision such a possibility in either the near or the distant future."[25] Later that year, the *Evangel* cited Dan Gilbert in *World-Wide Temple Evangelist* for the information that Russia was forming a "Committee of Free Germany" to provide Germany opportunity to become a junior partner in a northern European confederacy.[26] By February, 1944, the "Roving Reporter" in the *United Evangelical Action* was tossing off some flippant fatalism:

> Joe Stalin is running true to form. He is letting the United Nations know, in unmistakable terms, that he purposes to manage eastern Europe to suit himself. We had all better

> smile meekly and let him do it; he will anyway. By and by he will decide to run all of Europe and then the world. Let's hope for at least a decade of peace before he is ready. When it comes, the present conflict will resemble a Methodist love feast in comparison.[27]

Then in September, 1944, there was speculation that Russia was about to open a consulate in Jerusalem. The *Evangel* took the opportunity to recollect that Russia's claim to be a protector of Palestine had led to the Crimean War and declared that this renewed interest was significant.[28] A couple months later former Ambassador to Russia, William C. Bullitt, predicted in *Life* magazine a war between the United States and Russia within fifteen years.[29] Also in 1944, a diatribe against Russia by Dan Gilbert appeared, entitled *The Red Terror and Bible Prophecy.* He believed that Russia's battle against Germany was just a temporary diversion from Russia's true goal in Palestine. He declared that the war against Palestine had already begun with Russian persecution of the Jews. The objective was to desecrate the Holy Land and turn it into an "antireligious museum."[30] He claimed that already 22,000,000 Jewish and Christian believers had been killed by Russian Communists in their battle against God. This then was the background that premillenarians brought to the situation that developed after World War II. It was not necessary for Russia to act belligerently; her mere existence was sufficient provocation to the premillenarian mind which expected a postwar invasion of Palestine leading to Armageddon.

Armageddon had been a particular topic of interest at the beginning of the war. The popular author, Roger Babson, spoke of Russia as the controlling factor in the world crisis and of Stalin as the world's greatest statesman. This elicited the *Evangel's* comment that the reign of Antichrist and the battle of Armageddon were "swiftly approaching."[31] As the war spread to the Near East, and Britain had a million troops set to defend the Suez Canal, it was said, "With so much military activity in and around Palestine it seems that the nations are hastening on to their last great conflict at Armageddon."[32] Before the Russian alliance with Britain and the United States, the *Evangel* was saying that Russia *and her allies* would march upon Palestine and there meet destruction at the hands of God and His people. But after the alliance little was said about Russia's being defeated at Armageddon (except in theoretical discussions).

During the war a very confusing theological debate did develop about Armageddon. Was the battle of Armageddon of Revelation 16:16 the same as the battle in the Valley of Jehoshaphat of Joel 3:12? Was the Gog and Magog invasion of Revelation 20:8 the same as that in Ezekiel 38? The *Evangel* asserted the battle in the Valley of Jehoshaphat and the battle of Armageddon were the same, one of the first events to follow the rapture of the church.[33] Harry Rimmer, following Nathaniel West, taught that Armageddon would not take place until after the millennium, but that the battle of Hamon-Gog, or the battle of the Valley of Jehoshaphat, was the first battle on the agenda. This did not make his stand on Russia any different from the others. They all believed "the Russians are coming"; but instead of "Armageddon Now!" it was "Jehoshaphat Now!"[34] Later, Louis T. Talbot's system placed the battle of Armageddon at the end of the Great Tribulation which was to be the seven-year-period following Russia's defeat—that defeat being imminent in his expectation also.[35] Arno C. Gaebelein in *Our Hope* regarded Armageddon as the next battle in God's plan, but in his view Russia was not to be represented there. Her defeat was to come at the very beginning of the millennium. Although he did not believe Russia's invasion was to be immediate, he did believe that current events were leading toward that invasion and that if Russia won the war, Stalin would soon be a great universal dictator.[36] This was certainly a confusing array of prophetic interpretations; nevertheless they all maintained the continuity of premillenarian antipathies toward Russia, particularly as the Cold War began to develop.

Within a year after the end of the war, *Our Hope* was lashing out against the conduct of American foreign policy toward Russia. Gaebelein's periodical was the most vocal of the major premillenarian magazines, probably because it was not an official organ of any institution. Accordingly, he was concerned only with his subscribers' opinions rather than with those of a constituency that might possibly be offended by his political stance. He was later accused of "harping too much on Russia," but he vowed to continue.[37] He pointed out that "by God's grace" America had the greatest army and navy in the world, and yet by American consent, Russia had become a threat to the whole world.[38] The Yalta conference he declared to be a major tragedy and lamented the continued presence of Russian troops in Iran. "To appease the U.S.S.R. now can only bring disaster, another Munich. If the UNO is firm, however, and if other powers show a willingness to back up their words with weapons, we have no doubt that Stalin will come down off his high horse."[39] At the outset of World War II, Gaebelein had prophesied that Stalin would rule the world, but now it seemed to him too early for that to happen.[40] In retrospect he condemned the wartime policy: "To form a league with a God-defying government was sin, and nothing less."[41]

At about this same time, the *Evangel* drew its readers' attention to David Lawrence's prediction in *United States News* that current international trends made war possible in ten or fifteen years and probable within fifteen or twenty.[42] But the *Evangel* found an even more imminent threat in the appeal of some Arabs for Russian assistance in the Palestine situation.[43]

After Winston Churchill had tagged the split in Europe the "Iron Curtain," Arno C. Gaebelein called it an "interesting frontier" to students of prophecy because it approximated the dividing line between the northern confederacy of Ezekiel and the revived Roman Empire of Daniel and Revelation.[44] Similar statements were made in response to the announcement of the Truman Doctrine in March, 1947 (which committed America to defend nations against the spread of communism), and the development of the Marshall Plan after June, 1947 (Russia and her satellites having rejected the plan for the rehabilitation of Europe).[45] With regard to the Truman Doctrine, the *Evangel* cited a sister publication:

> A year ago, effort was exerted to get Russia out of Iran. Now pressure is put forth to keep her out of Greece and Turkey. But Russia is determined to reach the Mediterranean, and if she is blocked through other lands, she may by-pass them and come through the Holy Land.[46]

Under the heading, "The Menace of Russia," the *Evangel* spoke of Russia and Eastern Europe's rejection of the Marshall Plan, saying that it was little wonder that anti-God Russia was singled out by God in Ezekiel 38:3: "I am against *thee* O Rosh!" (RV).[47] A week later it was also pointed out that although worship was professedly tolerated in Russia, no member of the Communist Party was permitted even to believe in God.[48]

In view of this kind of concern among premillenarians, *The King's Business* saw fit to begin in October, 1947, a major series of ten articles by Louis T. Talbot on Palestine, Russia, and Ezekiel 36-39. He based his identification of Russia in Ezekiel 38 on the work of the nineteenth-century German philologist, Wilhelm Gesenius, who had no doubt that the Hebrew *Rosh* was Russia, *Meshech* was Moscow, and *Tubal* was Tobolsk.[49] One might well ask: If Gesenius and other German scholars had not been writing in an age of intense German nationalism (in the post-Napoleonic era following the Treaty of Tilsit by which Czar Alexander I and Napoleon had carved up Prussia), would they have been quite as certain about their identification? In discussing the expected great northern alliance, Talbot commented on the defunct Nazi-Soviet Pact of 1939, saying that "it only proved that there is nothing far-fetched or impossible in the prophecies about these amazing alliances"—if it happened before, it could happen again.[50] Similar material had been presented by the *Evangel* in citing D. M. Panton's remark in the British premillenarian monthly *Dawn:* "Gomer is to be a satellite of Rosh in the final invasion of Palestine (Ezek. 38:6), and Germany is already heading toward that Satanic ideal."[51] Talbot commented that the aggressive foreign policy that would lead the confederation into Palestine was comparable to the events of the past year.[52] He analyzed the motives of Russia.

> The Soviet Union has always been against God, but at the time of the fulfillment of this prophecy, it will form a diabolical expedition to wipe from the face of the earth every last vestige of the worship of God symbolized first by the Jewish people, and then by their promised Land, with its capital city of Jerusalem. Therefore, judgment swift and complete will come upon Gog and all his hordes, because our all-powerful God will Himself defend His name, His people, and His chosen city. He will bring irrevocable doom upon all who oppose Him in that day.[53]

In November, 1947, the recently established (1946) magazine *Christian Life* carried an article, "Russia in the News and Prophecy," by Merril T. MacPherson, pastor of the Church of the Open Door in Philadelphia and former president of the Independent Fundamental Churches of America. He categorically stated that the next world war would involve Palestine, and cited former Governor of Pennsylvania, George Earle, who had warned that unless America struck the first blow before Russia had perfected her atomic bomb, very likely within five years there would not be more than 10 per cent of the American people left. MacPherson believed that only the threat of massive atomic retaliation had contained Russia's aggressive plan so far. He concluded by asking:

> When will Russia strike? This we do not know, but we believe that it will be as soon as she judges herself to be capable of making some sneak atomic attacks upon our own great nation. One thing certain, according to God's Word, is that one day—perhaps in the near future—Russia will strike.[54]

There is no doubt that anti-Russianism was rampant among all Americans in late 1947. In this same issue, *Christian Life* editors quoted figures from a September 26 Gallup Poll which showed that 53 per cent of all American adults believed that World War III would break out within ten years. *Christian Life* had made its own poll of its readers which showed a comparable figure of 49 per cent. Though no figure is available for the general public, 26 per cent of the Christians expected war in five years, while 25 per cent of the readers did not expect war with Russia at all in the foreseeable future. One of the latter group responded: "Who thought up this hate-mongering?"[55]

Probably the worst example of "hate-mongering" appeared as an editorial in *The Southern Presbyterian Journal* by L. Nelson Bell, father-in-law of evangelist Billy Graham and eventually the first executive editor of the periodical *Christianity Today.* The editorial, entitled "Christian Realism," began with the premise that communism would continue until it was stopped by force, and then concluded:

> The solution—let the American Government issue notice to Russia that she is to start the immediate evacuation of all territories into which she has expanded since 1942. Further that at the end of one week one atomic bomb will be dropped in a sparsely settled area of European Russia

> and another in a like section in Siberia—to prove that we can and will carry out our ultimatum. Then, unless there is clear evidence that our demands are being carried out, at the end of five more days the next bomb will be dropped on the Kremlin with immediate and continued use of the bomb until the present Communist regime is replaced by men who are willing to comply with our demands.

After that shocker, he added:

> We do not expect this suggestion to be put into practice but we make bold to predict that not many years hence we will wish with all our hearts that we had done just this thing.[56]

No Scriptural basis was offered for such "realism." This statement of international ethics brought an avalanche of criticism in Christian journals throughout the country. Bell found it expedient to apologize, but not for the ideas, only for their expression: "It is our considered but belated judgment, that this journal was not the proper medium for the expression of a personal opinion on secular problems by a member of the editorial staff."[57] He had been guilty of violating the taboo against the social gospel, not of subverting the Beatitude, "Blessed are the peacemakers."

This attitude was not unique with Bell. Erling Jorstad in his 1970 book, *The Politics of Doomsday,* gave as an example the executive board of the ultrafundamentalist American Council of Christian Churches, which in 1948 called for war, saying America had "a moral responsibility to strike first using adequate and necessary ways to thwart the maddened purpose of the enemy." Jorstad's analysis of one of the bases for this frame of mind does seem appropriate: "Apocalyptic premillenialism assured them that their call for war with Russia was not really warmongering; since only God could destroy this planet and since that would not happen until after the Final Judgment, Americans need not fear any form of nuclear warfare."[58] In this philosophy the overlapping of morality and determinism was apparent. True, this selective morality was an appeal to a sort of "civil disobedience" in international law, especially the situation where Bell found it justified to meddle in the internal affairs of Russia to replace the present communist regime—his appeal was to some higher law of universal human welfare. Unfortunately, because of the deterministic element this moral crusade was not moderated by any realistic fear of retaliation or martyrdom. It was antinomianism—while refusing to leave everything fatalistically in the hands of God (since everything was predetermined according to prophecy anyway), proponents of this philosophy failed to nourish any healthy skepticism (of their own moral crusade) that could have produced sensible caution. Since all was predetermined, how could they possibly go wrong?

As the Cold War began to develop, detailed analyses appeared, such as Dan Gilbert's *Russia's Next Move: In the Light of Bible Prophecy.* He noted that secular writers could not understand Russia's interest in moving against Iran, but prophecy students knew that it was in fulfillment of Ezekiel's prophecy (38:5) that Persia would be an ally of Russia. One of Russia's next moves would be an occupation of Turkey as she moved south to annex Ethiopia and Libya, another fulfillment of Ezekiel 38:5. "A study of Soviet diplomacy indicates that Stalin is *now* in the process of building the very Empire outlined in Ezekiel 38-39."[59]

This sense of impending crisis paralleled the growing hostilities in Palestine and resulted in renewed expectations of Armageddon. The *Evangel* underscored columnist Dorothy Thompson's piece headed "Armageddon" which had stated: "It is entirely possible that World War III will start in ninety days."[60] In April, 1948, an *Evangel* article, "God and the World Crisis," stated that very likely the Arabs would ask help from Russia, and Russia would accept the opportunity. "Nine countries of Eastern Europe are already united. The stage is setting for the great battle of Armageddon." This supposedly meant that the United Nations was doomed.[61] Anticipation heightened in 1948 as Israel declared her independence, the Communists took over Czechoslovakia, and the Berlin blockade was established. *Our Hope's* observation on the blockade was that the end might be near, and "the Moscow Bear's paw will crush all opposition east and southeast, but not toward the west."[62] At the end of November, the *Evangel* was explaining why the nations of the world were insanely spending one-third of their incomes on the arms race: they were under the diabolic influence of the three unclean spirits of Revelation 16:13 which were gathering the nations to the battle of Armageddon.[63]

The *Evangel* relentlessly continued this battle cry through the first half of 1949. It cited the prediction in *Review of World Affairs* that Russia would move towards Palestine in the next decade. A quotation from the *Bible and the News* observed that "whether this invasion will occur in 1949 or later, is a question that is much discussed."[64] One article, "Things to Come," quoted the Truman Committee's report: "Atomic war will start on, before, or at least by January 1953."[65] All this self-induced excitement finally climaxed in D. P. Holloway's "Russia and Armageddon": "That we are nearing the great battle of Armageddon there can be very little doubt."[66]

In the summer of 1949 a series by Harry A. Ironside appeared in *Our Hope* under the title, "Setting the Stage for the Last Act of the Great World Drama." He, too, had the same sense of urgency about Russia and Germany forming a confederation:

> Has not this almost taken shape already? Now look at the northern part of the stage. Is there no significance in the apparent determination of Russia to dominate Germany? Take the Church of God out of the world tomorrow, and that confederation might spring into existence at once.[67]

Yet Ironside did not foresee the culmination of all this for at least another thousand years. According to his unique scheme the northern confederacy was to be destroyed at the end of the millennium.[68] Amazingly, even though the last act was still a millennium away, by noting that Russia and Germany were already on the stage he was able to generate excited expectancy of the rapture of the church.

In September, 1949, the Russians exploded their first atomic bomb. Curiously enough, the premillenarian response was subdued, in fact, nearly nonexistent. Perhaps after a couple of years of frantically crying, "Armageddon Now!" they were suffering from emotional battle fatigue, or maybe the awareness that the enemy also had the bomb was a sobering experience. *The King's Business,* which had said little about Russia, blandly headed an editorial: "Russia Has It—Now What?" The editor said that this was "but another step in the advance of Russia toward the goal of this Northern Confederacy" and that the proper response for the Christian was not to get alarmed, but to "rest upon his divinely-given knowledge of coming events."[69]

The recurring issue of who would oppose the rise of Russia and the northern confederacy had taken some interesting twists during the war and after. Louis S. Bauman in 1940 had continued to see a revived Roman Empire headed up by Mussolini as the outcome of the war. The war was to be a final struggle between democracy and autocracy, and autocracy would win and establish the Empire. According to Bauman, most premillenarians saw this as the interpretation of the image's iron and clay feet in the vision of Daniel 2.[70] Bauman explained that it was necessary for Mussolini to drop out of the Rome-Berlin-Tokyo axis in order to fulfill the prophecies.[71] The whole subject was quietly dropped as the tide of war turned against Italy.

Other premillenarians had better luck with their predictions. In *Our Hope,* W. W. Fereday predicted an alliance between Britain and Italy after World War II as part of the anticipated revival of the Roman Empire; and although it did not come about until 1973 when Britain joined the European Economic Community, it could be said that he was not completely wrong.[72] Harry Rimmer in 1940 forecast a new League of Nations as a result of the war—and the rise of a universal dictator.[73] The United Nations has arrived, but there is no dictator yet.

After the war, Arno C. Gaebelein projected a United Nations of Europe as the embodiment of the revived Roman Empire.[74] The East-West split of Europe foreshadowed for him the outlines of the two confederacies.[75] The formation of the North Atlantic Treaty Organization (NATO) was interpreted to be the alliance of ten kings in the empire.[76] Harry A. Ironside, with reference to NATO and the United Nations, asserted that "the ten kingdoms are already in process of organization."[77] Gaebelein suggested in 1949 a kind of revisionist interpretation of NATO and the Cold War when he said:

> These defense measures being taken by the nations of the West may be the very thing that will incite Russia to war eventually. . . .
>
> In a way, the Atlantic Pact is a step toward a world of peace, but not in the manner that Mr. Truman expects; for it may easily be an instrument in bringing about the aggression on the part of the East which will precede the coming of the Lord. Actually, then, the Atlantic Pact may be, first of all, the first step toward war![78]

There continued to be occasional speculation as to where the United States fitted into this scheme. In 1940 a discussion on Armageddon by Louis S. Bauman in *The Sunday School Times* brought forth this covering comment from the editor, Charles G. Trumbull: "It is to be noted carefully that Dr. Bauman does not say that Mussolini is the Antichrist, nor does he say that the activities of the Antichrist have begun in the present European War, nor that Britain will be defeated in the present war."[79] But very careful examination will show that those were exactly the things that Bauman was saying; but since this was the twenty-third article in a series, Trumbull would have found it inconvenient to reject the article even if he had wished to. Bauman specifically included the *allies* of Britain in this defeat.[80] But in 1942, after the United States was allied to Britain, Bauman reversed himself and rejoiced that the Stars and Stripes would float aloft in the millennial kingdom.[81]

> If our interpretation is correct, then thank God for this divine assurance that Great Britain and her young cubs, Canada, Australia, New Zealand, *and America* will be found protesting to the very end of the age against the ravages of the great Bolshevistic colossus of the north and its atheistic allies.[82]

After the war, *Our Hope's* analysis of the East-West split in Europe included the possibility that the revived Roman Empire might include the whole Western Hemisphere.[83] It seemed to Gaebelein that the United States would actually be "the moving and most powerful factor" in this Western Alliance opposing Russia; he did not, however, in 1947 expect war for eight to ten years.[84] Evangelist H. E. Fisher, whose Doctor of Theology thesis was "The Destiny of Soviet Russia," explained that Russia's invasion of Palestine, in support of the Arabs, would be opposed by Italy, England, and America, who would support the Jews. This latter union was to be a Catholic confederation which would defeat the Russians, and its great leader would become the first president of a world government.[85] This was presented as "The Plan," without any hedging whatsoever. Another article by Merril T. MacPherson in *Christian Life* in 1948 said the empire would "undoubtedly" include the British dominions and the United States, and that the Iron Curtain was a line placed there by God—so it must be held.[86] In Gaebelein's system, the Roman Empire, including the United States, would be destroyed by God at the battle of Armageddon; Russia would be destroyed after the battle.[87] Future prospects were most bluntly expressed by Dan Gilbert in *Will Russia Fight America? The Question Considered in the Light of Bible Prophecy:*

> The Red leadership is acting upon the assumption that it can never get into final position to launch the assault on Palestine until *"American opposition is neutralized."*
>
> The answer to the question, "Will Russia Fight America?" is *yes.*[88]

Although all these conflicting schemes may leave one confused, they do not obscure the basic fact that the premillenarians expected, if not welcomed, a fight with Russia. This predisposition was in part an ideological conflict with communistic socialism, but the driving force of the idea stemmed from their interpretation of prophecy.

To the premillenarian mind the formation of the United Nations was also a foreboding evil. It presaged the revival of the Roman Empire which was to be led by the Antichrist. This tone had been set by Harry Rimmer as early as 1940 when he predicted that a new League of Nations would appear after the war along with a universal dictator.[89] The very term *United Nations* sounded ominous to the *Evangel,* and the organization's ability to wield power justly was questioned.[90] Wilbur M. Smith in two timely articles, "How Antichrist Will Rule" and "The Shaping of One World," saw international affairs leading to the dictatorship of Revelation 13.[91] This skepticism toward anything associated with the United Nations resulted in a preference among premillenarians for unilateral action vis-à-vis Russia or Israel—there was great fear of submitting the sovereignty of the United States to the domain of the Antichrist.

The Far East continued to be assigned roles in prophetic schemes too. Asiatic nations were usually included among "the kings of the east" of Revelation 16:12 or the "many people with thee" accompanying the northern confederacy in Ezekiel 38:6. Japan was given priority in the early 40s: "Scriptures clearly indicated that great Oriental armies will invade Palestine from the east and the entry of Japan into the war seems to be a step in that direction."[92] But Japan's star quickly dimmed. After the war, *Our Hope* suggested China and India as likely candidates, because communism was making rapid strides there.[93] The advent of the Cold War shifted attention to eastern Europe, and the Russian satellites, as well as the Far East, were included among the "many people with thee."[94] Louis T. Talbot in *The King's Business* gave a different twist than others; in his system, Japan, China, and India would be *opposed* to the Russian confederation.[95] With the fall of China to the Communists, attention tended to center upon that nation as the dominant figure in the Far East: "It is possible that the sweeping victories of the Communist army in China indicate the groundwork for the federation of these northern and eastern nations is being laid."[96] In a message at the 1949 Founder's Week Conference at Moody Bible Institute, Wilbur M. Smith drew attention to an article on Gog and Magog by Walter Scott in the June 1888 issue of *The Prophetic News and Israel's Watch:*

> Russia has for ages meditated on the conquest of Asia and India and China. Great Britain, with the United States, stands face to face with this Russian power, and these two sides will come into one final awful struggle. We judge that the tide of Russian conquest will flow on to the frontiers of China.... We believe, from the place assigned to Russia in the Word of God, that her legions will sweep over the plains and mountains of Asia and become the dominant power over all the East until she falls forever on the mountains of Judea.[97]

The point Smith made was that only the inspired Word of God could have enabled Scott to make such an accurate prediction. (Smith did not suggest what spirit inspired another writer he quoted to identify in 1844 "the kings of the east" as the officers of the East India Company.)

The Certainty of Survival

A whole world in a very frenzy of preparation for the greatest of all wars! Such is the divine revelation of the days immediately preceding the Armageddon. No human being need be told that exactly that *describes our day!*

—Louis S. Bauman, *The King's Business,* 1950

Is the United States to be the next nation to fall from her present exalted position through her failure to help Israel in this crucial hour when she is surrounded by foes bent on her destruction?

—George T. B. Davis, *The Sunday School Times,* 1957

Today we see precisely this setup: Russia about to move on the Middle East; Israel in its place, regathered; the wealth, the spoil of the nations there; the need for possessing the Middle East perfectly obvious to Russia; and the only thing deterring her the fear of our military might.

—John F. Walvoord, *Moody Monthly,* 1959

As the premillenarians arrived at mid-century, they faced a situation in which Israel was precariously back in the Promised

Land, and an atomic Armageddon was prevented only by a tenuous balance of power. Nonetheless, they were confident—confident that nothing could dislodge the chosen people from His land, and certain that an atomic doomsday for humanity could not occur until all Biblical prophecy had been fulfilled. In the decade that lay ahead, their expectations were tantalized as Israel expanded toward Suez, and Russia showed belligerent hands in East Germany and Hungary.

The rebirth of Israel continued to be cause for celebration; it was spoken of as the most significant sign of the times and (as the Balfour Declaration before) as "a red-letter day." In an article in *The King's Business,* "Israel Lives Again!" Louis S. Bauman exclaimed, "But, behold, we who now live are seeing the most significant event of all the ages—Israel revives—still *spiritually* dead, yet in his very deadness he stands upon his feet, awaiting the breath of God!" This "most significant event" must have eclipsed even the resurrection of Jesus—traditionally the most highly esteemed event in Christian history. Bauman, however, drew the analogy that just as Christ was in the grave for three days, Israel had now been dead for three millennia (since Nebuchadnezzar had dethroned Zedekiah), and her resurrection was due. Bauman's literalism was based upon Hosea 6:2: "After two days will he revive us; *in the third day* he will raise us up, and we shall live in his sight." He also based his analogy on II Peter 3:8: "One day is with the Lord as a thousand years, and a thousand years as one day." Pursuing a similar argument, he averred that since six thousand years of history had transpired, the earth was due for a millennial sabbath of rest.[1]

Israel's success was attributed wholly to God's work in history. In support of this belief, the *Evangel* passed along an anecdote from *Israel Speaks*—the Commander-in-Chief of the British Mediterranean fleet had paid a visit to the Israeli Chief of Staff and had been presented with a Bible, which the Israeli had referred to as Israel's "secret weapon."[2] On his nationwide "Radio Bible Class," Martin R. DeHaan pleaded for the nations to get in step with God's program of history. The basic problem of the whole world was that "Palestine, the Holy Land, is also still God's chosen land, and there can be no peace in this world until the nation and the land, according to God's purpose, are again fully united." He repeatedly asked Christians not for political action, but for prayer: "Let us pray, therefore, that the leaders of the nation and our own nation may see that God is on the side of those who recognize this program."[3] Some premillenarians, however, recognized that if God were to answer such prayers for peace, then the prophecies of tribulation and Armageddon could never come to pass. W. E. Vine writing on "The Future of Israel" in *The Alliance Witness* pointed out that Israel's tendency to trust in national and material developments would lead to a period of unprecedented tribulation for the country.[4]

These issues were part of the larger question of whether the present return to Palestine was the prophesied restoration or not. The president of Moody Bible Institute, William Culbertson, expressed his awareness that some saw no connection between what was going on in the Holy Land and the Biblical prophecies, but he sided with those who believed in at least a partial return before the second coming of Christ.[5] Charles L. Feinberg of the Biola faculty expressed a similar view.[6] The *Evangel* thought the present restoration was the coming together of Ezekiel's "Dry Bones" and that an eventual repentance would invite the Breath of God to instill new life in them.[7] As Louis H. Hauff, pastor of the San Bernardino, California, Assembly of God expressed it:

> Some have been disturbed because there have not been signs of religious awakening in Israel. . . . The spiritual awakening will come later. . . . It seems logical to expect that Israel as a nation will continue in blindness and ungodliness until the Lord returns.

He believed that the Great Tribulation might be the "crushing" that would cause the Jews to cry out in repentance and accept Christ as the Messiah.[8] This position allowed premillenarians to take the edge off the criticism which attended Israel's unrighteous acts. They taught that even though the Jews were still evil, they were fulfilling the will of God, and, therefore, should not be opposed.

New insight was available to premillenarians in May and July of 1955 as *Moody Monthly* opened its pages to spokesmen for both the Israeli and Arab views. Isaac D. Unna, vice-consul of the Consulate of Israel in Chicago, and Fayez A. Sayegh, an

Arab spokesman on leave of absence from the United Nations Secretariat, each were given opportunity to express their views and offer rebuttals. It was particularly unusual for readers to be provided with the Arab view.

Unna in his presentation said that he did not feel that it was too much to ask that out of 2,022,200 square miles of land a tiny strip of 8,000 square miles be returned to a people who had been driven out two thousand years before. He claimed that repatriation of Arab refugees was not practical and that they must be resettled in Arab lands, pointing out that Israel itself had absorbed 350,000 Jewish refugees from Arab lands. He reminded readers that although Israel had been accused of aggressive acts, Egypt had been condemned forty times by the United Nations Mixed Armistice Commission for various acts of murder and violence between August 1954, and March 1955.[9]

On the Arab side, Sayegh recounted that Jews and Arabs had lived peaceably together until Zionists began to boycott the use of Arab labor and that such exclusiveness was expressly stated by Zionist leader Chaim Weizmann to have the objective of making Palestine "as Jewish as England was English." Sayegh claimed that the only way the Jews had been able to purchase Arab land, as Weizmann had confessed, was "sometimes through straw men, sometimes by bribes." During the 1948 war, the only reason Arabs fled their homes, Sayegh said, was fear of the Jewish troops and terrorists. They had not fled in response to appeals by Arab leaders as the Jews had claimed. He cited the opinion of historian Arnold J. Toynbee:

> If the heinousness of sin is to be measured by the degree to which the sinner is sinning against the light that God has vouchsafed to him, the Jews had even less excuse in A.D. 1948 for evicting Palestinian Arabs from their homes than Nebuchadnezzar and Titus and Hadrian and the Spanish and Portuguese inquisition had for uprooting, persecuting, and exterminating Jews in Palestine and elsewhere at divers times in the past. In A.D. 1948 the Jews knew, from personal experience, what they were doing; and it was their supreme tragedy that the lesson learnt by them from their encounter with the Nazi German Gentiles should have been not to eschew but to imitate some of the evil deeds that the Nazis had committed against the Jews.

Sayegh recalled that Israel had been condemned by the Mixed Armistice Commission no less than twenty times for raids across the armistice lines, and claimed that no Arab state had ever been condemned by any United Nations organ for such raids on Jewish territory. He decried the discrimination against Arabs who had remained in Israel, being subjected to military government, suffering discrimination in citizenship requirements, receiving depressed wages, and being sentenced without trial. He supported his contentions from a Jewish source, William Zukerman's *Jewish Newsletter:* "A more flagrant case of discrimination is hard to find even in the annals of the chauvinistic twentieth century."[10]

Moody Monthly's July 1955 issue carried the rebuttals of Karl Baehr, executive director of the American Christian Palestine Committee, and Mr. Unna. Unna accused the Arabs of responsibility for the 1948 war by refusing to accept partition, or any compromise, and by invading Israeli territory. He failed to offer any reason why they should wish to compromise on the confiscation of their homeland. One telling point was his ridiculing of Sayegh's claim that no Arab state had been condemned: "I fail to see any difference in the wordings of the respective United Nations Mixed Armistice Commission resolutions which frequently condemned the various Arab countries and those which much less frequently condemned Israel for defending its borders." Arab claims of peaceful intentions were belied, he said, by statements such as that by Major Salah Salem, Egypt's minister of propaganda, printed in the *Manchester Guardian:* "Egypt will strive to erase the shame of the Palestinian war, even if Israel should fulfill the United Nations resolutions." Karl Baehr observed that Sayegh had failed to remember the Arab massacre of seventy-six Hadassah doctors and nurses and the Security Council's double condemnation of the Arab blockade of Israeli shipping on the Suez Canal. His analysis was particularly acute when he observed that "in the Arab-Israel impasse, we are not dealing with an issue in which one side is all white and the other all black. We have here a conflict of rights as well as a confusion of wrongs." Even that much of a concession was enlightening to premillenarian readers.[11]

In his rebuttal Sayegh chose to reinforce his earlier arguments and attempted to show that the official Zionist policy had been to dispossess Arabs of their land even before 1948. He cited the King-Crane Commission report to President Woodrow Wilson in 1919 which had mentioned the Jewish objective of complete dispossession. On the refugee issue, he quoted an American missionary's eyewitness report that the Jews had sent trucks equipped with loud-speakers through the Arab areas threatening Arabs with annihilation if they did not leave. United Nations documents were offered as evidence that the Israelis had continued to expel and displace thousands of Arabs from the border zones even after the 1949 armistice agreements.[12] Such presentations did not suddenly flush premillenarian prejudices away, but they did begin slightly to erode confidence in the righteousness of Israeli expansion. This broadening process of new knowledge undermined the self-confidence of narrow-mindedness.

The *Evangel* attempted to dull the cutting edge of Toynbee's criticism by reporting the response of Abba Eban, the Israeli Ambassador to the United States. Toynbee claimed that the traditional Jewish view had been that any restoration had to stem from divine initiative—not from human endeavor. Eban had replied: "It is true that the Hebrew orthodox doctrine of history describes the restoration as a Divine purpose, but it also describes it as a Divine purpose which human effort should strive to accelerate. . . . If something is willed by God, then it is the duty of man in his material life to strive for its fulfillment."[13]

Striving for fulfillment included conspiring with the former imperialistic powers, Britain and France, to attack Egyptian territory in 1956. Britain hoped to regain control of the Suez Canal which had been nationalized by Egypt; France hoped to eliminate Egyptian support of Algerian rebels in North Africa; and Israel wished to eliminate the Egyptian military threat and harassment and to annex more territory. Egypt's President Nasser had been building his military might with Czechoslovakian armaments and, as a consequence, the United States had withdrawn American financing of the Aswan Dam. Nasser had, in turn, responded by nationalizing the canal to get revenue and to assert his independence of the West. In accordance with a secret agreement signed at Sèvres, France, on October 23, the Israelis attacked Egypt on October 29 and the British and French occupied the canal zone on November 5. The United Nations General Assembly had passed a cease-fire resolution on November 1, however, which had been supported both by Russia and the United States. The United States had very cautiously avoided participation in the Suez adventure because of her own criticism of the recent Russian intrusion in Hungary. Finally, the threat of Russian atomic retaliation brought a truce agreement which lengthened into a peace which lasted until 1967.

The premillenarian reaction to the Suez Crisis was based upon their belief in an extended millennial kingdom of Israel, which would reach from the Euphrates to the Nile. Back in 1950, Biola's Vice-president William W. Orr had commented on a border dispute which Israel was having with Jordan, the Arabs claiming Israel had invaded the land in violation of the truce agreement: "It is to be expected that by one means or another the Israeli government will come into full possession of the borders of the ancient Holy Land, according to the Scriptures!"[14] Seemingly, this implied that the predetermined ends justified "one means or another." W. E. Vine writing in the British Plymouth Brethren journal, *The Witness,* spoke of the ultimate expansion to the Euphrates—even though he did not believe in the Zionist movement as the road to national redemption.[15]

Israeli expansion was also inherent in the premillenarian expectation of the rebuilding of the Temple. A 1952 editorial in *The King's Business* bluntly stated: "Next in order for Israel will be the complete jurisdiction over Jerusalem, the destruction of the Mosque of Omar, the building of a great temple and the re-establishment of their ancient worship." The writer believed that his own generation would witness those "thrilling events."[16] Moody's President Culbertson in a 1953 article, "God's Clock Ticks On in the Holy Land," expressed this determinism—history guided not by an invisible hand, but by an invisible trumpet: "Someday—perhaps much sooner than we think—an invisible trumpet may sound and modern Israel, perhaps not quite knowing why, will move into old Jerusalem as its ruler." That would then bring to an end the times of the Gentiles.[17] This was the background that predisposed the premillenarian mind to accept an expanding Israel.

The Sunday School Times gave the strongest support to Israel's actual attack on Egypt and the strongest criticism to the failure of the United States to support the Israeli expansion. George T. B. Davis claimed that the reason Britain had lost her empire and was on the verge of bankruptcy was that she had failed to "bless the Jews." He also had dire predictions for the United States:

> Is the United States to be the next nation to fall from her present exalted position through her failure to help Israel in this crucial hour when she is surrounded by foes bent on her destruction?
>
> We are standing at the crossroads at this very moment! Will our leaders believe God's Word and take the road of blessing that will lead our nation to still greater glory and victory; or will we forsake God's Word and take a stand against the Jews and so bring upon us terrible judgments of God as in the case of Egypt, Spain, Germany and Great Britain?

Davis was not able to rise above measuring greatness only in terms of materialism and nationalism, assuming that God, not greed, had made the nation rich and powerful. But he now impugned the motives of the United States: "Is the oil of the Middle East more important than the blessing of God? As a nation let us take a firm stand to help and strengthen the Jews in the State of Israel." (It did not necessarily follow, however, that the Arab cause was unjust. There was always the possibility that the United States might support the Arabs as much for the justice of their cause as for oil interests.) Davis appealed to readers to pray that the leaders of the United States would have the right attitude toward Israel in this crisis hour in order to bring blessing on America.[18]

Another writer in *The Sunday School Times* in a series in late 1957 said that prior to the Suez Crisis an attack on Israel from Egyptian-held Gaza was a constant threat; and, consequently, even if the Israeli attack was not justifiable, it was understandable. He observed that if Israel was not able to cultivate the Negev in the south then it would be "natural" for her to seize some land from Jordan which did so little with it. He went further to say, "War seems inevitable and the extension of Israel's borders as a result is probably unavoidable."[19] Such expressions prepared the premillenarian mind for further land grabs in 1967.

The editor of the *Evangel* spoke of Israel's bitter feeling because of the leniency of the United Nations toward the Arabs. He lamented that Israel had to face the threat of sanctions, but nothing had come of Arab violations of international law. "Evidently they were too big, too hard to handle, whereas little Israel was at the mercy of the UN so it could be pressured to help salve a bad UN conscience." He called the Israeli attack a "rash decision" which put them in a worse predicament than before—because now the Arabs and the Russians were united against them. Nevertheless, he explained this as possibly a part of God's plan which might hasten the day of Russia's prophetic invasion of Palestine. God had secret weapons in reserve for that battle and He would rescue little Israel from the monster Gog.[20] A later article entitled "Israel Today and Tomorrow" expressed confidence that the Jews would never be uprooted from the land and recalled the 1948 statement of one of the pastors in the city of Jerusalem: "I saw miracles of God's intervention in behalf of the Jews just as great as anything that happened in the campaigns under Joshua!" It would certainly be fascinating to know what that pastor saw that compared to the battle of Jericho or the sun standing still. The author's comment, however, showed no sign of cynicism: "God gave the Jews the victory! And, He will do it again."[21]

Christianity Today, the recently-launched evangelical periodical, gave space to both sides of the issue. The widely respected conservative theologian and former professor of Old Testament at Princeton Theological Seminary, Oswald T. Allis, in "Israel's Transgression in Palestine" referred to the Jewish return as "an unjust restoration."

> Palestine did not belong to the British. It did not and does not belong to the United Nations. The persecution of the Jews in Europe was a grievous act of injustice. But allowing the Jews to take possession of a large part of Palestine and to force hundreds of thousands of Arabs out of it is an equally grievous wrong. Two wrongs do not make a right. Israel's demand that her occupation of part of Palestine be accepted as a *fait accompli* and her obvious intention to bring in many more Jews and to increase her holdings in the land as need requires and opportunity offers naturally incense the Arabs. How could it be otherwise?

Allis compared the restoration to the Crusades, and said the verdict of history was that the misguided Crusaders had not deserved to win.

> Does the Israeli cause deserve to succeed? Should Christians be willing to plunge the nations into a third world conflict just to restore unbelieving Jews to, and maintain them in, a land from which they were driven nearly two thousand years ago? We believe the verdict of history will be, No! May God grant that this verdict not be written in rivers of blood![22]

Taking the pro-Israel side of the debate was Wilbur H. Smith of Fuller Theological Seminary. He pleaded the legitimacy of the restoration on the basis of Scripture and quoted the 1937 words of David Ben-Gurion, then Chairman of the Executive of the Jewish Agency for Palestine, as he testified before the British Royal Commission: "The Bible is our mandate. The mandate of the League is only a recognition of this right and did not establish new things." On a more practical level, Smith argued that anyone who compared the former barrenness of the land with its recent productivity would know that "the Arab was a curse to the land." Beyond such materialism, though, the gist of his argument was determinism: "Not Antichrist himself will be able to prevent fulfillment of the divinely given promises."[23]

There were those who took a slightly different tack. These were premillenarians who accepted the prophetic predictions as traditionally interpreted, but yet held the nations involved in strict moral accountability. One such person was Paul S. Allen, the president of Simpson Bible College, San Francisco, a Christian and Missionary Alliance school. His statement in *The Alliance Witness* is a noteworthy milestone in the premillenarian response to an ever more aggressive Israel, and must be quoted at length.

> Regardless of our expectations of fulfillment of the prophecies concerning Israel's future, the Christian must not lose his perspective of right and wrong. The Israel of today must justify its acts, not in terms of its ultimate destiny (which is not universally recognized or accepted) but in terms of the moral conscience of the nations of today. The Christian, even while sympathizing with the ultimate objectives of the reestablishing of a national home for this people, must yet remember that there as elsewhere the end does not justify the means. If Israel's reactions to probing along its borders

> seem out of proportion to the provocations suffered—admittedly a two-eyes-for-an-eye policy of retaliation—the Christian is duty-bound to apply the measuring stick of moral values as he knows them.
>
> God does not need to use questionable methods in bringing about the fulfillment of prophecy. Prophecy is history seen in advance, but it is not necessarily morally desirable or approved. Israel's return to its land is clearly foretold in the prophetic Scriptures. Prophetic students can detect in the record indications that the return will be in unbelief. Possibly that unbelief will encourage methods incompatible with the Christian sense of justice. Such events, even though prophesied in advance, need not confuse the Christian. The fulfillment of God's promise will be an Isaac of miracle rather than an Ishmael of improvisation.[24]

Such moderation was the exception rather than the rule, however. A 1957 book by William L. Hull was more in keeping with most premillenarian views; it interpreted American policy in the Suez Crisis as encouraging Russia's inevitable invasion of Palestine, and asserted dogmatically, on the basis of the setting up of the state of Israel, "We live in the *last days*."[25] The liberal Protestant press on the other hand continued to criticize the immoral behavior of Israel in creating the refugee problem and to impugn the morality of Israel's very existence. John C. Bennett, editor of *Christianity and Crisis* and a professor at Union Theological Seminary, commented on the Suez struggle: "Israel's aggression was provoked, but the existence of Israel has been a continuous source of provocation."[26]

In 1958 Israel celebrated the tenth anniversary of its independence. The *Evangel* provided commemorative comment in an editorial, "The Miracle of Israel." The editor observed that no matter what view one might take of the Arab-Israeli dispute, he could not help but be impressed with the progress made in ten years. He then castigated those who criticized the restoration as "a political scheme concocted by materialistic Jews," and observed that "God's hand works where it is not seen." For him, it was truly God who had brought these Jews together and provided them sanctuary; in the struggle God was "standing in the shadows keeping watch above His own." "We must look beyond the passions of men in this struggle for the Holy Land and see the restoration of Israel as a fulfillment of His great plan."[27] The same issue of the *Evangel* carried a commemorative article by Louis H. Hauff. Hauff's tone was more anti-Arab than the editor's —he observed that if the 650,000 Jews in Palestine ten years ago had been able to absorb nearly twice that many more, surely forty million Arabs should be able to absorb and resettle only one million Arab refugees.[28]

Similar anti-Arab attitudes were reflected throughout the 50s in an era of growing Arab nationalism. These attitudes were, in part, derived from applying to the Arabs Obadiah's warning (to Edom) of divine judgment upon those who mistreated God's chosen people.[29] The refugee problem was often depicted as a result of the Palestinian Arabs' own folly in leaving their homes in response to the call of Arab leaders. Even if this were true (it may have been in a few areas), the question was never dealt with in terms of the justice or injustice of the Palestinian demands. It was claimed that the Arabs were better off under Israeli leadership than they had ever been before and that they enjoyed the same freedom and equality as Jews. An article in *Moody Monthly* recounted the usual arguments, but the author then inadvertently revealed the true situation in a footnote:

> We have been told that 5,000 Arabs have left Beersheba, an Israeli city, and that perhaps eventually more from all over Israel will leave. Room must be made for the ten or fifteen thousand Jewish immigrants arriving every month. We not only hope, but judging from the attitude of the Jews in the land, feel certain that the exit of more Arabs will not cause too great a hardship and loss to them.[30]

One would certainly also hope that this was an expression of naiveté and not of cynicism.

The King's Business referred to the Arabs who occupied old Jerusalem as "victims of a blindness which only Satan can produce" —but eventually they would have to give way in face of God's purposes.[31] Commenting on the Saudi Arabian monarch's statement calling on the Arab states to be prepared to sacrifice a million men in the process of exterminating Israel, the *Evangel* observed that the attempt to destroy the Jews had been tried many times before, but it always resulted in a boomerang effect:

"All such efforts have turned upon the would-be destroyer to destroy him!"[32] Premillenarians depicted Arab nationalism as a sinister demonic force, whereas Israeli nationalism was an ennobling divine call back to the Holy Land. If nationalism, however, can be equated with pride, then in terms of a truly Christian ethic it would seem that Arnold Toynbee's analysis of nationalism as the greatest sin of the twentieth century is particularly appropriate.[33]

The Arab position in prophetic history was given a new twist in a 1956 book by Charles E. Pont, *The World's Collision.* This work was honored with an introduction by E. Schuyler English, the new editor of *Our Hope* after the death of Arno C. Gaebelein (and later an editor of the revised *Scofield Reference Bible*). Pont believed that the Arabs would not be allied with Russia at the time of her invasion of Palestine, as most writers said, but rather would be on the side of the United States and Britain.[34] The variety of possibilities which these Biblical scholars were able to come up with was truly amazing, especially in light of the confident dogmatism with which they asserted their own particular views.

Prior to the Suez Crisis, the *Evangel* had shown some sympathy for the cause of the Palestinian refugees, refusing to ascribe blame for the situation. The editor extolled the peace that would eventually exist between Israel, Egypt and Assyria according to Isaiah 19:25. But there were inherent anti-Arab feelings even in this attempted expression of moderation: "As we look into Bible prophecy we see many dire predictions concerning Egypt's future and many golden prophecies regarding Israel." Whatever predisposition that one might have to sympathize with either side in the dispute would be overridden, however, by the anti-social gospel admonishment, "Our responsibility as Christians is not to worry over international affairs but to preach the gospel to every human being."[35] After the Suez Crisis, though, the bedrock of the true premillenarian attitude was thrust to the surface as the editor said: "Today the Arabs are charging that the Jews are trespassing on land that has been Arab for centuries. Is it not more correct to say that the Arabs for centuries have been trespassing on land that God gave to the Jews millenniums ago!"[36]

Parallel to the anti-Arab disposition was a continuing stream of pro-Jewish sentiment. This attitude was synthesized in *The King's Business* in an article by Biola's Charles L. Feinberg entitled "Israel—The Apple of God's Eye." Drawing upon Zechariah 2:8, "He that toucheth you toucheth the apple of his eye," Feinberg claimed that when Israel was mistreated, God considered it a personal blasphemy, and that whoever touched Israel for ill would be punished.[37] As for anti-Semitism, it was not a major topic for discussion among premillenarians during the 50s since flagrant anti-Semitism had declined due to the reaction to the excesses of the Nazis. Yet, occasional comments indicated a continuation of traditional ideas. The *Evangel* continued to see the hand of the Lord in the Nazi episode, interpreting it as a fulfillment of Jeremiah 16:16; the Germans had been hunters and fishers sent by God to hunt out His people and cause them to return.[38] What was to develop later as a major topic of discussion was Russian anti-Semitism. In 1950 *The Sunday School Times* explained Russia's prohibition against Jews leaving the Soviet Union as a response to the defeat of communist candidates in the Israeli elections following independence—totally ignoring the long tradition of anti-Semitic expression in Russia.[39] The *Evangel* carried on the conventional attitude of regarding anti-Semitism as God's punishment for the Jews' iniquity. In speaking of the restoration, Milton R. Lindberg said that the final regathering could not take place until the Jews acknowledged their sin which had brought on the 1,900-year dispersion.[40]

The premillenarian response to the supposed Russian threat in the 50s was, as before, not carried on at an ideological or economic level, but was based upon the atheism of communism and upon the identification of Russia as the invading Gog of Ezekiel 38. Premillenarian interest definitely centered upon the prophetic aspects of the Russian threat; although their paths often crossed, the activism and witch-hunting of the political right wing in the McCarthy era was not the mainstream thrust of premillenarianism as reflected in the sources under study. The main objective of the premillenarians was not to eliminate the threat of a communist takeover, but to scare people into the Kingdom of God and goad them on to greater service by demonstrating from current events that the end was near.

Leaders of religious right-wing movements such as Fred C. Schwarz were speakers at premillenarian meetings and conventions, but their single-mindedness never became the reason for existence within mainstream premillennialism. The caption to Schwarz's speech at Moody, which was printed in *Moody Monthly,* revealed the editor's interests: "Communism lies across the world in 1951 like a huge colossus. This article reveals it for what it is—Satan's substitute for God's salvation." In the text, Schwarz claimed that atheism was the basic fiber in the construction of communistic ideology. He quoted from *Lenin, on Religion:* "Atheism is a fundamental portion of Marxism, of the theory and practice of scientific socialism."[41]

Similarly, a couple months later *The King's Business* quoted extensively from a speech by Charles Habib Malik presented in *Christian Century.* Malik was the United Nations delegate from Lebanon, and an avowed Christian. The quotation began with what was the core of his statement: "Communism is predicated on the emphatic rejection of God." On the question of the possibility of peaceful co-existence with communism, Malik was quoted as saying, "Obviously I cannot get along with one whose whole being not only contradicts mine, but is bent on destroying mine." The conclusion that the editor drew was that this great threat of communism would stir Christian people out of their lethargy and force them to return to the great principles and ideals of Christianity. Noting that Malik was not a premillennialist, the editor took pains to make the proper premillenarian application of Malik's thesis: that (according to Ezekiel 38 and 39) things were going to get worse until God came and utterly blasted Russia to the ground.[42]

An article in *The Sunday School Times* at the end of 1955 dealt with "Communism's Unchanged Heart," its antagonism toward religion. The author quoted from a United States Information Agency propaganda bulletin a purported quotation from the Communists themselves, namely, from the Odessa radio: "It is the duty of party organizations to pay the most serious attention to the intensification of anti-religious propaganda, and to make it militant and aggressive."[43] These, then, were the continuing concerns of the premillenarian mind vis-à-vis communism; other issues, such as the individual versus the state or capitalism versus collectivism, simply were not the bases of extended discussions.

As before, resistance to Russia mainly focused on the national identity of Russia, rather than on Soviet ideology. The problem which premillenarians faced was still that of determinism on one hand and moral responsibility on the other, although most were not aware of the dilemma. Just as in the case of Israel, though, there were those occasional souls in the 50s who became conscious of the dilemma.

One of the determinists, D. M. Panton, was cited in the *Evangel* to the effect that if Russia knew anything of prophecy, the last country in the world she would approach would be Palestine, which was to be the crux of her doom. He said that in spite of any political or military disinclination, God would *compel* Russia to invade Palestine.[44] No mention was made of the philosophical problem of what good it would do for Russia to know about the prophecy—if she were going to be compelled to invade Palestine even against her will. With similar obliviousness, Leonard Sale-Harrison in *The Sunday School Times* quoted with approval the declaration of one missionary, "We must fight communism with all power at our command," and then in the same article observed that it was thrilling to see Russia's advancements and actions which clearly pointed to her later attack on Palestine.[45] According to his system, Sale-Harrison was actually advocating fighting against the will of God.

In June, 1950, just a week before the outbreak of the Korean War, there appeared in the *Evangel* an article, "Russia in Prophecy," by Frank M. Boyd of the faculty of Central Bible Institute, Springfield, Missouri. He pointed out that the result of World War II was the ascension of Russia to power and he predicted that sooner or later Russia would withdraw from the United Nations as she had withdrawn from the League—thus dividing the world into two opposing camps. Boyd regarded Ezekiel 38 as a prophecy of the ultimate doom of Russia; the reason given for her fate was her future attempt to exterminate Israel.[46] This impending struggle was granted the highest priority as Moody Bible Institute devoted an entire correspondence course by Wilbur

M. Smith to the subject, "World Crises and the Prophetic Scriptures." The first lesson recalled the early prophetic conferences of the twentieth century and observed: "Then students of prophecy talked about a *coming* world crisis; now we are in a world crisis."[47]

"The Russian Bear Prowls Forth to His Doom" was one subject in a series of prophetic articles in the latter half of 1950 by Louis S. Bauman, who was now pastor of the First Brethren Church, Washington, D.C. He, too, looked to the past and recalled that in the December 30, 1939, issue of *The Sunday School Times* he had claimed that Ezekiel 38 and 39 referred to Russia. He noted that *The Presbyterian Guardian* had countered in the February 25, 1940, issue with the statement: "If . . . Rosh [RV] is taken as a proper name, with what country is it to be identified? *We confess that we do not know.*" Bauman ridiculed such honest indecisiveness and reaffirmed his earlier position; he pointed out that even before Russia was a major power, the editors of *The Scofield Reference Bible* in 1909 had identified Gog as Russia. He then affirmed, "How recent years have proven them to be absolutely right!" He did not explain by what twist of logic their position had been proved, but went right ahead to remind his readers that more than ten years ago in *Russian Events in the Light of Prophecy* he had predicted that Stalin and not Hitler would win the war. And now with equal confidence he was predicting the ultimate doom of Russia. He evidently had no fear of Russia nor any qualm that America's policy of containing communism by means of atomic threats to the brink of war might stimulate retaliation. He was certain; and he admonished his readers, "Instead of being distressed, arouse, ye saints, the sight *is* glorious!"[48]

The Great World Crisis was the title of a 1950 book by Douglas Ober. He traced the identification of Rosh and Meshech as Russia back to the fifth century, claiming that the Patriarch Proclus' association of Ezekiel 38 and 39 with the invasion by the barbarian Huns supported this identification.[49] In reality what it supported was a long line of mistaken identity, which should have been a lesson of caution for the confident prophets of the mid-twentieth century. This security continued to be reflected, however, as *The King's Business* editorially spoke in 1951 of the "inevitability" of Russia's future raid on Palestine.[50] The grandfather of actor-evangelist Marjoe Gortner and former president of Glad Tidings Bible Institute, J. Narver Gortner, wrote in 1952 of "Russia's Origin, Character, and Doom," assuring his readers that Germany would be associated with Russia in the invasion of Palestine, and that "we need not be in doubt as to the ultimate outcome of the controversy that is now going on."[51]

Concerning the threat of war, *Our Hope* was not quite as pessimistic as others; it responded in 1955 to rumors of impending atomic attack by predicting that there would be war, but probably not *now*. The editor somehow discovered military realism at work in history along with the hand of God: "The present military strength in America is a reasonable assurance of peace for the time being, that is, with Russia."[52] Hopeful optimism took still another form in an article which three months later spoke of atomic activity, somber figures in the Kremlin, and world-wide subversion: "Yet the present ominous signs, though evident tokens of perdition for the ungodly, are harbingers of redemption for the children of God. . . . The dark hour precedes the dawn."[53]

Even prior to the interest stimulated by the Suez Crisis and the Hungarian revolt, *The Sunday School Times* was pleading God's case against Gog. Six accusations were listed: (1) Russia leads the world in atheism; (2) Russia leads the world in blasphemy; (3) Russia leads the world in defiance of Almighty God; (4) Russia is the greatest persecutor of Christians the world has ever known; (5) Russia is the greatest persecutor of the Jews; (6) Russia leads the world today in mass immorality.[54] After Suez and Hungary, the case against Russia was even greater in the premillenarian mind. The *Evangel* asserted confidently that Russia would march into Palestine against the Jews and there meet her doom.[55] A lengthy article title proclaimed: "Ambitious Russia: Without Doubt Her Greed Will Lead to Her Downfall on the Mountains of Israel." The author believed that it was clear that Russia had decided to oppose Israel, but he knew from Scripture that Israel was going to be Russia's undoing.[56]

One attempt to grapple with the problem of moral responsibility versus determinism was presented in the *Evangel* in a reprint of an article by Kenneth de Courcy, editor of the *Intelligence Digest*. His concern was evidently stimulated by the renewed threat of atomic attack as the result of Russia's launching of the satellite *Sputnik* in October, 1957. He explained that Christians expected, of course, divine intervention in world affairs, but that this was no excuse for "suidical folly in public affairs."

> Many think that these are the closing days of that era, and that it will end with the manifestation promised to the Church by the prophets.
>
> Those who do so believe, nevertheless, likewise believe that the judgment of the irresponsible at that point will prove to be far graver for them than either the consequences of nuclear war or of surrender to Communist tyranny; and while, therefore, there is a consolation to be had from Christian conviction, a mere acceptance of the inevitability of Divine intervention is not a thing lightly to accept, since it may well prove to be worse for those guilty of irresponsibility than any other outcome of human affairs.

His plea was for the western powers to resist Russia, and for Christians to get actively involved in political action. "It is active minorities which change historical courses."[57] De Courcy was holding the Christian world morally responsible to enforce morality. In this he was, of course, following the policy of many others; his contribution was a philosophical rationale for bypassing determinism.

Toward the end of the decade, though, while holding Russia morally responsible, most premillenarians continued to see the future of the world strictly from the standpoint of determinism. In *The King's Business,* evangelist Merv Rosell wrote "God Pre-Writes the Headlines."

> Let me remind you, man cannot annihilate the entire human race as many claim. Read your Bible! We will not obliterate all mankind within the "next 40 years" as British Philosopher Bertrand Russell has said. It is impossible to annihilate all humanity before Jesus comes for according to the Word of God, some will be "alive."[58]

Survival was certain.

Writing in the last *Moody Monthly* of the decade, John F. Walvoord, president of Dallas Theological Seminary, saw in the Middle East "a situation shaping up that will lead precisely to the scene described in Ezekiel."

> The widespread fear of Russia conquering the world does not seem to be in the foreview of prophecy. . . .
>
> Today we see precisely this setup: Russia about to move on the Middle East; Israel in its place, regathered; the wealth, the spoil of the nations there; the need for possessing the Middle East perfectly obvious to Russia; and the only thing deterring her the fear of our own military might.[59]

According to this analysis, the United States was the "only thing" preventing "Armageddon Now!"

This attitude may be contrasted with that of the few pro-Israel liberal Protestants (such as the co-editor of *Christianity and Crisis,* Reinhold Niebuhr), who, while they supported the existence of Israel and advocated American support for Israel, did not do so from deterministic certainty of survival, but from a position of a calculated risk involving moral responsibility. Niebuhr criticized American public opinion in the Suez Crisis for its pacifistic fear of Russian reprisal, and advocated that America "must risk war to protect people from tyranny."[60]

Russia's allies in the impending invasion were also the topic of some discussion. It was a foregone conclusion to most writers that the Soviet Bloc was the great northern confederacy of Ezekiel. In 1950, Douglas Ober in *The Great World Crisis* drew attention to the fact that five or ten years earlier no one would have dreamed that parts of Austria and Germany would be under Soviet control. He found it particularly significant that the sections that Russia controlled were areas that had not been in the ancient Roman Empire.[61] Evangelist Merv Rosell identified the other allies of the Soviet Bloc as Persia (portions of Iran and Iraq), Libya, Ethiopia, Germany (at least a portion), and Turkey, together with the Arab nations.[62]

There continued to be confusion, however, as to whether this invasion by the Russians and their satellites was, or was not, the battle of Armageddon. Biola's president, Louis T. Talbot, had apparently made up his mind that Russia would fight at Armageddon for the book which he had written in the 1930s with the title, *Russia, Her Invasion of Palestine in the Last Days,* was rewritten with the more timely title, *Russia Mobilizes for Armageddon.*[63] Moody's President Culbertson believed that present tensions in the Holy Land might erupt any moment into "Armageddon Now!"[64] Radio evangelist C. M. Ward of the "Revivaltime" broadcast expressed it dramatically:

> The eyes of the whole world are upon the East. Will we or will we not make a "do or die" stand against the Communists? When and where will this matter be resolved between East and West? God marks the spot and gives the name—Armageddon! . . .
>
> God's hour is upon us, neighbor! Mankind is marching inexorably toward ARMAGEDDON.[65]

Our Hope apparently shifted its position under its new editor, E. Schuyler English. Commenting on an article in the December 2, 1955, issue of *U.S. News and World Report* which discussed communist expansion, English stated: "Armageddon is still on the horizon—perhaps not as far off as some would have us believe!" Evangelist Merv Rosell explained in detail that "right now" NATO was a possible nucleus for a Mediterranean bloc of nations which would move east through the Mediterranean, land at Haifa harbor, and meet the Russians on the plain of Megiddo for the battle of Armageddon.[66]

Other premillenarians—though all believed the end was near, and most believed that a Russian invasion of Palestine was upon them—did not identify the immediate battle as Armageddon. The last article that Louis S. Bauman wrote before he died was "The Nations Marshalling for Armageddon." In it he listed the "Present Signs of the Battle." One sign was the armament race:

> A whole world in a very frenzy of preparation for the greatest of all wars! Such is the divine revelation of the days immediately preceding the Armageddon. No human being need to be told that exactly *that* describes our day!

Another sign was the formation of the United Nations. On the basis of these signs, Bauman believed that the overthrow of Russia would soon be brought about by a great military alliance of noncommunist nations, which would in turn be the power that would invade Palestine and be defeated at the true Armageddon by God Himself.[67] So he believed that Armageddon was coming soon, but that the Russians were coming even sooner.

In *The Great World Crisis,* Douglas Ober explained that there would be two invasions by Gog, neither of which was called Armageddon; the point he was making was that a quick and peaceful settlement of the Palestinian issue should not be expected. Any apparent peace settlements should be considered mere forebodings of the more intense struggle to come with the invasions from the north.[68] "Shadow of Armageddon" was the title of a presentation made at the 1955 International Congress on Prophecy at New York City. The message was that the attempted communist takeover of the United States was making the situation ripe for the appearance of the Antichrist who would defeat the Russians and then, in turn, be defeated himself at the battle of Armageddon.[69] The invasion of Palestine by Russia was, then, only the "prelude to Armageddon"—not Armageddon now, but "prelude" now! A similar scenario was given to readers of the *Evangel* by Frank M. Boyd.[70]

Somewhat different was the sequence of events described in *The Sunday School Times* by Edgar Ainslie. In his scenario, Russia would not invade Palestine until *after* the battle of Armageddon, her purpose being to "grab the immense spoil" that had been brought there by the nations defeated by the Messiah at Armageddon.[71] This system rounded out the kaleidoscope of confusing interpretations of end-time events, demonstrating the great difficulty of attempting literal interpretation of Biblical prophecy.

Various motives for Russia's invading Palestine were offered. It was claimed that reforestation and irrigation projects were making the land attractive in addition to the "amazing increase" in rainfall during the past generation.[72] The oil beneath the desert and the chemicals in the Dead Sea were depicted as necessities for the resource-hungry industrial giant out of the north. The strategic position of Israel made its invasion a necessity for any world conqueror. Moreover, Palestine was the cradle of three great religions, Christian, Jewish, and Mohammedan—all opposed to communism. Russia desired to destroy their very roots.[73]

The means of that invasion evoked a curious discussion due to the literalist bent of the premillenarian interpreters. Ezekiel 38:15 described the invasion as follows: "And thou shalt come from thy place out of the north parts, thou, and many people with thee, all of them riding upon horses." The problem was to somehow fit cavalry into an era when war was characterized by atomic bombs and blitzkrieg. It was claimed that the Russians were still dependent upon cavalry, and a stamp of the 1930s commemorating the tenth anniversary of the Red cavalry was offered as supporting evidence.[74] In *The King's Business,* Louis S. Bauman claimed in 1950 that the Russians owned half of the world's horses. "Other nations may put their trust in gasoline for mobile purposes if they wish to do so. But the wily old northern bear scents the possibility of bombs breaking up the oil fields of the earth to such an extent that the great gas-propelled war machines will be stalled in their tracks—'out of gas'!"[75] In the same magazine in 1958 Merv Rosell was claiming that the Russians now had 70 per cent of the world's horseflesh.[76] The *Evangel* carried a report of an officer from World War II recounting in the *London Times* that almost all the Russian divisions depended upon horse transport.[77] Evangelist Bill Lewis in the *Evangel* placed the reference to horses alongside Ezekiel 38:9, "Thou shalt ascend and come like a storm," and concluded the invasion was to be by horses and airplanes.[78] It was all too much, however, for William L. Hull, who arrived at a compromise solution:

> We have read descriptions of how Russia is buying up horses all over the world and that this is in preparation for the fulfillment of this prophecy. However, the prophet was merely indicating that this great force would be carried, it would not walk on its own feet. Horses were the chief means, in Ezekiel's day, of transport so he used that picture. But the emphasis was on riding, and not on what they rode. It is very doubtful whether there will be a single horse used by the Russian army in this attack.[79]

The threat of Russian expansion also brought increased speculation about who would lead the resistance to this invader from the north. Although somewhat complicated by the various chronologies discussed above, the various premillenarian schemes generally depicted a revived Roman Empire led by the Beast (Antichrist) as the focus of this resistance. William K. Harrison in *Christianity Today* discussed the circumstances that might bring such a leader to power. He felt that the threat of war and chaos to an industrial civilization might cause the nations to surrender their sovereignty to a brilliant leader who seemed to offer peace and prosperity. The United Nations and collectivism were movements that perhaps foreshadowed just such an arrangement.[80] Various organizations and institutions were suggested as possible harbingers of the coming western confederation that was to fulfill the prophecy of a revived Roman Empire, including NATO, the United Nations, and the United States of Europe.

Louis S. Bauman in 1950 regarded NATO as the power that would prevent Russia from invading Europe in her program of expansion, thus forcing her into Palestine. A few years later Charles E. Pont in *The World's Collision* credited Bauman with predicting even many years before NATO the rise of such a power: "We believe the North Atlantic Pact a potent forerunner of the 'ten kings' if not the real ten."[81] A plan for a European Defense Community was developed in 1952 to meet the Russian threat, but by 1954 it became obvious that, because of fear of a rearmed Germany, France would not ratify the plan. After EDC failed, *Our Hope* observed that it was the passing of another shadow, but that it did demonstrate how a western confederation might develop.[82] Later it was said that the EDC had come to life in the new form of NATO and that it was a shadow of the coming revived Roman Empire.[83]

A fear of the United Nations colossus continued to haunt all premillenarians, as they feared the universal government of the coming Antichrist. Even if they cast him in the role of protagonist against the monster Gog, they also cast him as the Beast which the Messiah would defeat and cast into hell. Louis S. Bauman remarked: "When the Antichrist shall attain this 'power' over the 'nations,' then the whole world will become indeed 'United Nations,' united in one great super-government."[84]

As early as 1950, Bauman had spoken also of a United States of Europe as a possible fulfillment of the revived empire. And in 1956, during negotiations prior to the Treaty of Rome in 1957 which formed the European Economic Community, *Our Hope* made the following observation:

> Thus, when we see six nations of Europe (France, West Germany, Italy, Belgium, Luxembourg, and the Netherlands) uniting in common economic and defense schemes, and more than that number considering seriously the formation of a union of their nations, we think of the ten-kingdom

> power that will come into being and play such an important part in the prophetic Scriptures—the revived Roman Empire.[85]

Every development in Europe or the United Nations that could somehow be credibly interpreted as fulfillment of these fringe-area prophecies served to reinforce premillenarian belief in the great drama of Russia's impending invasion of Israel.

Some premillenarians carried on in the 50s the attempt to find a specific reference to the United States in the prophesied program of end-time events. The United States as one of Britain's "young lions" continued as a favorite theme. Louis T. Talbot included the United States in prophecies that he ascribed to England. England was to be one of the ten toes in Nebuchadnezzar's dream:

> There are, of course, two great toes and eight lesser ones. So, also, in that great ten-toed kingdom, there will be ten nations of different powers and strength. And the two great nations will doubtless be England and Italy. The Antichrist will be head over the government in Italy, ruling from Rome.[86]

Perhaps Charles E. Pont was a little self-conscious as he asked his readers in *The World's Collision:* "Does this sound like a lot of symbol stretching? We do not think so." Pont believed that World War III was inevitable and was strongly opposed to any nuclear disarmament, fearing it would be to the disadvantage of the United States.[87]

That the old Stars and Stripes would float aloft in the millennial kingdom had been Louis S. Bauman's belief in 1942, but in 1950 he was predicting the submergence of the United States into the United Nations under the leadership of the Antichrist: "*Already* 'Old Glory' is battling to maintain its pre-eminence above the flag; in that day of international control, the old emblem of human freedom will have to fold its wings and perish with Liberty! Nothing less than this will satisfy the prophetic picture."[88] Much more optimistic was William L. Hull in *Israel—Key to Prophecy.* He did not believe that Russia and America would fight at all; the United States had shown in the Suez Crisis that Russia could bluff and get what she wanted without fighting.[89] Another totally different view was that of retired Lieutenant General William K.

Harrison, Jr., in *The Sunday School Times* article, "Is the United States in Prophecy?" His answer was *yes, probably.* He found the United States in Revelation 8:8, 9—she was to be destroyed in a surprise atomic attack by Russia before Russia went off to fight the Beast. It may be assumed that Harrison was advocating preparedness, although the article did not say explicitly.[90]

Another participant in the drama of the end was to be China, which took on new significance after the communist takeover in 1949. Leonard Sale-Harrison explained in *The Sunday School Times* that Russia wanted to use the "vast hordes" of China for her future warfare and wanted Ho Chi Minh's Indo-China for resources.[91] Louis S. Bauman claimed that the recent events in China did not surprise him, for he saw them prophesied in Daniel 11:44, where the Antichrist's enemies come "out of the east and out of the north."[92] *Our Hope* observed that the establishment of Russian-Japanese diplomatic relations was in line with Biblical prophecy—all Asia would be aligned with the Russians in a great northwestern confederacy.[93] However, Merv Rosell evidently took a different route of exegesis as he predicted: "I do not believe that China will be the permanent ally of the Soviet." He foresaw an independent role for the "kings of the east" when they arrive at Armageddon—where God would smash them all.[94]

The unfathomable element in all this premillenarian Armageddon-mongering is to what extent it affected their attitudes toward foreign affairs and to what extent it influenced their voting patterns. Admittedly the evidence for any political behavior has been spotty at best, but any instrument that attempts to plumb the depths of anti-Russian feeling among these people must be calibrated to compensate for their anti-social gospel bias. Premillenarians saw themselves as wayfaring strangers temporarily passing through this "vale of tears" on their way to the Promised Land of heaven. This predisposed them to be nonactive politically; their citizenship was in the Kingdom of God. The premillenarian press found political questions taboo, especially those journals that were tied to particular institutions and constituencies. To the extent that they were premillenarians, these people saw Russia in a demonic role, an evil to be resisted. To the extent that they were Americans, they saw America as a morally pure crusader whose manifest destiny was to right all wrongs and set the captives free. Since both political parties in America were anti-Russian, there was probably little effect on voting patterns, with the possible exception of the 1956 election when Adlai Stevenson openly advocated a unilateral ban on nuclear testing. Even that is merely guessing for premillenarians avoided public statements on such social-political issues.

Jerusalem! What Now?

This, then, said Ezekiel 2,500 years ago, would comprise the great northern federation of Gog and Magog, and we are today living in the very day of the fulfillment of these prophecies.

—Martin R. DeHaan, *The King's Business,* 1961

That for the first time in more than 2,000 years Jerusalem is now completely in the hands of the Jews gives a student of the Bible a thrill and a renewed faith in the accuracy and validity of the Bible.

—L. Nelson Bell, *Christianity Today,* 1967

The current build-up of Russian ships in the Mediterranean serves as another significant sign of the possible nearness of Armageddon.

—Hal Lindsey, *The Late Great Planet Earth,* 1970

Since the 1950s the most significant event for the premillenarian was Israel's conquest of Jerusalem in the Six-Day War of June, 1967. John F. Walvoord, the president of Dallas Theological Seminary, called it "one of the most remarkable fulfillments of biblical prophecy since the destruction of Jerusalem in A.D. 70."[1] This event ranks second only to the 1948 establishment of the state of Israel in the premillenarian dramatic drive toward Armageddon.

After the Israeli conquest of the Sinai Peninsula in the 1956 Suez Crisis, Israel had been induced to withdraw in exchange for a guarantee by the United States and other nations of the right of free passage through the Straits of Tiran to the Israeli port of Eilat on the Gulf of Aqaba. For a few years after the crisis, the conflict was relatively quiet, even though a treaty was never established—the Arabs still refusing even to recognize the existence of Israel as a state. By 1967, the Arabs' confidence had grown because of the addition of Soviet arms and the self-deception of their own propaganda. When rumors developed of a retaliatory strike by Israel against Syria, the Arab nations massed their troops on Israel's borders and Egypt's President Gamal Abdel Nasser declared a blockade of the Tiran Straits. Israelis considered this an act of war (there had also been threats to annihilate their state). On June 5, 1967, the Israelis suddenly attacked and within two hours had destroyed most of Egypt's air force and within six days had captured 80 per cent of Egypt's armored equipment and had defeated the entire Arab coalition. The conquered territory included the whole Sinai Peninsula, the West Bank of the Jordan, the Gaza Strip, the Golan Heights, and most significant of all—Jerusalem. Jews had not even been allowed to visit the city since the 1948 war, and the victory brought not only a euphoria, but a rebirth of the Jewish spirit, particularly for those who had grown to adulthood since the war of independence.

The renewed hostilities were a surprise to no one as the heightened tension of ever more frequent incidents had anticipated the ultimate explosion. While some may have trembled with fear at the prospect that the coming war might escalate into an atomic confrontation between East and West, premillenarians trembled with anticipation at the promise of exciting new developments in the Holy Land. As early as October, 1963, an article in *Moody Monthly* quoted *The Intelligence Digest* to the effect that the Arab nations had decided to invade Israel and that Russia was committed to supply arms. "We are going to see an invasion of Israel and we shall see great pressure upon America, Britain and France to intervene." The author, Moody's vice-president S. Maxwell Coder, cited with approval President John F. Kennedy's affirmation of support for Israel's security.[2]

The premillenarian response to actual hostilities was given public expression only four days after the war began. Moody Bible Institute's radio station WMBI presented a two-hour broadcast in which faculty member Alan Johnson said, "To me these events confirm the literal interpretation of Old Testament and New Testament prophecies. The entire city of Jerusalem, for instance, has now come under at least temporary control by Israeli forces." He reminded listeners of Jesus' prophecy in Luke 21:24: Jerusalem would be trodden down of the Gentiles until the times of the Gentiles were fulfilled. Johnson could not be sure that these events were a direct fulfillment, but interpreted them as indications of the *possibility* that the return of Christ would come soon.[3]

"It was the story of David and Goliath all over again," was the analysis of the *Evangel* editorial headlined "The Miracle of Israel." But certainly it was not an "immoral miracle"; the war was depicted as a reminder of the "indestructibility of Israel."[4] L. Nelson Bell editorialized in *Christianity Today* under the caption "Unfolding Destiny": "That for the first time in more than 2,000 years Jerusalem is now completely in the hands of the Jews gives a student of the Bible a thrill and a renewed faith in the accuracy and validity of the Bible." Bell believed that the overwhelming victory did not just happen, but that "God was working out his own purposes, far above and beyond the capabilities of men or nations!" As he concluded his remarks, he again spoke of the *thrill* of seeing prophecy fulfilled.[5] This twin sense of destiny and thrill was truly the epitome of the general premillenarian feeling associated with the Israeli victory in the Six-Day War.

The war was offered as a final proof of the legitimacy of the restoration. A week after the above *Christianity Today* editorial, the former General Superintendent of the Assemblies of God, Ralph M. Riggs, asked, "Who is the rightful owner of Palestine?" and answered that the war looked like a confirmation that God had given Palestine to the Jews.[6] *Moody Monthly* responded to the war and the conquest of Jerusalem with a special issue on Israel. In one article, President John F. Walvoord of Dallas Theological Seminary claimed the occupation of Jerusalem offered proof of the miraculous preservation of the Jews, and he observed, "Surely this is the finger of God indicating the approaching end of the age."[7] This special issue also offered excerpts from Wilbur M. Smith's new book, *Israeli/Arab Conflict and the Bible,* the preface of which stated, "The Christians believe that the events of these recent days are part of God's plan of the ages."[8] Another article expressed the philosophy of history that God is in control of all events and that the nations are merely a drop in the bucket or dust on the scales.[9] The entire concern was with fulfillment of prophecy and destiny; the issue of the morality of war or the justice of the Israeli attack was not even a consideration.

One observer in Jerusalem just a few days prior to the hostilities was the president of the Evangelical Free Church, Arnold T. Olson, whose inexpensive paperback, *Inside Jerusalem, City of Destiny,* appeared the following year. Olson spoke of the unification of Jerusalem as the most exciting headline of the war and as a sign of the end. He believed, as his title implied, "Jerusalem has a rendezvous with destiny."[10] A special point was made criticizing the extreme orthodox sect of the Jews which opposed the establishment of the state of Israel.[11] This view had been reflected by Rabbi Amram Blau who called the Israeli victory a disaster:

> God promised he will redeem Zion with the Messiah. That redemption is to come in a manner and in circumstances clearly specified in Jewish tradition. The Messiah has not arrived. The specified circumstances do not exist. The creation of an independent Jewish state by men, not God in his own way and time, is a grave sin. It is faithlessness.

Olson found it quite ironic that this group that called themselves "the Guardians of the City" were fleeing the country in the crisis days just prior to the war. Although their refusal to fight was logically consistent with their theological position, he bitingly observed, "It filled me with disgust to note such a display of cowardice and disloyalty."[12]

Attitudes toward the war were the subject of a study by Arnold Ages, a professor in the Department of Classics and Romance Languages of the University of Waterloo. He showed that the fundamentalist, literalist churches had become more favorably disposed toward Israel since the Six-Day War, even though earlier studies had revealed such groups to be more anti-Semitic in their attitudes than liberal Christian groups. In contrast to the trend among fundamentalist, literalist groups, Ages observed that "many of the liberal Christian groups (including the United Church of Canada) have either adopted ambivalent attitudes toward Israel or been openly hostile."[13] Rabbi Marc H. Tanenbaum, National Director of the Inter-Religious Affairs Department of the American Jewish Committee, spoke of this shift in a *Newsweek* interview: "Many liberal Protestant organizations remained silent or took an outright anti-Israel position." In contrast, he happily observed that "Evangelical Protestants were the first to offer us sympathy during the war."[14]

The initial response of the premillenarians has solidified into an enduring disposition in favor of the war and Israel. A 1973 article in *Christian Life* claimed that the war was a fulfillment of Psalm 83:1-8 and that the territories conquered (Jerusalem, the West Bank, the Gaza Strip, and the old city of Samaria) had been predicted by Obadiah 17-20. Isaiah 19:1-17 was interpreted as a prophecy of Egypt's economic plight as a result of the war.[15] S. Maxwell Coder in an article entitled "Jerusalem: Key to the Future" emphasized the war's significance: "Gentile times were fulfilled when Gentiles ceased to control Jerusalem in 1967." The world, he said, was now in a period of transition which would bring the time of the Gentiles to its ultimate end.[16]

Not all the Evangelical press was entirely one-sided; *Christianity Today* also reported opposing interpretations of the war. James L. Kelso, former moderator of the United Presbyterian Church, informed readers of the atrocities of the Jews—they had looted the YMCA, badly damaged a Lutheran hospital, wrecked an Episcopal boys' school, and shot up an Episcopal girls' school, killing some of the girls. One missionary was quoted as saying that the war was "perhaps the most serious setback that Christendom has had since the fall of Constantinople in 1453." Kelso claimed that the first crime of the Zionists was to make the Balfour Declaration apply to *all* of Palestine in spite of its specific guarantees to existing non-Jewish communities. Another crime was the Israeli refusal to do anything about the refugee problem.

He asked, "How can a Christian applaud the murder of a brother Christian by Zionist Jews?" and then wryly commented, "An equal or even greater horror is that so many Christians applaud crimes against the Arab Muslim."[17] His article reflected the view of many missionaries and scholars who had been in direct contact with Arab Christian communities, but their pleas made little impact on the general premillenarian mind-set.

Israel has made a conscious attempt to exploit the reservoir of good will among the premillenarians in addition to courting the favor of all Christian communities. Evangelist Oral Roberts in his 1963 book, *The Drama of the End-Time,* recalls that when he was a guest of the Israeli government, several government officials sat with him all day long because they wanted to assure him of his welcome, even though Prime Minister David Ben-Gurion had been unable to keep an earlier appointment due to an emergency. Roberts' appointment was postponed, whereas others were simply canceled. The Israelis' time was not spent in vain; the television evangelist returned to vibrantly spread the message:

> When I departed from Israel, I did not lose the spell that had fallen over me. Even now I feel the surge, the rise, the swell, the thrill of deep emotion. There is something going on in Israel. It is of eternal consequence, and the spiritual significance of that something leaps in my blood like a flame. God's ancient people are carving out an empire. They are literally creating it with their own hands. That's what the Bible told us they would do. The meaning of it in terms of a coming great world revival and the Second Coming of Jesus has thrilled me to the very fiber and core of my being.[18]

Evangelist Billy Graham's associate, Cliff Barrows, recounts a similar extraordinary welcome at a special showing of the Billy Graham film *His Land* for Prime Minister Golda Meir.[19] This film has been criticized for portraying an unfavorable image of the Arabs while profiling the Jews in glowing terms.[20] But Rabbi Tanenbaum called the film "perhaps the most beautiful, sympathetic portrayal of the people of Israel restored to their ancestral land that had been made by any Christian since the creation of the Jewish State."[21]

Just two months after the Six-Day War, the Israeli government sent Dr. Yonah Malachy, a member of the Department of Christian Ministries of the Department of Religious Affairs, to the United States to study Christian attitudes toward Israel. Dr. Malachy knew more Christian eschatology than most theology professors and was familiar with all the leading premillenarian authors. He was released from active duty with the army of occupation in order to work on a book about Christian prophetic writings concerning the restoration of Israel. In a visit to Biola College he expressed appreciation to the faculty for their support of the Israeli cause, but was critical of the fact that there had not been more tangible support from Protestant sources during the Six-Day War. An example of the type of active support that appealed to Dr. Malachy was the "Manifesto of the Fundamentalists of America to the Jews of the World," which denounced anti-Semitism in the 1930s. This document had been signed by fifty-one leading fundamentalists, fifteen of whom were associated with Biola at one time or another.[22] As a result of this Israeli goading, Biola issued "A Proclamation Concerning Israel and the Nations." The opening paragraph provided firm, but cautious, support.

> Recent events have focused the attention of the world upon biblical prophecies relating to the fulfillment of Israel's destiny. Prominent among predicted end-time events related to the coming of Jesus the Messiah is the return of the Jews to their land and their redemption. It appears that recent developments in the Middle East may be preparing the way for these great prophetic events. Analysts of contemporary developments should exercise caution at this point, however, in equating particular events with the fulfillments per se of specific prophecies.

Included was a word of warning for those who were not warm enough in their support of Israel.

> Throughout its history the nation Israel has been the object of opposition and attack by Satan the archenemy of God's purpose and program. Untaught and unholy men have unwittingly cooperated with the devil in this. It is our conviction that the true people of God should not be found in league with those who oppose the will and work of God for Israel.

If Israel's critics were demonic, it would seem to follow that Israel's enemies, the Arabs, were too. But the proclamation made a special point of heading off Arab antipathy:

> God's purpose for the Arab world includes promises of national enlargement and blessing. They along with all Gentiles are the objects of God's love and of the proclamation of His grace. Therefore, we acknowledge our indebtedness to them, as to all nations, and desire to contribute to their spiritual, social, and material needs.[23]

The document conspicuously avoided comment on the rightness or wrongness of the Israeli occupation.

The premillenarians' support for the Israeli cause and their belief in its righteousness were a natural outgrowth of the attitudes developed prior to the June War. It made little difference to them whether Israel or Egypt instigated the conflict; it was all part of God's great plan, and they were the fortunate witnesses of the greatest events of the ages. In 1960 Louis H. Hauff wrote in the *Evangel* on "Israel—The Budding of the Fig Tree": "Should we not rejoice that we have been privileged to see this in our generation? Truly the fig tree has budded and is producing fruit." A speaker at the West Coast Prophetic Congress in Los Angeles in 1961 spoke of the "incredible" progress of Israel since 1948—just as Ezekiel had anticipated.[24] This was also a theme of Louis T. Talbot, who in a 1964 issue of *The King's Business* wrote on "The National Resurrection of Israel and Her Future Glory." He revived the idea of the restoration of the latter rains in Palestine and passed along estimates of the wealth of the Dead Sea, all for the purpose of demonstrating God's blessing upon the restored nation. He reminded his readers that the land promised to the seed of Abraham was fifty times as great as had been conquered under Joshua. "Therefore, we need not fear about the man-made schemes to drive Israel from her homeland."[25] Wilbur M. Smith, writing "Concluding Words on the Signs of the Times" in the year prior to the war, spoke of the return of the Jews (along with the rise of Russia) as being a "universally agreed upon" sign among prophetic students.[26] The war came as a logical extension of these popular expectations.

These same views then became, after the war, the justification of the Israeli position. Immediately after the fighting, the *Evangel* editor pointed out that the restoration of Israel was not a new idea, citing James H. McConkey's *The End of the Age,* which was copyrighted in 1897. The fulfillment of a particular interpretation of a prophecy was purportedly the same as the fulfillment of the prophecy itself. "Atheists have ridiculed this idea. Liberal clergymen have scoffed at it. But today it is being fulfilled before our eyes, indicating that these are indeed the 'last days' both for Israel and for the Church."[27] Arnold T. Olson supported Israel's occupation of Jerusalem and approved various assertions by the Israelis that they would never leave the city. He saw no "justification for proposals that would again break up the unity of the city."[28] A 1973 *Christian Life* article directly asserted that the reason Israel would not give up the Golan Heights or the Sinai Peninsula was that God had promised all that territory to the Jews, and went further to say that "as yet, the Israelite only has his foot in the door in the Middle East."[29] The *Evangel* on the occasion of the 1974 Geneva Conference on the disengagement of troops in the Golan Heights recalled that God's program had been announced thousands of years before when He said that the land of Canaan would be given to Jacob and his descendants.[30] Obviously, his uncle Ishmael's children were to be left out. The latter rain also continued to be heralded as proof of God's blessing—only this time the increase was said to have begun with the establishment of the state of Israel in 1948. Actually, average rainfall in the decade of the 50s was next to the lowest on record.[31]

Although support of the Israeli position was widespread among premillenarians after the war, it was not unanimous, and even some of the supporters were selective in their approval. Some found themselves in an ambivalent position; they believed in the ultimate restoration of Israel, but they could not conscientiously endorse the method or the arrogance of Israel. These nagging doubts about Zionism had been expressed earlier in *The King's Business* in 1960 by radio preacher William Ward Ayer, the former pastor of the Calvary Baptist Church, New York City. He pointed out that Zionism was an enigma to Bible scholars because it was difficult to believe that modern Zionism was fully in keeping with what the Bible revealed the restored Jews were to be like, but nevertheless it appeared that God was using the Zionist movement to bring about His purposes.[32] When Israeli territory was tripled by the 1967 conquests, people with these kinds of doubts found their misgivings greatly reinforced. In the September issue following the June War, *Eternity* carried an article by Bernard Ramm expressing his personal ambivalence. On the basis of Romans 11, he believed that there was a great future ahead for the Jews, but it was not clear to him what political pattern that future would take.

> I can only express my own way of understanding this question. First, no Christian is wise enough nor learned enough to be able to say that *this* hour or *these* events are the prophetic hours and events. We must emphatically say that times and seasons are in God's hands,—not ours—so Acts 1:7.
>
> Second, those promises yet awaiting fulfillment, will be fulfilled in God's *way* and in God's *time* and therefore I myself may not use such promises to form *present* political theory.[33]

On the first anniversary of the war, Moody's President Culbertson expressed the view in *Christianity Today* that although he expected the return of the Jews according to prophecy, he was not ready to defend every last action taken by the Israelis.[34] And even such a staunch pro-Israeli as Arnold T. Olson admitted that some Christians were apt to be so enthusiastic about the rebirth of Israel that they were blind to the injustices inflicted upon the Arabs by the Jews. "The fact that one believes the prophecies of the Bible include the restored nation, does not warrant his approval of the methods used in achieving the goals."[35]

In 1970 a leading Evangelical publisher, William B. Eerdmans, published a major criticism of the Israeli position and of the premillenarian attitude—*Whose Land Is Palestine?* by Frank H. Epp. It was probably not widely influential among premillenarians, but those who cared to pursue the question found trenchant passages like this:

> Christians should remind themselves that the various prophetic schemes that have had credence within the Christian

> community all arose in specific political contexts in which Christ and anti-Christ were related to the political powers of the day struggling against each other. The schemes changed with the changing of the powers. At the moment many Christians see Christ allied with America and the anti-Christ with Russia and the Arabs.[36]

The book had telling arguments, but as a whole it was not likely to find acceptance among premillenarians because it rejected the foundations of a literalist interpretation. Epp universalized the promises of the Holy Land and interpreted the Nile-to-the-Euphrates borders as only symbolic.[37]

Charles C. Ryrie, professor of systematic theology and dean of doctoral studies at Dallas Theological Seminary, made a more effective type of presentation in *Christianity Today*. Speaking of premillennialists, he noted that they thought the Six-Day War to be another step toward eventual occupation by Israel of the territory from the Euphrates to the river of Egypt. "Every such gain is generally viewed with rejoicing, for the furthering of God's purpose for Israel seems to indicate that the coming of the Lord draws near." Reminding his readers that no side was entirely blameless, he went on to say, "And while the efforts of a political state may ultimately be used by God in the mysterious accomplishing of his purpose, his use of the wrath of men does not excuse that wrath or make right the wrongs that the state may commit. In other words, we must not assume that the end justifies the means." Using the analogy of the crucifixion, he remarked that those who crucified Christ were not without blame just because they were doing the will of God. "Likewise, the state of Israel is not relieved of its obligation to act responsibly in the community of nations even though the secret purpose of God may be brought to fruition through its actions. Any premillennialist's rejoicing over the apparent nearness of the Lord's return will have to be coupled with sadness over current events."[38] Even the *Evangel* voiced a similar position. Ralph W. Harris indicated that even though the outcome of the Arab-Israeli conflict was predestined, that did not mean one side was entirely right or wrong; the Scripture merely indicated the final outcome.[39]

The conquest of Jerusalem brought a flourish of speculation about the rebuilding of the Temple. The *Evangel's* initial comment upon the war included an observation of Israeli Defense Minister Moshe Dayan: "If I may say so, we felt we were fighting to prevent the fall of the Third Temple."[40] An article a month later quoted a Florida rabbi's statement that "the time has come when the Temple should be restored in fulfillment of the promise Jews have made in their prayers for centuries, 'Bring us back to our land and we will rebuild Thy house.' "[41]

Various paperback books since the Six-Day War have referred to the rebuilding of the Temple. Wilbur M. Smith's *Israeli/Arab Conflict and the Bible* included a discussion of the Temple that was to be built in Jerusalem and pointed out that it was to be built where the Moslem Dome of the Rock stood.[42] Arnold T. Olson, in *Inside Jerusalem, City of Destiny,* was more dogmatic:

> The Temple will be rebuilt. Israel has the will, access to the means, and now the site. What remains is the problem of how to occupy that site without bringing on themselves the wrath of the Arabs stirred up to what would be to them a real holy war. But build she will.[43]

The most influential of these paperbacks was Hal Lindsey's national best-seller, *The Late Great Planet Earth,* which has reportedly sold five million copies.[44] Lindsey also took a strong line on the Temple: "Obstacle or no obstacle, it is certain that the Temple will be rebuilt. Prophecy demands it." But he went even further and predicted, "If this is the time this writer believes it is, there will soon begin the construction of this Temple." He recounted that in an interview just after the war, the Israeli historian Israel Eldad had said, "From the time that King David first conquered Jerusalem until Solomon built the Temple, just one generation passed. So it will be with us." When asked about the Dome of the Rock, Eldad responded, "Who knows, maybe there will be an earthquake."[45]

Lindsey had also used this interview with Eldad for his article in *Moody Monthly's* special issue on Israel just after the war. In "The Pieces Fall Together" he said that for centuries it appeared that the Jews had no chance of returning to the Holy Land, but within twenty years the state had developed, and in recent months Jerusalem had been repossessed. "We only await the rebuilding of the temple and this piece of the puzzle will be complete."[46] This feeling was not unique; John F. Walvoord also observed in this same issue that many were predicting an early erection of the Temple.[47] In a news section headed "Israel: Things to Come" *Christianity Today* reported on an advertisement in the *Washington Post* asserting that a project to rebuild the Temple had begun and inviting inquiries from those who were willing to help. *Christianity Today* also cited a London periodical, *The Christian and Christianity Today,* which reported that to build the Temple the Israeli government had ordered 60,000 tons of stone from Bedford, Indiana, and that it was being handled by Pier 26 in New York. The cornerstones were supposedly already in Israel.[48] Such information was never verified.

Eternity magazine carried an article, "Time for the Temple?" by Raymond L. Cox which recounted that Jewish soldiers had placed a sign at the newly-captured Wailing Wall proclaiming, "This is a temple!" Cox noted that some Jewish religious leaders said that nothing could be done about rebuilding the Temple until the Messiah came, but that others such as Menachem Begin, leader of Israel's Freedom Party, had announced, "The Third Temple outlined by Ezekiel will assuredly be rebuilt in our own generation." This was all offered as evidence of the direction of Israeli thinking. Although Israeli officials had promised that Moslem holy places would not be disturbed, Cox observed that "not even the government of Israel can forever restrain the fulfillment of prophecy."[49] A later article in *Eternity,* however, pointed out that the Israelis had been misunderstood, that the sign at the Wailing Wall, *Beyt Knesset,* should have been translated, "This is a synagogue." To assume that the building of the Temple was next on the agenda was unwarranted.[50] J. Dwight Pentecost in 1971 reported in *Moody Monthly* that on his trip to the Middle East he could uncover no plans for the rebuilding of the Temple (much to the consternation of his premillenarian inquirers). The point he was making was that it was not necessary for the rebuilding to precede the rapture of the church.[51]

A new twist was offered by Malcom Couch in a 1973 article in *Moody Monthly* entitled "When Will the Jews Rebuild Their Temple?" Couch was the producer of *The Temple,* a film based upon the book *Satan in the Sanctuary* by Thomas S. McCall and

Zola Levitt. According to the article, recent archaeological excavations filmed by Couch had proved that the Holy of Holies, the inner sanctum of the Temple, was located fifty yards or more east of the Dome of the Rock—the Temple could be rebuilt without destroying the mosque. Couch said, "What I saw and heard there, plus our research of past months, convinces me that within the next ten years Israel could move to rebuild the temple."[52] All of this fascination with the Temple assumed the permanency and legitimacy of the Israeli control of Jerusalem; the justice of the conquest was not even given a second thought.

The Six-Day War also stimulated a revival of the premillenarians' antipathy toward the Arabs. The month after the war, William Ward Ayer claimed that the Arabs were proof of Biblical inspiration. The Bible had said of Ishmael, "His hand shall be against every man, and every man's hand against him." Ayer commented, "This had been proved correct because the Arabs had lived in continual warfare with the rest of the world."[53] One chapter in Wilbur M. Smith's *Israeli/Arab Conflict and the Bible* was titled "The 'Perpetual Hatred' of the Arabs." Speaking of the Arab, Smith said, "He cannot be said to be distinguished for amiability and love of peace. He personally shall be the aggressor against all others."[54] God's judgment against Mount Seir in Ezekiel 35 was applied to the Arabs: "This particular paragraph regarding Edom in Chapter 35 relates particularly to the events occurring at the end of this age, and what we have seen in the June of 1967 only adds evidence to the truthfulness of this ancient prophecy."[55] Biola's Charles L. Feinberg spoke of the perpetual belligerency of the Arabs and concluded: "God will in His own good time cast out the sons of Ishmael, despite all their devisings and intrigues, and will settle the sons of Isaac."[56] A *Christian Life* article in essence denied the legitimacy of the Arabs' very existence, tracing the problem back to Ishmael's father, Abraham, and Abraham's wife, Sarah. "Had the pair put their trust in God to solve their problem, instead of mixing blood with an Egyptian, Ishmael would never have been born. Today, there would be no controversial birthright over which to shed streams of human blood."[57] Such wistful musing was characteristic of premillenarian thinking; it had no relation to reality and, even if accepted as an explanation of the problem, made no suggestion toward a solution.

Russian involvement in supplying arms to the Arabs before and after the Six-Day War led to increased speculation of the future relationship of Russia and the Arabs as Armageddon approached. According to *The Late Great Planet Earth,* the Arabs would ally with all the Moslem nations of Africa and with Russia's great northern confederacy against Israel. Current events in the Middle East had supposedly prepared the stage for Egypt's last great act. But Egypt was to be double-crossed by the Russians and would herself, along with the African nations, fall subject to Russia. It would all turn out in the end, however, for Egypt in her extremity would turn to Christ for salvation. Hal Lindsey concluded his chapter on the Arabs ("Sheik to Sheik") with the usual sense of premillenarian urgency:

> It's happening. God is putting it all together. God may have His meaning for the "now generation" which will have a greater effect on mankind than anything since Genesis 1.[58]

The "Jesus Freaks" and "Jesus People" of the early 1970s may have taken their name from Christianity's founder, but Hal Lindsey became their high prophet.[59]

Another facet to the Arab problem was being taught by radio evangelist C. M. Ward of "Revival Time." According to Ward the moment in history seemed to be approaching when there would be an Arab-Israeli reconciliation. "Russia is going to discover that Jacob and Esau are *twin brothers,* and there is a limit to how much misunderstanding and strife can be promoted between them." He predicted that Suez and Sinai would be negotiated because there were promises to Esau as well as to Jacob, but he did not claim to see any current signs of reconciliation.[60]

America's relations with Russia progressed from the crises of the early 1960s, the U-2 spy plane incident (1960) and the Cuban missile crisis (1962), through the Test Ban Treaty (1963) to the spirit of détente of the early 1970s. There seems to be evidence of this détente in the premillenarian literature; Russia was not as frequent a topic as before—it had lost its newsworthiness—but the slant did not change. Russia has continued to be depicted as a demonic power that is about to pounce on the poor Jews in the Middle East or is about to come to blows with the Antichrist leading the European Common Market as the revived Roman Empire.

Martin R. DeHaan, director of the "Radio Bible Class," wrote in 1960 in *The King's Business* on "Russian Communism and God's Timetable." He used the time-honored equation of "Magog equals Russia," saying that this identification had been the consensus of Bible expositors since Russia's earliest times. He claimed that only a few years earlier the fulfillment of Ezekiel's prophecy had seemed remote, but "we are today living in the very day of the fulfillment of these prophecies." For further emphasis, he proclaimed:

> God has clearly foretold that Russia will meet her doom, only in Palestine, when she meets up with the Western Alliance of nations under the leadership of a Super-man upon the mountains of Israel. . . . We are, and dare to be, dogmatic about this fact, for we have the clear teaching of the Word of God in this matter. Russia's program of aggression, bit by bit, is running true to form according to prophecy. . . . Oh, that men would turn to this Book for their information and guidance in dealing with the present Russian crisis.

Unfortunately, DeHaan offered his reader no suggestion of what should be done, even though he was party to the revealed wisdom of the ages. He concluded by simply announcing, "The stage is all set, Israel is in the land, Russia is on the march, the United Nations described in Ezekiel 38 are seeking to organize, waiting only for one man, the Super-man of the last days to unite them against the King of the North."[61] DeHaan's dogmatism, however, was in disagreement with a speaker at the West Coast Prophetic Congress at Los Angeles in 1961 who taught that the Russians would not be destroyed by an opposing army, but by the direct, supernatural intervention of God Himself.[62]

Evangelist Billy Graham in his 1965 book dramatically entitled *World Aflame* wisely avoided any specific identification of nations, but on the very first page observed the world around him and lamented, "We seem to be plunging madly toward Armageddon."[63] Such warnings of doom in this national best-seller by one so highly esteemed in America served to reinforce the general acceptance of lesser men's systems of interpretation which made more hazardous identifications.

An interesting presentation on the identification of Russia with Ezekiel's *Rosh* was developed by Wilbur M. Smith. This was described in "The Future of Russia," an article appearing in the October 1963 issue of *Moody Monthly*. Moody's vice-president, S. Maxwell Coder, cited Smith's claim that the Byzantine Empire had been invaded by northern barbarians in the ninth century and that Photius, the Patriarch of Constantinople, called these invaders by the Biblical name *Rosh*. According to Smith's argument, the term spread into the Russian language. The thrust of the presentation was to prove that the subject of Ezekiel's prophecy was identical with the modern state of Russia. Photius identified the invaders from the north as the *Rosh* of Ezekiel's prophecy—and the name stuck. He was wrong, and so every argument based upon that identification since that time is also wrong.[64]

A similar question was also the concern of Richard DeHaan of the "Radio Bible Class" in a 1968 book, *Israel and the Nations in Prophecy*. DeHaan admitted that the identification of Russia, Moscow, and Tobolsk with terms in Ezekiel was not unanimously accepted by scholars, but he concluded that no supporting evidence was necessary, for Russia's location in the "north" made such an identification positive.[65] He also offered a further refinement of the end-time chronology, arguing that the battle of Armageddon would come at the end of a seven-year tribulation period, but that the invasion by Russia would occur at the middle of that tribulation.[66] Hence, he was able to claim, "We are not looking for the Battle of Gog and Magog but for the Son of God"; current events were, nevertheless, emphatic signs of the end.[67]

Radio preacher C. M. Ward was teaching in 1969 that Israel had the capacity to develop an atomic bomb and might have nuclear warheads by 1970. He felt that this would cause Russia to rattle her atomic weapons in the Mediterranean and the United States might reply in kind. Referring to the Russian threat to Israel, Ward said, "Hell is mobilizing its final efforts to pull down this flag of promise and hope to mankind and to raise its own banner of slavery." Russia was testing God's promises to Abraham: "I will bless them that bless thee, and him that curseth thee will I curse" (Gen. 12:3, ASV).[68] In early 1971 Ward speculated that the Strategic Arms Limitation Talks (SALT) between Russia and the United States might trigger a Soviet move into the Middle East, since she already occupied Egypt and could (if the talks were successful) depend on conventional weapons without fear of atomic retaliation by the United States.[69]

Another adjunct of the anti-Russian attitudes among premillenarians during the late 60s and early 70s was the growing concern about Soviet anti-Semitism. Due to the protest of world Jewry it became a newsworthy issue, and premillenarians made the most of it—as a sign of impending conflict between Russia and Israel. There was, however, virtually no program of opposition to the Russian anti-Semitism. Curiously enough, the Russians in this case were not subjected to the standard of ethics. Since American interests were not at stake this time, the premillenarians returned to the pre-World War II standard of sometimes tolerating Russian developments in a deterministic frame of reference as they usually tolerated Israel.

The groundwork for this predisposition had been laid in the early 60s as anti-Semitism persistently was spoken of as a normal phenomenon. An article in *The King's Business* in 1960 referred to the coming "time of Jacob's trouble" when more Jews would perish than had been liquidated under Hitler.[70] Another article a couple years later spoke of anti-Semitism as a potent force in stimulating the continuing restoration of the Jews.[71] Besides being something to be expected, anti-Jewish feeling was still depicted as a well-deserved punishment. A 1964 article on "The Future Glory of Israel" exulted, "Well may every believer today praise God for His great people and promise concerning Israel," but then drew the contrast: "Well may every Jew ponder the decision of the rabbinical council in rejecting their Messiah almost 2000 years ago and bringing such suffering upon this poor nation while the Gentile nations have entered into Israel's blessing."[72] Louis T. Talbot, now the chancellor at Biola, did not focus upon the crucifixion of Jesus, but rather upon Israel's apostasy in general as the source of her just chastisement.[73] President John F. Walvoord of Dallas Theological Seminary, on the other hand, blamed the Jews' troubles more directly upon Satan than upon God's chastisement, saying, "It should be noted that through the centuries the trials of Israel have stemmed from the basic conflict between divine purpose and satanic opposition. The very fact that God selected Israel as a special means of divine revelation has made the nation the object of special satanic attack."[74] Both men most likely would have glossed over this apparent disagreement by explaining that God had *allowed* Satan's attack as a just punishment—but still one wonders, "Which came first? The Satanic attack, or the decision to sin?" Whichever way the premillenarian might view it, anti-Semitism was still a product of the great forces of the universe at work—for Christians to get involved in a great humanitarian struggle against it would be pointless.

As the issue of Soviet anti-Semitism gained popular interest, evangelist C. M. Ward in 1971 accused the Russians of using their anti-Semitism to blackmail the Arabs: "In essence, Moscow blusters toward Araby, 'If you are having trouble with two or three million Jews in Israel, how would you like to face the release of three million more from within our border?' "[75] Ward explained that this was one of the devices Russia was using to expand her power in the Middle East. A few months later in "Fuses Ignited—Explosion Ahead!" Ward charged:

> The leaders of the Kremlin are seeking favorable world opinion that will permit aggression toward Israel. It is the same virus—anti-Semitism. Now, as in Czarist and Stalinist times, anti-Semitic incitements are the desperate resort of frightened men.
>
> Soviet leaders are gingerly testing world sentiment. They want to ascertain whether a world will stand by numbly and allow a repeat of Nazi crimes against Jews—a wholesale butchering. Will the world dismiss it as "a Jewish problem"?
>
> So the uneasy status remains within the Soviet border until this finding is made—a kind of permanent "house arrest" for all Soviet Jews.[76]

Admittedly these are overly dramatic expressions, but they illustrate, nevertheless, the premillenarian penchant to treat the issue not as a problem to be solved, but as a foreboding sign of the end—a sign to be expected and welcomed, since it was prophesied.

This attitude was not universal among premillenarians, however, as the editors of *Christian Life* in 1974 opened their pages to an appeal by Harold B. Light, the chairman of the Bay Area Council on Soviet Jewry and national chairman of the Union of Councils for Soviet Jews. In his article, "Let My People Go," he pleaded for Christians to persuade their congressmen to use economic pressure on Russia to wring concessions for the Russian Jews.[77] This could possibly be interpreted as a symptom of a growing "neo-evangelicalism" which demonstrated some humanitarian concern and social action in spite of the social gospel onus, but more likely it was only one small cry in the wilderness, not an omen of a popular ground swell of premillenarian social involvement.

As the fear of an imminent Russian invasion declined in the United States, mention of the battle of Armageddon was also greatly reduced. Another reason for the lessened interest in Armageddon was that the theology that had evolved did not necessarily identify the Russian invasion as that particular battle. Armageddon was still impending, however, and was not forgotten. As the Vietnam War developed, the question arose whether this new war would lead to Armageddon. An article in *The King's Business* assured readers that it would not, but explained the prophetic significance of the current crisis:

> Well, for one thing, we are feeling intensely the threat of Red China. We have seen the development of the great northern power Russia. Egypt is presently a developed power engulfed in an Arab alliance. We are witnessing the development of a great western confederacy in the form of a European Common Market. And now we are faced with the recognition of a vast Eastern power that is not only communistic but also atheistic. Is not the stage set?[78]

The Late Great Planet Earth had an extensive discussion of the battle of Armageddon. Lindsey said that the current build-up of the Russian navy in the Mediterranean Sea was another significant sign of the possible nearness of Armageddon.[79] The Russians, however, were to be defeated by supernatural power at the very beginning of the actual battle of Armageddon which was to be fought by the combined forces of western civilization under the leadership of the Antichrist against the vast hordes of the Orient under the leadership of the Red Chinese.[80] The eastern powers alone would wipe out one-third of the earth's population, but then Christ would appear to save mankind from self-destruction and would set up an earthly millennial kingdom.[81]

Russia's allies in the end-time battles continued to be topics for discussion. Germany remained nearly a unanimous choice, but there was bewildering debate over the others. *Moody Monthly* argued that the confederation would include Persia, Ethiopia, and Libya; but Martin R. DeHaan in *The King's Business* claimed the Biblical *Cush* was not modern Ethiopia but a neighbor of Persia.[82] Another *Moody* author compromised by proclaiming that there were both an African and an Asian *Cush;* he also included China as an ally on the argument that there was no other place from which Ezekiel's "many people with thee" (38:6, 9; 39:4) could be drawn.[83] Wilbur M. Smith in "A Prediction Concerning India" in *Moody Monthly* forecast Russia's future control over an alliance with India.[84] Richard DeHaan identified Turkey along with Germany as the potential Russian allies.[85] Hal Lindsey recognized the developing Third World forces by claiming that the Arab nations of black Africa would be the future supporters of Russia in the northern confederacy.[86] All in all, the varied interpretations presented a fascinating jigsaw of nations.

During the 60s and 70s the theme of communism and atheism in Russia was also greatly diminished in the premillenarian literature. Communism and Russia were differentiated in a 1964 article in *Moody Monthly* by John F. Walvoord, "Converging Signs of Our Times." He predicted on the basis of Scripture that although Russia would eventually be defeated, nearly the whole world would come to embrace the atheistic religion of communism.[87] This view was in agreement with a presentation made at the 1961 West Coast Prophetic Conference in Los Angeles.[88] But in another 1964 article, "Russia's Cold War on Christians," *Moody Monthly* claimed that Russia was engaged in a grim new push toward atheism by establishing an Institute of Scientific Atheism to direct a coordinated effort to eliminate all religion from Russia.[89] There was, however, very little of this type of anti-Russian harangue after that time—the *Evangel* reported that the Soviets were easing their pressure on religion and that although in 1961 a target date of 1980 had been set for the elimination of religion, there was no longer any mention of such a goal.[90] Without the popular fear of subversive communism, as in the McCarthy era, premillenarians could not exploit anti-Russian fear on the basis of the ideological conflict, but had to rely more upon what remained of the big-power threat of Russia.

The continued drive toward European unity has served to fertilize premillenarian speculation on the revived Roman Empire which under the Antichrist would ultimately resist Russia or play some other great role at the end. At the beginning of the decade of the 60s *The King's Business,* still fascinated by the role of the United Nations, spoke of a pattern that was emerging on the international scene that could easily be the setting for the advent of the Antichrist.[91] In 1963 John F. Walvoord in *The Sunday School Times* wrote of Europe's economic revival as a prerequisite to political revival and of the possibility of a ten-nation unification.[92] This pattern foreshadowed for him the fulfillment of end-time prophecies. Richard DeHaan emphasized the significance of the formation of the Common Market as the revived Roman Empire.[93] Hal Lindsey in 1970 said he believed the Common Market to be the revived Roman Empire and that predictions of a United States of Europe by the year 1980 might need to be foreshortened in view of rapid developments. He asked, "Is it any wonder that men who have studied prophecy for many years believe that the basic beginning of the unification of Europe has begun?"[94] In spite of setbacks to European unity in the years following, *Moody Monthly* in a 1974 article, "Prophecy and the Common Market," was still optimistic about the probable revival of the Roman Empire.[95]

Where the United States was to fit into all these rapidly approaching events continued to be of interest to some writers. "Is the United States in Prophecy?" was extensively discussed in *The King's Business* by the president of Detroit Bible College, Roy L. Aldrich. After commenting on various scholars' identification of Tarshish in Ezekiel 38:13 as Great Britain, Aldrich concluded:

> The idea that Great Britain is to be identified as Tarshish, and that the United States is one of the young lions, is only a theory; and one which is contradicted by most of the evidence. It would seem to be the part of wisdom not to attempt to identify any modern nation as Tarshish; at least, not until more definite evidence is available.[96]

He believed that the identification of Tarshish as Spain was more in keeping with what little evidence there was. A few years later, Frank M. Boyd in the *Evangel* identified Tarshish as Tartessus in southern Spain near Gibraltar, and reconciled the two views: "In either case, we know who has possessed Gibraltar for many years, and we are acquainted with the 'lion' symbol of our passage as referring to Britain—'The British lion.' "[97]

The Late Great Planet Earth was very definite in its predictions; the United States was to decline in power until it became only an adjunct of the European power and would succumb to the leadership of the Antichrist fighting against China in the great battle of Armageddon.[98] Implicit in Hal Lindsey's chronology was the conclusion that the United States will have nothing to fear from the Soviet Union at that time. Russia was to be destroyed by God at the very beginning of the Armageddon struggle, whereas the United States would be around later to participate in the Armageddon main event.

1973 was the twenty-fifth anniversary of Israel's independence, and many magazines offered commemorative pieces which characterized the premillenarian response to Israel (as well as to Russia occasionally). The *Evangel* began the memorial year by editorializing the old determinism.

> As a race they are unique, because they have a divinely determined destiny. God chose them for a purpose, and that purpose must be fulfilled. Until then, the nation may be despised, and it may even be decimated, but it cannot be destroyed.[99]

Moody Monthly explained that Evangelicals identified with the Israelis because of the Jews' initiative, the common Old Testament roots, sympathy for the persecuted, and their prophetic significance. This self-analysis closely parallels that of Nadav Safran cited earlier.[100] *United Evangelical Action,* the publication of the National Association of Evangelicals, took the occasion to castigate the liberals and particularly the World Council of Churches for their unfriendly attitude toward Israel, citing Rabbi Marc Tanenbaum's censure of the liberal Protestant community for failing to support their Jewish neighbors on nearly every priority Jewish concern except for the problem of Soviet Jewry. The author,

Arnold T. Olson, summarized his indictment by saying, "The Arabs, the community of nations, and the church are all guilty of making Israel's survival during these 25 years more difficult—yet there is the miracle of survival."[101] *Christian Life* proclaimed that the occupation of Jerusalem and the Temple site as a result of the miracle of the 1967 war was a sign that the Gentile domination over Israel would rapidly come to an end.[102]

On the other hand, there were expressions of doubt about the moral position of the Israelis after twenty-five years. *Eternity* endorsed the "incredible historical record of Israel's revival and the weight of biblical prophecy," but gave a two-part warning to "our fellow premillennial believers." The first was that excessive dogmatism on prophetic details should be avoided: "History is littered with the torn-up pages of prophetic scholars who have linked antichrists, wars and other biblical elements with specific historical events." The author was clearly concerned with the ever-expanding history of the premillennialists' credibility problem. The second warning was to avoid glorifying the state of Israel. In the midst of the Watergate scandal, the invidious comparison was drawn: "Politically Israel is no purer than Washington, D.C." The author pointedly observed that Israel's leaders were not inerrantly inspired and that they needed occasional rebuke and rebuff just like all political chieftains.[103]

Christianity Today similarly editorialized that although Americans might admire the determination and decisiveness of Israeli foreign policy, they should recognize that an inflexible pro-Israel stand might not always correspond with justice. The editor also pointed out that Arab control of oil production meant that an inflexible pro-Israel stand might not always correspond with the American national interest either.[104] Such realistic assessments evoked criticism from the Jews at the time of the oil embargo by Arabs after the 1973 Yom Kippur War. Jews assumed that the only explanation for opposition to the Israeli position was a caving-in to the Arab blackmail—it never occurred to them that there might be a sincere resistance to Israel's stubbornness in retaining Jerusalem and other conquered lands. Among the premillenarian press, however, there was never any questioning of the right of Israel to exist as a nation in Palestine.

In October, 1973, on the holiest of Hebrew holidays, Yom Kippur, Israel was suddenly attacked by Syria and Egypt. The Israelis were nearly defeated in the early days of the war, and most likely would have been if Syria had not failed to follow up her initial thrust. But after a counterinvasion of Egypt by the Israeli army, a cease-fire was arranged. Both sides were recipients of massive military aid—the United States resupplying Israel after some hesitation, and the Soviet Union energetically supporting the Arabs. The result was a temporary Arab embargo on oil supplied to many western nations, creating a distressing energy shortage.

Some premillenarians slid into the traditional deterministic response, the *Evangel* observing confidently that no one had solved the problem yet, but God would eventually, and *Christianity Today* reporting John F. Walvoord's assertion that Israel would never be destroyed.[105] Others, however, feared for the very existence of Israel.

A few liberal Protestant voices continued to question the very right of the state of Israel to exist. One of them said, "It is quite conceivable that Israel may have to die for world peace."[106] But although officers of national organizations were usually officially quiet, there was more support for Israel at the local level than there had been in 1967.[107] Judith Banki writing for the American Jewish Committee has explained the continued official antipathy of liberal Protestant bodies:

> It may derive from Christian theological presuppositions about the mission of Judaism—not so much the "old" Christian anti-Semitism, which held that the Jews must remain despised and dispersed throughout the earth because of their murder and rejection of the Messiah, but the "new" theological anti-Semitism, which holds, in effect, that Jews should not be permitted the trappings of normal nationhood to which other peoples are entitled because their prophetic tradition calls them to a more universal mission.[108]

Polls of general opinion showed the same pattern of response as in the June War; 47 per cent were sympathetic to Israel, 6 per cent to the Arabs, and the rest were uncommitted. A *Commentary* writer observed, "In the gross, Americans sympathize with Israel, but not so intensely that they are ready to sacrifice a great deal to save her."[109]

Among premillenarians, though, the threat to Israeli existence brought appeals for active support and sacrifice. Donald Barnhouse in *Eternity* called for American aid, asking, "Have we no practical obligation under the biblical commandments about loving Jerusalem to help bear the cost of fighting off attacks against it?"[110] He advocated cutting back on energy use by forming car pools and using mass transit in order to free American foreign policy from Arab pressure. The First Baptist Church of Dallas, the largest church in Christendom, took an advertisement in *The Dallas Morning News* urging Christians to write their congressmen in support of Israel and to donate to the Jewish Welfare Federation.[111] Although Malcolm Couch did not claim that everything Israel said and did was right, in *Moody Monthly* he called for a letter campaign to congressmen and editors and attributed Britain's difficulties in the energy crisis to divine punishment for British treatment of the Jews in the 1930s and 40s.[112]

Among the veritable explosion of prophetic literature that has appeared since the 1967 war, one book was devoted exclusively to the Yom Kippur War. George Otis' *The Ghost of Hagar* was the result of his special trip to Israel during the war to get firsthand premillenarian coverage. Otis explained, "We Christians believe in fighting for God's people, the Jews, as well as praying for them."[113] He called for continued national sacrifices:

> The test of our willingness to bless the Jews will come as the novelty of the energy sacrifices wears thin. *Beware of growing anti-Israel sentiments.* The "spreading effect" of the oil shortage has brought more than inconvenience: lost jobs, shortages, higher prices, and recession. If we can hold steady we will see the salvation of the Lord![114]

Otis further hinted that the peacemaker of the Yom Kippur War, Secretary of State Henry Kissinger, might possibly be the Antichrist. Such speculation was rampant in premillenarian circles.[115]

These appeals to action, in spite of the traditional taboos against the social gospel, may be attributed to the new threat to the very existence of Israel—such a situation had never occurred before. But on the other hand, these appeals may be as explained above: an indication of a neo-evangelical trend toward social action on all levels.

In recent years some premillenarians have developed a more discriminating criticism of Israel's actions, but in times of crisis such as the Yom Kippur War, many are quick to revert to their standard twentieth-century response: a nonmoral, deterministic support of Israel and a belligerent prejudice toward a demonic Russia.

Epilogue

God predicts in His word what He does not applaud in His law.

John Cumming, *The End,* 1855

Prophecy is history seen in advance, but it is not necessarily morally desirable or approved.

—Paul S. Allen, *The Alliance Witness,* 1957

Any premillennialist's rejoicing over the apparent nearness of the Lord's return will have to be coupled with sadness over current events.

—Charles C. Ryrie, *Christianity Today,* 1969

"Armageddon Now!" has been the premillenarians' cry since 1917—to what avail? An analytical review of the problems inherent in their response to Russia and Israel may be categorized under literalism, determinism, and opportunism. No attempt has been made to evaluate or criticize the theological positions of the premillennial system in contrast to other systems of eschatology, but any set of beliefs may be expected to demonstrate in practice an internal consistency *within* that body of ideas.

Literalism. If the premillenarians espouse an interpretation of Scripture that expects a literal, precise fulfillment of prophecy, then one may expect precise, accurate definitions of the fulfillment of those prophecies, or lacking such precision, one may expect an admission of indefiniteness which would at least have the advantage of avoiding false identifications and gross error. The premillenarians' history, however, is strewn with a mass of erroneous speculations which have undermined their credibility. Sometimes false identifications have been made dogmatically, at other times only as probabilities or possibilities, but the net result has always been the same—an increased skepticism toward premillennialism.

Those persons confronted with premillenarians' presentations need to be conscious of the composite past of prophetic interpretation which has included the following phenomena. The current crisis was always identified as a sign of the end, whether it was the Russo-Japanese War, the First World War, the Second World War, the Palestine War, the Suez Crisis, the June War, or the Yom Kippur War. The revival of the Roman Empire has been identified variously as Mussolini's empire, the League of Nations, the United Nations, the European Defense Community, the Common Market, and NATO. Speculation on the Antichrist has included Napoleon, Mussolini, Hitler, and Henry Kissinger. The northern confederation was supposedly formed by the Treaty of Brest-Litovsk, the Rapallo Treaty, the Nazi-Soviet Pact, and then the Soviet Bloc. The "kings of the east" have been variously the Turks, the lost tribes of Israel, Japan, India, and China. The supposed restoration of Israel has confused the problem of whether the Jews are to be restored before or after the coming of the Messiah. The restoration of the latter rain has been pinpointed to have begun in 1897, 1917, and 1948. The end of the "times of the Gentiles" has been placed in 1895, 1917, 1948, and 1967. "Gog" has been an impending threat since the Crimean War, both under the Czars and the Communists.

Such loose literalism when considered as a whole is no more precise than the figurative interpretations of which these literalists are so critical. The breadth of interpretations might even be compared to the obscure, Platonic, allegorical interpretations of the early Greek church fathers.

In commenting on Hal Lindsey's *The Late Great Planet Earth,* a premillenarian writer in the *United Evangelical Action* has charged, "Lindsey may be so busy looking to the future that he hasn't profited from the past."[1] Premillenarians could profit immensely from a greater consciousness of their own history.

Determinism. The response to Jews and Israel has demonstrated that the premillenarians are guilty of the charge of determinism even to the extent of heretical antinomianism. They have expected and condoned anti-Semitic behavior because it was prophesied by Jesus. Their consent (even though given while spewing pro-Zionism out the other side of their mouths) makes them blameworthy with regard to American as well as Nazi and Soviet anti-Semitism. Neither as a body nor as individuals has their cry against such inhumanity been more than a whimper. On the other hand, the establishment of the state of Israel has been unquestioningly approved with little or no consideration of the effect on the native Arab population. Even if the right of Israel to exist as a nation is granted, the situation still demands that the decision be made on the basis of just and moral considerations rather than merely on the grounds that it fulfills prophecy. Israeli conquests have been applauded as proof of the legitimacy of literalism—the nation was compelled toward prophetic borders. Usual definitions of aggression and violation of international law have been ignored in favor of prophecy.

If Russian aggression had been consistently treated with the same determinism as Israel was, the Iron Curtain would have been hailed as a wonderful sign of the end. This might have been the case had America not been involved on the European front in World War II and had the Cold War not been depicted as a direct threat to the United States. Premillenarians also found themselves in the dilemma of approving the prophetic expansion of Russia while disapproving the Russian threat to Israel at Armageddon. This is evidently the explanation for the confused role assigned to the United States in the various writings on prophecy. In general, premillenarians called for resistance to every hint of Russian expansion, demanding conformity to international law and justice, rather than consenting to prophetic considerations.

Opportunism. The premillenarians' credibility is at a low ebb because they succumbed to the temptation to exploit every conceivably possible prophetic fulfillment for the sake of their prime objective: evangelism. The doomsaying cry of "Armageddon Now!" was an effective evangelistic tool of terror to scare people into making decisions for Christ and to stimulate believers to "witness for Christ" to add stars to their heavenly crowns before it was everlastingly too late. Voices of moderation were less likely to find mass appeal. Times of crisis tend to produce feelings of insecurity in the general populace as a matter of course. The evangelistic message was found to be most effective when couched in terms of confident, dogmatic overstatements, rather than in a carefully reasoned, moderate theology that offered indefinite conclusions. The success of such evangelistic approaches was to the premillenarians well worth the risk of false identifications in the interpretation of prophecy. It would be unfair to accuse any one preacher or writer of such insincerity; they were True Believers (sometimes caught up in the snare of their overly zealous rhetoric), but, nevertheless, the result as a whole has been gross opportunism.

It is not likely that the situation will change greatly. Although within the movement there are many moderate voices that will continue to speak out against this irresponsibility, these voices will go unheeded since they do not offer any hope of greater success in the primary goal of evangelism. As a matter of fact, these voices that in the name of truth and integrity cry aloud against opportunism will find their message muted by their own realization that their principal thrust must continue to be evangelism, not the reform of their brothers' methods. The premillenarians see evangelism as the means to save the world and will continue to use this means as a justification to misuse the end.

Notes

CHAPTER 2

1. Cyrus Ingerson Scofield, ed., *The Scofield Reference Bible* (New York: Oxford University Press, 1909).

2. Ernest R. Sandeen, *The Roots of Fundamentalism: British and American Millenarianism, 1800-1930,* p. 222.

3. James M. Morton, Jr., "The Millenarian Movement in America and Its Effect upon the Faith and Fellowship of the Southern Baptist Convention," p. 44.

4. *Scofield Bible,* Isaiah 10:12, n.

5. Ezekiel 38:2, 3.

6. For Scofield, "kingdom-age" equals the millennium.

7. Peter Toon, ed., *Puritans, The Millennium and the Future of Israel: Puritan Eschatology, 1600-1660,* p. 126. Sir Henry Finch, *The World's Great Restauration, or The Calling of the Jews,* pp. 2-3.

8. R. G. Clouse, "The Rebirth of Millenarianism," in *Puritan Eschatology,* ed. Peter Toon, p. 49.

9. Ibid., p. 62.

10. Daniel 2:44.

11. B. S. Capp, "Extreme Millenarianism," in *Puritan Eschatology,* ed. Peter Toon, p. 68.

12. Ibid., pp. 70-71.

13. Ibid., p. 69.

14. Toon, *Puritan Eschatology,* p. 127.

15. Increase Mather, *The Mystery of Israel's Salvation Explained and Applyed, or A Discourse Concerning the General Conversion of the Israelitish Nation,* pp. 8, 11-12; Leroy Edwin Froom, *The Prophetic Faith of Our Fathers: The Historical Development of Prophetic Interpretation,* III, pp. 125-134.

16. Clarence C. Goen, "Jonathan Edwards: A New Departure in Eschatology," *Church History* XXVIII (March, 1959), 37-38.

17. Ibid., pp. 32-33.

18. Sandeen, *The Roots of Fundamentalism,* p. 7.

19. Ibid., pp. 6-7.

20. Ibid., pp. 10-11.

21. George Stanley Faber, *A Dissertation on the Prophecies,* I, p. 240.

22. Ibid., II, p. 200.

23. Ibid., p. 218.

24. Ibid., pp. 219-20.

25. Ibid., p. 218.

26. George Stanley Faber, *A General and Connected View of the Prophecies,* p. 4.

27. Ibid., p. 251 n.

28. Ibid., p. 45.

29. Ibid., p. 44.

30. Ibid., pp. 44-45 n.

31. Ibid., p. 275.

32. Ibid., pp. 274-75.

33. Ibid., p. 239.

34. Ibid., p. 230 n.

35. Ibid.,

36. Ibid., p. 231 n.

37. Sandeen, *The Roots of Fundamentalism,* pp. 22-23.

38. Ibid., pp. 11-12.

39. Samuel Taylor Coleridge, *Notes on English Divines,* II, p. 337.

40. Frank H. Epp, *Whose Land Is Palestine? The Middle East Problem in Historical Perspective,* p. 125.

41. Milton Plesur, "The American Press and Jewish Restoration During the Nineteenth Century," in *Early History of Zionism in America,* ed. Isidore S. Meyer, pp. 55-75.

42. Sandeen, *The Roots of Fundamentalism,* p. 42.

43. Ibid., p. 44.

44. Ibid., p. 55.

45. Ibid., p. 49.

46. Jacob J. Janeway, *Hope for the Jews,* p. 205.

47. Ibid., p. 226.

48. George Vernadsky, *Ancient Russia,* pp. 138-39.

49. Arnold E. Ehlert, *A Bibliographic History of Dispensationalism,* p. 56.

50. John Cumming, *Signs of the Times; or Present, Past, and Future,* p. 73.

51. John Cumming, *The End: or The Proximate Signs of the Close of This Dispensation,* pp. 92-94.
52. Ibid., pp. 95-96.
53. Cumming, *Signs of the Times,* pp. 142-43.
54. Ibid., p. 152.
55. Cumming, *The End,* p. 213.
56. Ibid., p. 212.
57. Ibid., p. 214.
58. Ibid., pp. 260-62.
59. Ibid., p. 267.
60. Ibid., p. 264.
61. Ibid., pp. 264-65.
62. Ibid., p. 269.
63. Ibid., p. 274.
64. Ibid., p. 286.
65. Ibid., p. 276.
66. Ibid., p. 275.
67. Ibid., p. 276.
68. Ibid., p. 277.
69. Ibid., p. 280.
70. John Cumming, *The Great Preparation; or Redemption Draweth Nigh,* pp. xli-xlii.
71. Ibid., p. xlii.
72. Ibid., p. xliii.
73. Ibid., p. 166.
74. Sandeen, *The Roots of Fundamentalism,* pp. 59, 98.
75. James H. Brookes, *Maranatha: Or, The Lord Cometh,* p. 418.
76. Ibid., pp. 392-96. See Genesis 13:14-17, 17:8, and 48:4.
77. Ibid., p. 424. See Daniel 9:24.
78. Ibid., p. 426.
79. Ibid., p. 430.
80. Ibid., p. 436.
81. Ibid., pp. 443-45.
82. Sandeen, *The Roots of Fundamentalism,* p. 134.
83. Ibid., pp. 94-96.
84. Ibid., pp. 276-77.
85. Nathaniel West, ed., *Premillennial Essays,* p. 239.
86. H. Grattan Guinness, *The Approaching End of the Age,* p. 368.
87. Ibid., p. ix.
88. Ibid., p. 348.
89. Sandeen, *The Roots of Fundamentalism,* p. 157.
90. George C. Needham, ed., *Prophetic Studies of the International Prophetic Conference,* pp. 122-23.
91. Ibid., p. 107.

92. Wilbur M. Smith, *Israeli/Arab Conflict and the Bible,* pp. 288-89.

93. Alfred H. Burton, *The Future of Europe: Religiously and Politically, In the Light of Holy Scripture,* pp. 60-61.

94. Cyrus Ingerson Scofield, *Addresses on Prophecy,* p. 62.

95. James M. Gray, *Great Epochs of Sacred History,* p. 107.

96. Ibid., p. 113.

97. Isaac Massey Haldeman, *The Signs of the Times,* p. 441.

98. Ibid., pp. 452-53.

99. A. B. Simpson, *The Coming One,* pp. 191-92.

100. Ibid., pp. 71-72.

101. William Appleman Williams, *American-Russian Relations, 1781-1947,* pp. 3-90.

CHAPTER 3

1. Reuben A. Torrey, *The Return of the Lord Jesus,* p. 89.

2. *Our Hope,* XXV (1918-19), 81.

3. *Our Hope,* XXIV (1917-18), 582.

4. Harris Franklin Rall, "Premillennialism," *The Biblical World,* LIII (1919), 341.

5. *The Weekly Evangel,* April 10, 1917, p. 3. The Assemblies of God was formed as a Pentecostal or charismatic organization by people mainly out of the holiness tradition; it has become the largest denomination committed to premillenarianism.

6. C. I. Scofield, "The War in the Light of Prophecy," *The Weekly Evangel,* October 28, 1916, pp. 6-7.

7. *The King's Business,* (August, 1919), 786.

8. Rall, "Premillennialism," p. 346.

9. Walter Scott, *At Hand: Or, Things Which Must Shortly Come to Pass,* p. 129.

10. Arno C. Gaebelein, ed., *Christ and Glory, Addresses Delivered at the New York Prophetic Conference, Carnegie Hall, November 25-28, 1918,* p. 156.

11. *The Weekly Evangel,* April 10, 1917, p. 3.

12. *The King's Business, V* (December, 1914), 685-86. Biola had been established by the wealthy businessman Lyman Stewart, hence the appropriate title for its magazine.

13. *The King's Business,* VI (April, 1915), 273-74.

14. *The Weekly Evangel,* August 12, 1916, p. 7.

15. Albert Norton, "The Year 1917 in Prophecy," *The Weekly Evangel,* October 13, 1917, p. 4.

16. *Our Hope,* XXIII (1916-17), 184-85.

17. *The Christian Workers Magazine,* XVII (1916-17), 180, 795.

18. *Our Hope,* XXIV (1917-18), 366.

19. *The Weekly Evangel,* February 26, 1916, p. 6.

20. *The Weekly Evangel,* April 28, 1917, p. 7.

21. *Our Hope, XXIV* (1917-18), 290.

22. *The Weekly Evangel,* February 3, 1917, p. 11.
23. Scott, *At Hand,* p. 77.
24. W. E. Blackstone, "The Times of the Gentiles," *The Weekly Evangel,* May 13, 1916, pp. 6-9.
25. *The Weekly Evangel,* May 19, 1917, p. 7.
26. Hawthorne Quinn Mills, "American Zionism and Foreign Policy," p. 28.
27. Stephen Wise, *Challenging Years: The Autobiography of Stephen Wise,* pp. 186-87.
28. Ibid., p. 197.
29. *The Weekly Evangel,* January 5, 1918, p. 5.
30. W. Fuller Gooch, "The Termination of This Age," *The Weekly Evangel,* March 23, 1918, p. 12.
31. Reuben A. Torrey, *What War Teaches: The Greatest Lessons of the Year* 1917, p. 4.
32. *Our Hope,* XXIV (1917-18), 438.
33. W. W. Fereday, "After the Great War," *Our Hope,* XXVI (1919-20), 34.
34. Hertzel Fishman, *American Protestantism and a Jewish State,* p. 28.
35. *The Weekly Evangel,* December 22, 1917, p. 3.
36. A. B. Simpson, Editorial, *The Alliance Weekly,* XLIX (December 22, 1917), 177.
37. A. B. Simpson, "The Fall of Jerusalem in the Light of Prophecy," *The Alliance Weekly,* XLIX (February 16, 1918), 306-7.
38. F. I. Langston, "The Chosen People and the Chosen Land," *The Weekly Evangel,* March 23, 1918, pp. 2-3.
39. A. E. Thompson, "The Capture of Jerusalem," *Light on Prophecy: A Coordinated, Constructive Teaching, Being the Proceedings and Addresses at the Philadelphia Prophetic Conference, May 28-30, 1918,* p. 160.
40. Gaebelein, *Christ and Glory,* p. 157.
41. *The King's Business,* X (October, 1919), 927. See also *The Christian Workers Magazine,* XIX (1918-19), 807.
42. *The King's Business,* X (August, 1919), 786; Dov Ashbel, *One Hundred and Seventeen Years (1845-1962) of Rainfall Observations,* p. 118.
43. *The Weekly Evangel,* February 26, 1916, p. 6.
44. Joseph W. Kemp, "The Jewish Tragedy," *The Christian Workers Magazine,* XVII (1916-17), 180.
45. *Our Hope,* XXIII (1916-17), 751.
46. *Our Hope,* XXV (1918-19), 140.
47. F. A. Wight, "The Restoration of the Jews," *The Alliance Weekly,* XLIX (January 12, 1918), 230-31.
48. *The King's Business,* X (October, 1919), 927.
49. *Our Hope,* XXVI (1919-20), 506.
50. Scott, *At Hand,* p. 77.
51. Ibid., p. 70.
52. *Our Hope,* XXIII (1916-17), 44.
53. *Our Hope,* XXIII (1916-17), 110-13.
54. *Our Hope,* XXIII (1916-17), 185, 559.

55. Arno C. Gaebelein, "The Prophet Ezekiel," *Our Hope,* XXIV (November, 1917), 281.
56. Andrew D. Ursham, *The Weekly Evangel,* March 24, 1917, p. 1.
57. *The King's Business,* IX (October, 1918), 835.
58. *The King's Business,* X (August, 1919), 785.
59. *Our Hope,* XXIV (1917-18), 492.
60. *Our Hope,* XXVI (1919-20), 534.
61. *The King's Business,* X (October, 1919), 926.
62. *Our Hope,* XXV (1918-19), 116.
63. Thompson, "The Capture of Jerusalem," p. 160.
64. Gaebelein, "The Prophet Ezekiel," p. 281.
65. Isaac Massey Haldeman, *The Signs of the Times,* pp. 641-47.
66. *The Christian Workers Magazine,* XVII (1916-17), 722. Reader Harris, "Nearing the End of the Pentecostal Age," *The Weekly Evangel,* July 15, 1916, pp. 7-9.
67. Shirley Jackson Case, "The Premillennial Menace," *The Biblical World,* LII (1918), 17.
68. Scott, *At Hand,* p. 47.
69. Case, "The Premillennial Menace," p. 22.
70. T. Valentine Parker, "Premillenarianism: An Interpretation and an Evaluation," *The Biblical World,* LIII (1919), 40.
71. *The Christian Workers Magazine,* XX (1919-20), 113.
72. *Our Hope,* XXV (1919-20), 205.
73. *Our Hope,* XVI (1919-20), 414.
74. *Our Hope,* XXV (1919-20), 230.
75. Haldeman, *The Signs of the Times,* pp. 383-84.
76. *Our Hope,* XXVI (1919-20), 414.
77. Ibid.
78. *The King's Business,* X (June, 1919), 38.
79. Gaebelein, *Christ and Glory,* pp. 156-57.
80. Case, "The Premillennial Menace," p. 20.
81. Parker, "Premillenarianism," p. 37.
82. James H. Snowden, "Summary of Objections to Premillenarianism," *The Biblical World,* LIII (1919), 165.
83. Harris Franklin Rall, "Premillennialism: II. Premillennialism and the Bible," *The Biblical World,* LIII (1919), 339.
84. *Our Hope,* XXIV (1917-18), 267.
85. Nathaniel West, *The Thousand Years,* p. 448.
86. Harrison Franklin Rall, "Premillennialism: III. Where Premillennialism Leads," *The Biblical World,* LIII (1919), 623.

CHAPTER 4

1. *The King's Business,* XI (October, 1920), 947.
2. Thomas M. Chalmers, "Palestinian Mandate Approved," *The King's Business,* XIII (November, 1922), 1137.

3. E. L. Langston, "Signs of the Times," *The Pentecostal Evangel,* March 3, 1923, p. 3. (Formerly *The Weekly Evangel, The Pentecostal Evangel* is hereafter cited as *Evangel.*)

4. *Evangel,* November 29, 1924, p. 10.

5. F. E. Howitt, "Israel and Other Lands in Prophecy," *Evangel,* March 10, 1928, pp. 2-3.

6. Edward C. Porter, "How the Nations Are Made Ready for the End of the Age," *Moody Bible Institute Monthly,* XXIV (August, 1924), 598. (*Moody Bible Institute Monthly* is hereafter cited as *Moody Monthly.*)

7. Thomas M. Chalmers, "The Shadow of Armageddon: Will America Take Part in the Conflict?" *Evangel,* January 15, 1927, p. 6 (Reprint from *Jewish Missionary Magazine*).

8. *Moody Monthly,* XXII (August, 1922), 1132-33.

9. *The King's Business,* XI (April, 1920), 370.

10. French E. Oliver, "The League of Nations and Prophecy's Program: Its Place in Scripture, Its Necessity in the World, and Its Outcome," *The King's Business,* XI (October, 1920), 927-28.

11. C. E. Robinson, "What of the Jews?" *Evangel,* December 12, 1925, p. 11; "Shadows of Coming Events," *Evangel,* March 27, 1926, p. 6.

12. Dov Ashbel, *One Hundred and Seventeen Years (1845-1962) of Rainfall Observations,* pp. 118-31.

13. *The King's Business,* XI (June, 1920), 563.

14. *The King's Business,* XIV (June, 1923), 589.

15. *The King's Business,* XI (April, 1920), 370.

16. *The King's Business,* XI (August, 1920), 761.

17. Christabel Pankhurst, *The Lord Cometh! The World Crisis Explained,* p. 93.

18. *New York Times,* January 5, 1925, p. 9.

19. *Watchman Examiner,* XIII (January 15, 1925), 71.

20. Christabel Pankhurst, "Christabel Pankhurst to the London Police: An Address by Miss Christabel Pankhurst at the Annual Meeting of the International Christian Police Association, London, Eng." *Moody Monthly,* XXVIII (September, 1927), 14.

21. Doreen Ingrams, "Palestine Papers: 1917-1918," in *The Zionist Movement in Palestine and World Politics, 1880-1918,* ed. N. Gordon Levin, Jr., p. 147.

22. Frank Manuel, *The Realities of American-Palestine Relations,* p. 249. The commission was led by the president of Oberlin College, Henry C. King, who had been a religious director of the American Expeditionary Forces, and Charles Crane, the vice-chairman of the Democratic Party's finance committee in 1912.

23. Thomas M. Chalmers, "Palestinian Mandate Approved," *The King's Business,* XIII (November, 1922), 1137.

24. *The King's Business,* XIV (January, 1923), 40-41. On the muddled American foreign policy see Manuel, *Realities of American-Palestine Relations,* pp. 271, 289.

25. Chalmers, "Palestinian Mandate Approved," p. 1136.

26. Thomas M. Chalmers, "Israel's Title to Canaan," *The King's Business,* XVII (February, 1926), 94.

27. *The King's Business,* XI (August, 1920), 760.

28. Myer Pearlman, "The Jewish Question from the Viewpoint of a Converted Jew," *Evangel,* June 4, 1927, p. 8.

29. Harry J. Steil, "Two Million Signs of the Times," *Evangel,* July 30, 1967, pp. 2-4.

30. *Evangel,* August 23, 1928, pp. 2-3. There is a marked discrepancy with the *Evangel's* own figures of 30,000 immigrants per year (March 12, 1927), but they were probably based on the 1925 figure of 33,801. See Frank H. Epp, *Whose Land Is Palestine? The Middle East Problem in Historical Perspective,* p. 147.

31. *Moody Monthly,* XXIX (April, 1929), 376.

32. Charles C. Cook, "The International Jew: A Summary of the Recent Articles Concerning the Jews, with Some Scriptural Light," *The King's Business,* XII (November, 1921), 1088.

33. Chalmers, "Palestinian Mandate Approved," p. 1136.

34. *The King's Business,* XVII (May, 1926), 262.

35. J. A. Vaus, "Jewish News Notes," *The King's Business,* XVI (May, 1925), 239.

36. *Evangel,* February 5, 1927, p. 7.

37. Cited in Stanley H. Frodsham, "Signs of the Approaching End," *Evangel,* February 25, 1928, p. 2.

38. *The King's Business,* XII (June, 1921), 575.

39. *The King's Business,* XII (August, 1921), 795.

40. Cook, "The International Jew," pp. 1186-87.

41. *The King's Business,* XIV (June, 1923), 588.

42. S. A. Jamieson, "His Coming Draweth Nigh—Signs of the End," *Evangel,* November 28, 1925, pp. 2-3.

43. Eva Morton, "Behold the Fig Tree," *Evangel,* August 13, 1927, p. 6.

44. Frodsham, "Signs of the Approaching End," p. 2.

45. From the *Jewish Chronicle* as cited in *Evangel,* May 12, 1928, p. 1.

46. Frederick W. Childe, "The Sure Word of Prophecy," *Evangel,* September 9, 1928, p. 6.

47. A. Stacy Watson, "The Time of Jacob's Trouble," *Morning Star,* as reprinted in *Evangel,* September 30, 1922, p. 3.

48. *The King's Business,* XIV (June, 1923), 589.

49. S. B. Rohold, *Jewish Missionary Herald,* as cited in *The King's Business,* XV (January, 1924), 58.

50. *Moody Monthly,* XXX (October, 1929), 58.

51. *The King's Business,* XX (October, 1929), 490.

52. *Our Hope,* XXXVI (1929-30), 230.

53. *Evangel,* January 18, 1930, p. 8.

54. *Evangel,* February 1, 1930, pp. 4-5.

55. *Christian Century,* October 29, 1930, p. 1300, as cited in Hertzel Fishman, *American Protestantism and a Jewish State,* p. 28.

56. Fishman, *American Protestantism and a Jewish State,* p. 29.

57. Arno C. Gaebelein, *The Conflict of the Ages: The Mystery of Lawlessness: Its Origin, Historic Development and Coming Defeat,* p. 101.

58. Norman Cohn, *Warrant for Genocide: The Myth of the Jewish World-conspiracy and the "Protocols of the Elders of Zion,"* p. 158.

59. D. M. Panton, "Latest Preparations for the Anti-Christ," *Evangel,* September 4, 1920, pp. 6-7.

60. Cook, "The International Jew," p. 1087.

61. *The King's Business,* XII (August, 1921), 795.

62. *The King's Business,* XI (September, 1920), 858.

63. *The King's Business,* XII (June, 1921), 575.

64. *The King's Business,* XVII (May, 1926), 262.

65. Charles J. Waehlte [Waehlite?], "The Red Terror," *The King's Business,* XIII (September, 1922), 908-09.

66. O. R. Palmer, "Christ and Antichrist in Russia," *Moody Monthly,* XXIV (October, 1923), 59.

67. *The King's Business,* XV (March, 1924), 133.

68. Alton B. Parker, "Recognition of Soviet Russia?" *Moody Monthly,* XXIV (March, 1924), 347.

69. *Evangel,* February 21, 1925, pp. 6-7.

70. *Evangel,* November 29, 1924, p. 9.

71. *Evangel,* April 30, 1927, p. 3.

72. F. E. Howitt, "Israel and Other Lands in Prophecy," *Evangel,* March 10, 1928, pp. 2-3.

73. Frodsham, "Signs of the Approaching End," p. 2.

74. *Evangel,* December 13, 1924, pp. 6-7.

75. *The King's Business,* XIV (February, 1923), 136.

76. *Evangel,* July 26, 1925, pp. 6-7.

77. Stanley H. Frodsham, "The Revival of the Roman Empire," *Evangel,* December 11, 1926, pp. 4-5.

78. *Evangel,* April 30, 1927, p. 3.

79. Leonard Sale-Harrison, *The Coming Great Northern Confederacy: or The Future of Russia and Germany,* pp. 20-23.

80. I. R. Wall, "Christ and Antichrist," *The King's Business,* XX (November, 1929), 525.

81. D. Grether, "Disarmament and the Signs of the Times," *Moody Monthly,* XXII (February, 1922), 806.

82. James McAlister, "Startling Signs of the Times," *Evangel,* July 10, 1930, pp. 1-3.

83. *The King's Business,* XI (October, 1920), 926-27.

84. Arthur W. Frodsham, "The Return of the Lord. The Signs of the Times," *Evangel,* February 18, 1922, p. 3.

85. Pankhurst, *The Lord Cometh!,* p. 94.

86. *Evangel,* February 7, 1925, p. 6.

87. W. Percy Hicks, "Proposed Revival of the Old Roman Empire," *Evangel,* March 20, 1926, p. 4.

88. Wall, "Christ and Antichrist," pp. 524-25.

89. Oswald J. Smith, "Is Antichrist at Hand?" *Evangel,* October 30, 1926, pp. 2-3.

90. *Evangel,* March 12, 1927, p. 3.

91. J. N. Hoover, "Mussolini: Is the World Preparing for Antichrist?" *Evangel,* November 26, 1927, p. 1.

92. Chalmers, "The Shadow of Armageddon," p. 6.

93. Reginald T. Naish, *The Midnight Hour and After!,* pp. 172-73.

94. F. E. Howitt, "Does the United States Appear in Prophecy?" *The King's Business,* XXII (April, 1931), 153-54.

95. John H. Baxter, "The Spiritual Values of Armageddon," *Evangel,* April 13, 1929, pp. 2-3.

CHAPTER 5

1. *Prophecy,* III (October, 1931), 7.

2. Agnes Scott Kent, "Palestine Is for the Jew," *The King's Business,* XXII (November, 1931), 494.

3. Charles G. Trumbull, *Prophecy's Light on Today,* p. 72.

4. *The Pentecostal Evangel,* July 26, 1930, p. 4. (Hereafter cited as *Evangel*)

5. Aaron Judah Kligerman, "Israel and Palestine," *Moody Bible Institute Monthly,* XXX (August, 1930), 587-88. (Hereafter cited as *Moody Monthly*)

6. As cited in *Evangel,* December 13, 1930, p. 6.

7. *Evangel,* December 6, 1930, p. 4.

8. J. A. Huffman, "The Jew and Arab Controversy over Palestine," *The King's Business,* XXI (September, 1930), 417-18.

9. *The King's Business,* XXII (April, 1931), 149.

10. *Our Hope,* XLI (1934-35), 377.

11. *Evangel,* March 3, 1934, p. 5.

12. Myer Pearlman, "Jewish Notes," *Evangel,* August 20, 1932, p. 7.

13. Edward Hilary Moseley, *The Jew and His Destiny,* p. 10.

14. As cited in *Evangel,* February 1, 1936, p. 11.

15. *Evangel,* April 20, 1935, p. 5.

16. *Evangel,* February 24, 1934, p. 4.

17. *Evangel,* January 5, 1935, p. 5.

18. Frank H. Epp, *Whose Land Is Palestine? The Middle East Problem in Historical Perspective,* p. 147.

19. Jacob Gartenhaus, *What of the Jews?,* p. 47.

20. Jacob Gartenhaus, *The Rebirth of a Nation: Zionism in History and Prophecy,* p. 128.

21. Leonard Sale-Harrison, "The Approaching Combination of Nations As It Affects Palestine," *Moody Monthly,* XXXVII (September, 1936), 18.

22. *Evangel,* February 11, 1933, p. 5.

23. *Evangel,* November 15, 1930, p. 5.

24. Otto J. Klink, "The Jew—God's Great Timepiece," *Evangel,* May 9, 1931, p. 1.

25. *Evangel,* April 25, 1938, p. 4.

26. *Moody Monthly,* XXXI (January, 1931), 239.

27. *Moody Monthly,* XXXI (February, 1931), 346.
28. Louis S. Bauman, *Shirts and Sheets: or Anti-Semitism, a Present-day Sign of the First Magnitude,* pp. 41-44.
29. The social views of conservative Christians, of whom premillenarians may be considered a part, have been surveyed in Kenneth K. Bailey, *Southern White Protestantism in the Twentieth Century,* and in Lowell D. Streiker and Gerald S. Strober, *Religion and the New Majority: Billy Graham, Middle America, and the Politics of the 70's.*
30. Arthur D. Morse, *While Six Million Died: A Chronicle of American Apathy,* p. 169.
31. *Evangel,* September 23, 1933, p. 5.
32. *Evangel,* February 24, 1934, p. 5.
33. *Evangel,* August 31, 1935, p. 5.
34. Wilbur M. Smith, "With the Bible in the Land of the Book," *Moody Monthly,* XXXIX (October, 1938), 69. *(Moody Monthly* is now the official title.)
35. *The Alliance Weekly,* LXXIV (January 21, 1939), 34.
36. Bauman, *Shirts and Sheets,* p. 20.
37. Ibid., pp. 50-51.
38. Ibid., p. 50.
39. Arno C. Gaebelein, *The Conflict of the Ages: The Mystery of Lawlessness: Its Origin, Historic Development and Coming Defeat,* p. 100.
40. Thomas M. Chalmers, "The Present Situation in World Jewry," *The King's Business,* XXV (June, 1934), p. 216.
41. Bauman, *Shirts and Sheets,* p. 18.
42. *Time,* November 12, 1934.
43. *Evangel,* May 18, 1935, p. 1.
44. William Bell Riley, *Wanted—A World Leader!* Riley was president of the World's Christian Fundamentals Association.
45. S. A. Jamieson, "The Signs of the Times," *Evangel,* April 4, 1931, p. 9.
46. *The New York Times,* July 20, 1930, p. 8.
47. *Ammianus Marcellinus,* xxiii.1.2.
48. *Evangel,* March 12, 1932, p. 3.
49. Gaebelein, *Conflict of the Ages,* p. 30.
50. Cited in *Evangel,* February 1, 1936, p. 11.
51. *Evangel,* August 7, 1937, p. 7.
52. Charles S. Price, *The Battle of Armageddon,* p. 58.
53. Ibid., p. 42.
54. Cited in *Evangel,* August 22, 1936, p. 7.
55. Trumbull, *Prophecy's Light on Today,* p. 67.
56. Riley, *Wanted—A World Leader!,* p. 27.
57. *Evangel,* August 28, 1937, p. 7.
58. *Evangel,* November 6, 1937, p. 7, citing John C. Smith, *Advent Herald.*
59. *Evangel,* December 4, 1937, p. 7.
60. *Evangel,* February 17, 1940, p. 11.
61. Hertzel Fishman, *American Protestantism and a Jewish State,* p. 45.

62. *Christian Century,* November 17, 1937, p. 1412, as cited in Fishman, *American Protestantism and a Jewish State,* p. 48.
63. *Evangel,* February 1, 1930, p. 9.
64. Agnes Scott Kent, "Palestine Is for the Jew," *The King's Business,* XXII (November, 1931), 494. Louis S. Bauman, "Present-Day Fulfillment of Prophecy," *The King's Business,* XXIII (July, 1932), 313.
65. *Evangel,* February 4, 1933, p. 5.
66. Frederick Childe, "Christ's Answer to the Challenge of Communism and Fascism," *Evangel,* October 31, 1931, p. 1. *Evangel,* December 2, 1939, p. 7.
67. *Evangel,* December 5, 1931, p. 4, citing S. J. Williams, *Jewish Missionary Magazine.*
68. Bauman, "Present-Day Fulfillment of Prophecy," p. 314.
69. *Evangel,* July 4, 1936, p. 4, citing Keith L. Brooks, *Prophecy.*
70. *Evangel,* November 30, 1937, p. 7.
71. Arthur W. Payne, "Recent Progress in Palestine," *The King's Business,* XXI (March, 1930), 129.
72. W. F. Smalley, "Another View of the Palestine Situation," *The King's Business,* XXI (June, 1930), 290.
73. Ibid., p. 291.
74. Ibid.
75. Ibid., p. 292.
76. *Prophecy,* III (November, 1931), 23.
77. *Prophecy,* IV (November, 1932), 22. *Evangel,* June 23, 1934, p. 5, citing *Jewish Missionary Intelligence* in *Alliance Weekly.*
78. William H. Nagel, "Palestine—What of Its Progress? How Bible Promises Are Being Fulfilled," *Evangel,* October 31, 1936, pp. 8-9.
79. *Evangel,* August 7, 1937, p. 7, citing *Jewish Chronicle.*
80. *Evangel,* August 28, 1937, p. 7.
81. Childe, "Christ's Answer," p. 1. Bauman, "Present-Day Fulfillment of Prophecy," p. 313.
82. George T. B. Davis, *Rebuilding Palestine According to Prophecy,* p. 112.
83. *Evangel,* March 18, 1936, p. 6.
84. Oswald J. Smith, *Prophecy—What Lies Ahead?,* p. 85.
85. *Evangel,* March 26, 1938, p. 5, citing *The Hebrew Christian* (italics mine).
86. *Evangel,* August 12, 1939, p. 9.
87. *Our Hope,* XLVI (1939-40), 179.
88. *Christian Century,* May 31, 1939, pp. 695-96, as cited in Fishman, *American Protestantism and a Jewish State,* p. 51.

CHAPTER 6

1. *Prophecy,* IV (September, 1932), 22.
2. *Evangel,* November 12, 1932, p. 14, citing *The Life of Faith.*
3. As cited in *Evangel,* January 30, 1937, p. 7.

4. *Evangel,* February 12, 1938, p. 7.

5. Louis S. Bauman, "Socialism, Communism, Fascism," *The King's Business,* XXVI (July, 1935), 252.

6. N. J. Poysti, "What Is Bolshevism?" *Evangel,* February 1, 1936, p. 4.

7. Frederick Childe, "Christ's Answer to the Challenge of Communism and Fascism," *Evangel,* October 31, 1931, p. 1.

8. As cited in *Evangel,* February 22, 1930, pp. 4-5.

9. Paul B. Peterson, "A Desperate Situation in Russia," *Evangel,* March 8, 1930, p. 9.

10. As cited in *Evangel,* January 21, 1933, p. 5.

11. *Evangel,* May 13, 1933, p. 4. See I Kings 22:12.

12. *Prophecy,* III (December, 1931), 4-5.

13. *Evangel,* August 4, 1934, p. 7.

14. *Evangel,* August 1, 1936, p. 11.

15. John Robertson Macartney, "The Spread of Communism in Our Land," *Moody Monthly,* XXXV (May, 1935), 413.

16. Harry J. Steil, "The Trend Toward Armageddon," *Evangel,* July 18, 1936, pp. 2-3.

17. *Evangel,* July 2, 1932, p. 5.

18. *Prophecy,* IV (November, 1932), 22.

19. Louis S. Bauman, " 'Prepare *War*!' " *The King's Business,* XXV (December, 1934), p. 425.

20. Ibid., p. 424.

21. "Where Fundamentalists Stand," *The King's Business,* XXVIII (March, 1937), 90.

22. *Evangel,* October 2, 1937, p. 7.

23. Thomas M. Chalmers, "Russia and Armageddon," *Evangel,* April 14, 1934, p. 1.

24. See also Charles S. Price, *The Battle of Armageddon,* p. 59.

25. Louis S. Bauman, *God and Gog: or The Coming Meet Between Judah's Lion and Russia's Bear,* p. 38.

26. Louis S. Bauman, "Russia and Armageddon," *The King's Business,* XXIX (September, 1938), 286.

27. Price, *The Battle of Armageddon,* p. 49.

28. Louis T. Talbot, "Russia: Her Invasion of Palestine in the Last Days and Her Final Destruction at the Return of Christ," p. 18; "The Judgment of God upon the Russian Confederacy," p. 15. Both of these published sermons are available at the Biola College Library, La Mirada, California.

29. Bauman, "Russia and Armageddon," p. 287. Alva J. McClain, "The Four Great Powers of the End-Time," *The King's Business,* XXIX (February, 1938), 100.

30. Bauman, *God and Gog,* p. 35.

31. Price, *The Battle of Armageddon,* p. 5.

32. *Evangel,* October 11, 1930, p. 4.

33. Childe, "Christ's Answer," p. 8 (italics mine).

34. *Moody Monthly,* XXXII (March, 1932), 328.

35. Arno C. Gaebelein, *The Conflict of the Ages: The Mystery of Lawlessness: Its Origin, Historic Development and Coming Defeat,* p. 144.

36. Chalmers, "Russia and Armageddon," p. 6.

37. *Evangel,* August 4, 1934, p. 7 (italics mine).

38. Leonard Sale-Harrison, "The Approaching Combination of Nations As It Affects Palestine," *Moody Monthly,* XXXVII (September, 1936), 18.

39. *Evangel,* June 26, 1937, p. 9.

40. *Evangel,* October 23, 1937, p. 7, citing *Advent Witness.*

41. As cited in *Evangel,* December 11, 1937, p. 10.

42. As cited in *Evangel,* August 20, 1938, p. 5.

43. As cited in *Evangel,* February 25, 1939, p. 16.

44. *Evangel,* April 22, 1939, p. 9.

45. Bauman, "Russia and Armageddon," p. 287.

46. *Moody Monthly,* XXIX, (September, 1938), 287.

47. Dan Gilbert, "Views and Reviews of Current News," *The King's Business,* XXX (January, 1939), 8.

48. *Evangel,* September 16, 1939, p. 9.

49. Louis S. Bauman, "Gog & Gomer, Russia & Germany, and the War," *The Sunday School Times,* LXXXI (December 16, 1939), 911-12.

50. Arno C. Gaebelein, "The Great Coming North-Eastern Confederacy," *Our Hope,* XLVI (1939-40), 234-35.

51. *Evangel,* November 11, 1939, p. 6.

52. *Evangel,* December 23, 1939, p. 11.

53. *Prophecy,* III (December, 1931), 14.

54. *Evangel,* March 25, 1933, p. 5, and June 16, 1934, p. 5. Louis T. Talbot, "The Army of the Two Hundred Million," *The King's Business,* XXIII (October, 1932), 424.

55. *Evangel,* September 11, 1937, p. 7. See also *Evangel,* February 5, 1938, p. 5.

56. H. A. Ironside, "The Kings of the East," *The King's Business,* XXIX (January, 1938), 9.

57. Bauman, "Russia and Armageddon," p. 286.

58. *Prophecy,* III (November, 1931), 22 (italics mine).

59. As cited in *Evangel,* September 3, 1932, p. 10.

60. Louis S. Bauman, "Socialism, Communism, Fascism," *The King's Business,* XXVI (August, 1935), 293.

61. McClain, "The Four Great Powers of the End-Time," p. 97.

62. Gaebelein, *The Conflict of the Ages,* p. 144.

63. As cited in *Evangel,* June 5, 1937, p. 7.

64. *Our Hope,* XLI (1934-35), 377.

65. As cited in *Evangel,* August 8, 1936, p. 11.

66. Steil, "The Trend Toward Armageddon," pp. 2-3.

67. Bauman, "Socialism, Communism, Fascism," pp. 293-94.

68. McClain, "The Four Great Powers of the End-Time," pp. 96-100.

CHAPTER 7

1. *The Pentecostal Evangel,* January 10, 1942, p. 10. (hereafter cited as *Evangel)*
2. *Evangel,* November 25, 1944, p. 9.
3. *Evangel,* December 17, 1950, p. 13.
4. T. DeCourcy Rayner, "Hidden Hands in Palestine," *Moody Monthly,* XLVIII (December, 1947), 265.
5. *The Sunday School Times,* LXXXII (April 20, 1940), 319.
6. *Evangel,* February 17, 1940, p. 11.
7. *Our Hope,* LVII (1940-41), 341. Arno C. Gaebelein, "The Problem of Gog and Magog," *Our Hope,* XLVII (1940-41), 456-57.
8. H. A. Ironside, "Lesson for October 10, 1948," *The Sunday School Times,* XC (September 25, 1948), 835.
9. *Evangel,* November 22, 1941, p. 4.
10. *Evangel,* January 17, 1948, p. 10.
11. *Evangel,* March 20, 1948, p. 10.
12. Louis T. Talbot, "Palestine, Russia and Ezekiel 37," *The King's Business,* XXXVIII (November, 1947), 8.
13. H. A. Ironside, "Setting the Stage for the Last Act of the Great World Drama," *Our Hope,* LV (June, 1949), 724.
14. *Evangel,* March 2, 1940, p. 11.
15. *Evangel,* May 22, 1943, p. 16.
16. *The Sunday School Times,* LXXXIV (October 3, 1942), 781.
17. *Evangel,* January 2, 1943, p. 10.
18. *Evangel,* July 10, 1943, p. 16.
19. George T. B. Davis, "Why Are the Jews Returning to Palestine?" *The Sunday School Times,* LXXXVI (June 17, 1944), 435.
20. *Evangel,* April 22, 1944, p. 16.
21. *Evangel,* July 1, 1944, p. 16.
22. *Evangel,* December 9, 1944, p. 16. *The Sunday School Times,* LXXXVI (November 18, 1944), 837.
23. *Evangel,* February 17, 1940, p. 11.
24. *Evangel,* October 5, 1946, p. 18.
25. *Evangel,* December 27, 1947, p. 10.
26. *Evangel,* January 3, 1948, p. 10.
27. *The King's Business,* XXXIX (February, 1948), 4.
28. William L. Pettingill, "Signs of the End of the Age," *The Sunday School Times,* LXXXIX (April 12, 1947), 360.
29. *Evangel,* April 5, 1947, p. 10.
30. *Our Hope,* LIII (1946-47), 424.
31. *Our Hope,* LIV (1947-48), 355.
32. Rayner, "Hidden Hands in Palestine," p. 264.
33. Frank H. Epp, *Whose Land Is Palestine? The Middle East Problem in Historical Perspective,* p. 184.
34. *Moody Monthly,* XLVIII (May, 1948), 634.
35. *Evangel,* May 29, 1948, p. 10.

36. *Our Hope,* LIII (1946-47), 95-96; 172.

37. T. A. Lambie, "Palestine Focus of World Attention," *The Sunday School Times,* LXXXVII (May 4, 1946), 401 (italics mine).

38. Morris Zeidman, "The Restoration of the Kingdom," *Evangel,* May 1, 1948, p. 2 (italics mine).

39. Aaron J. Kligerman, "Palestine—Jewish Homeland," *The Southern Presbyterian Journal,* VII (June 1, 1948), 17.

40. Louis T. Talbot and William W. Orr, *The New Nation of Israel and the Word of God!* (Los Angeles: The Bible Institute of Los Angeles, [1948]), p. 8.

41. *The King's Business,* XXXIX (July, 1948), 4.

42. *Evangel,* June 12, 1948, p. 8.

43. *Evangel,* July 3, 1948, p. 8.

44. *Our Hope,* LV (1948-49), 27.

45. *Evangel,* June 5, 1948, p. 10.

46. *The King's Business,* XXXIX (October, 1948), 4.

47. *Evangel,* July 2, 1949, pp. 5-6.

48. *Annual of the Southern Baptist Convention, 1948* (Nashville: Executive Committee, Southern Baptist Convention, 1948), p. 34.

49. John G. Snetsinger, "Truman and the Creation of Israel," p. 139. On the struggle between the State Department and Congress see Frank E. Manuel, *The Realities of American-Palestine Relations,* particularly pp. 318-19.

50. *Evangel,* June 5, 1948, p. 10.

51. *Evangel,* September 25, 1948, p. 9.

52. Morris Zeidman, "The Commonwealth of Israel," *Evangel,* November 23, 1948, p. 3.

53. T. A. Lambie, "Future Blessings in Palestine," *The Sunday School Times,* XCI (July 16, 1949), 633.

54. *Alliance Weekly,* LXXXIV (March 5, 1949), 146.

55. *Evangel,* October 23, 1948, p. 12.

56. *Evangel,* April 30, 1949, p. 9.

57. William W. Orr, "The Bible in the News," *The King's Business,* XL (June, 1949), 6.

58. *Evangel,* September 4, 1948, p. 10.

59. George Carmichael, "Rebuilding Palestine," *Evangel,* February 19, 1949, p. 2.

60. U. S. Grant, "Things to Come," *Evangel,* May 21, 1949, p. 2.

61. *Our Hope,* LV (December, 1948), 627-28.

62. T. A. Lambie, "God's Answers to Questions on Palestine," *The Sunday School Times,* XCI (June 18, 1949), 557.

63. *Evangel,* December 28, 1940, p. 10.

64. *Evangel,* May 3, 1941, p. 10.

65. *Evangel,* January 2, 1943, p. 10.

66. *The King's Business,* XXXVIII (October, 1947), 4.

67. W. E. Vine, "An Ancient Prophecy," *Evangel,* June 18, 1949, p. 12.

68. E. L. Langston, "The Present War and Prophecy," *Evangel,* May 25, 1940, p. 5. Louis T. Talbot, "Palestine, Russia and Ezekiel 38," *The King's Business,* XXXIX (February, 1948), 17.

69. Louis S. Bauman, "Gog & Gomer, Russia & Germany, and the War," *The Sunday School Times,* LXXXI (December 16, 1939), 912.

70. *The Sunday School Times,* LXXXII (February 10, 1940), 124-25.

71. *Evangel,* May 29, 1943, p. 8.

72. *Evangel,* October 20, 1945, p. 4.

73. *Evangel,* August 20, 1949, p. 10.

74. Louis S. Bauman, *Russian Events in the Light of Bible Prophecy,* p. 130.

75. Harry Rimmer, *Palestine the Coming Storm Center,* pp. 33, 37.

76. *Alliance Weekly* as cited in *Evangel,* February 22, 1941, p. 10. *Evangel,* August 2, 1941, p. 10.

77. Rayner, "Hidden Hands in Palestine," p. 282.

78. Stanley H. Frodsham, "Man's Vain Attempts to Destroy Israel," *Evangel,* July 17, 1948, p. 4.

79. *Evangel,* September 18, 1948, p. 4; February 28, 1948, p. 10.

80. *Evangel,* May 14, 1949, p. 9.

81. Epp, *Whose Land Is Palestine?,* pp. 195, 202.

82. Hertzel Fishman, *American Protestantism and a Jewish State,* p. 146.

83. *Evangel,* May 21, 1949, p. 10.

84. *Evangel,* December 11, 1948, p. 7.

85. *Evangel,* July 16, 1949, p. 7.

86. *Christian Century,* December 6, 1950, p. 1445, as cited in Fishman, *American Protestantism and a Jewish State,* p. 146. See also Manuel, *Realities of American-Palestine Relations,* pp. 322-23.

87. Nadav Safran, *The United States and Israel,* p. 271.

88. Ibid.

89. *Christian Voice for a Jewish Palestine,* I (Summer, 1946), 6.

90. D. Malcomb Leith, "American Christian Support for a Jewish Palestine: From the Second World War to the Establishment of the State of Israel," p. 133.

91. Louis T. Talbot, "Palestine, Russia and Ezekiel 37," *The King's Business,* XXXVIII (November, 1947), p. 9.

92. *Evangel,* January 17, 1948, p. 10.

93. Louis S. Bauman, *Light from Prophecy as Related to the Present Crisis,* pp. 105-06.

94. *Evangel,* May 7, 1949, p. 9.

95. *Evangel,* January 23, 1943, p. 10.

96. *Evangel,* July 19, 1947, p. 10.

97. *Evangel,* January 28, 1948, p. 10.

98. As cited in *Evangel,* February 5, 1949, p. 10.

99. *Evangel,* March 26, 1949, p. 10.

100. *Alliance Weekly,* LXXXIV (May 14, 1949), 306-08.

101. Louis S. Bauman, "Europe's Triumvirate of Beasts," *The Sunday School Times,* LXXXII (July 20, 1940), 579.

102. *Evangel,* October 19, 1940, p. 10. Louis T. Talbot, "Palestine, Russia and Ezekiel 38," *The King's Business,* XXXIX (January, 1948), 16. Rayner, "Hidden Hands in Palestine," p. 264.

103. John Cumming, *The End: or The Proximate Signs of the Close of This Dispensation,* p. 275.

CHAPTER 8

1. Louis S. Bauman, "Gog & Gomer, Russia & Germany, and the War," *The Sunday School Times,* LXXXI (December 16, 1939), 912.
2. *The Pentecostal Evangel,* August 17, 1940, p. 7. (Hereafter cited as *Evangel*)
3. Arno C. Gaebelein, "The Problem of Gog and Magog," *Our Hope,* XLVII (1940-41), 455.
4. Louis S. Bauman, *Light from Prophecy as Related to the Present Crisis,* pp. 40, 42.
5. *Evangel,* February 24, 1940, p. 11. Bauman, "Gog & Gomer," pp. 911-12.
6. *Evangel,* August 17, 1940, p. 7.
7. John Hess McComb, "Europe and the Bible," *The King's Business,* XXXI (May, 1940), 167-68.
8. *Evangel,* October 5, 1940, p. 7; October 19, 1940, p. 10.
9. *Evangel,* December 28, 1940, p. 10.
10. Harry Rimmer, *The Coming War and the Rise of Russia,* pp. 59, 81.
11. W. W. Fereday, "Armageddon," *Our Hope,* XLVII (1940-41), 399.
12. *Evangel,* July 12, 1941, p. 10.
13. Arno C. Gaebelein, "The New Great World Crisis," *Our Hope,* XLVIII (1941-42), 89.
14. *Our Hope,* XLVI (1939-40), 234.
15. Gaebelein, "The New Great World Crisis," p. 91.
16. *Evangel,* August 9, 1941, p. 10.
17. *Evangel,* August 27, 1941, p. 13.
18. *Evangel,* October 4, 1941, p. 10.
19. Louis S. Bauman, *Russian Events in the Light of Bible Prophecy,* pp. 513-14. Ernest Gordon, "Russia and Christianity," *The Sunday School Times,* LXXXIV (June 27, 1942), 513.
20. *Evangel,* February 20, 1943, p. 16 (italics mine).
21. *Evangel,* January 10, 1942, p. 10.
22. Bauman, *Russian Events,* p. 84.
23. Ibid., p. 173.
24. *The Sunday School Times,* LXXXIV (November 21, 1942), 937-38.
25. *Evangel,* May 29, 1943, p. 8.
26. As cited in *Evangel,* September 11, 1943, p. 13.
27. As cited in *Evangel,* February 26, 1944, p. 8.
28. *Evangel,* September 30, 1944, p. 16.
29. As cited in *Evangel,* November 18, 1944, p. 16.
30. Dan Gilbert, *The Red Terror and Bible Prophecy,* pp. 18-20.
31. *Evangel,* January 6, 1940, p. 9.
32. *Evangel,* March 9, 1940, p. 11.

33. *Evangel,* September 14, 1940, p. 8.
34. Harry Rimmer, *Palestine the Coming Storm Center,* pp. 41, 71. See also Nathaniel West, *The Thousand Years: Studies in Eschatology in Both Testaments,* p. 19.
35. Louis T. Talbot, "Palestine, Russia and Ezekiel 39," *The King's Business,* XXXIX (July, 1948), 5.
36. Gaebelein, "The Problem of Gog and Magog," pp. 454-59; "The New Great World Crisis," pp. 91-92.
37. *Our Hope,* LV (1948-49), 294.
38. *Our Hope,* LII (1945-46), 617.
39. Ibid., pp. 690, 756.
40. Gaebelein, "The New Great World Crisis," p. 92. *Our Hope,* LII (1945-46), 617.
41. *Our Hope,* LIII (1946-47), 362.
42. *Evangel,* April 20, 1946, p. 11.
43. *Evangel,* May 23, 1946, p. 9.
44. *Our Hope,* LIII (1946-47), 22.
45. *Our Hope,* LIII (1946-47), 681. *Our Hope,* LIV (1947-48), 109.
46. *Evangel,* April 26, 1947, p. 10.
47. *Evangel,* December 13, 1947, p. 9.
48. *Evangel,* December 20, 1947, p. 10.
49. Louis T. Talbot, "Palestine, Russia and Ezekiel 39," *The King's Business,* XXXIX (January, 1948), 11.
50. Ibid., p. 16.
51. *Evangel,* September 13, 1947, p. 10.
52. Louis T. Talbot, "Palestine, Russia and Ezekiel 38," *The King's Business,* XXXIX (February, 1948), 13.
53. Louis T. Talbot, "Palestine, Russia and Ezekiel 38," *The King's Business,* XXXIX (January, 1948), 13.
54. Merril T. MacPherson, "Russia in the News and Prophecy," *Christian Life,* II (November, 1947), 25-28.
55. *Christian Life,* II (November, 1947), 58.
56. L. Nelson Bell, "Christian Realism," *The Southern Presbyterian Journal,* VI (January 1, 1948), 4-5.
57. *The Southern Presbyterian Journal,* VI (January 16, 1948), 4.
58. Erling Jorstad, *The Politics of Doomsday,* pp. 50-51.
59. Dan Gilbert, *Russia's Next Move: In the Light of Prophecy,* pp. 9-10.
60. *Evangel,* March 27, 1948, p. 8.
61. Mark Kagan, "God and the World Crisis," *Evangel,* April 24, 1948, p. 7.
62. *Our Hope,* LV (1948-49), 228.
63. *Evangel,* November 27, 1948, p. 15.
64. As cited in *Evangel,* April 30, 1949, p. 9.
65. *Evangel,* May 21, 1949, p. 2.
66. D. P. Holloway, "Russia and Armageddon," *Evangel,* June 4, 1949, pp. 5-6.
67. H. A. Ironside, "Setting the Stage for the Last Act of the Great World Drama," *Our Hope,* LVI (1949-50), 22.

68. H. A. Ironside, "Setting the Stage for the Last Act of the Great World Drama," *Our Hope,* LV (1948-49), 745.

69. *The King's Business,* XL (November, 1949), 6.

70. Louis S. Bauman, "The Iron Versus the Clay," *The Sunday School Times,* LXXXII (August 17, 1940), 647-48.

71. Bauman, *Light from Prophecy,* p. 49.

72. Fereday, "Armageddon," p. 398.

73. Rimmer, *The Coming War,* p. 83.

74. *Our Hope,* LIV (1947-48), p. 238.

75. *Our Hope,* LIII (1946-47), 536.

76. *Our Hope,* LV (1948-49), 673.

77. H. A. Ironside, "Setting the Stage for the Last Act of the Great World Drama," *Our Hope,* LVI (1949-50), 20.

78. *Our Hope,* LVI (1949-50), 160, 162.

79. Louis S. Bauman, "Armageddon—A War, Not a Battle," *The Sunday School Times,* LXXXII (September 7, 1940), 700.

80. Ibid.

81. Bauman, *Russian Events,* p. 147.

82. Ibid., pp. 147, 151.

83. *Our Hope,* LII (1945-46), 757; LIII (1946-47), 681.

84. *Our Hope,* LIII (1946-47), 681.

85. H. E. Fisher, *Soviet Russia and Palestine,* p. 67.

86. Merril T. MacPherson, "The Reign and Rule of Anti-Christ," *Christian Life,* III (February, 1948), 30.

87. *Our Hope,* LV (1948-49), 172; LVI (1949-50), 160. H. A. Ironside, "Setting the Stage for the Last Act of the Great World Drama," *Our Hope,* LVI (1949-50), 20.

88. Dan Gilbert, *Will Russia Fight America? The Question Considered in the Light of Bible Prophecy,* p. 27.

89. Rimmer, *The Coming War,* p. 83.

90. *Evangel,* February 19, 1944, p. 16.

91. Wilbur M. Smith, "How Antichrist Will Rule," *Moody Monthly,* XLVIII (February, 1948), 399-400; "The Shaping of One World," *The Sunday School Times,* XC (November 20, 1948), 1027-28.

92. *Evangel,* January 10, 1942, p. 10.

93. *Our Hope,* LII (1945-46), 757.

94. *Our Hope,* LIV (1947-48), 8.

95. Louis T. Talbot, "Palestine, Russia and Ezekiel 39," *The King's Business,* XXXIX (April, 1948), 8.

96. Donald M. Hunter, "China Today," *Our Hope,* LV (1948-49), 676.

97. Wilbur M. Smith, "The Testimony of Bible Prophecy," *Moody Monthly,* XLIX (September, 1949), 15.

CHAPTER 9

1. Louis S. Bauman, "Israel Lives Again!" *The King's Business,* XLI (September, 1950), 7.

2. *Evangel,* September 2, 1950, p. 7.
3. Martin R. DeHaan, *The Jew and Palestine in Prophecy,* pp. 64-65.
4. As cited in *Evangel,* May 17, 1951, pp. 4-6.
5. William Culbertson, "God's Clock Ticks On in the Holy Land," *Moody Monthly,* LIII (January, 1953), 348.
6. Charles L. Feinberg, "The Future of Israel," *Moody Monthly,* LIX (October, 1958), 27.
7. *Evangel,* August 28, 1955, p. 2.
8. Louis H. Hauff, "A Sign of the Times," *Evangel,* February 5, 1956, p. 2.
9. Isaac D. Unna, "Israel—Triumph of Spirit," *Moody Monthly,* LV (May, 1955), 16-19.
10. Fayez A. Sayegh, "The Arab Plight in the Holy Land," *Moody Monthly,* LV (May, 1955), 24-25.
11. Isaac D. Unna, "The Israeli View," *Moody Monthly,* LV (July, 1955), 9.
12. Fayez A. Sayegh, "The Arab View," *Moody Monthly,* LV (July, 1955), 8.
13. *Evangel,* March 25, 1956, p. 12.
14. William W. Orr, "The Bible in the News," *The King's Business,* XLI (November, 1950), 7.
15. As reprinted in *Evangel,* May 17, 1951, pp. 4-6.
16. *The King's Business,* XLIII (March, 1952), 7.
17. Culbertson, "God's Clock," p. 379.
18. George T. B. Davis, "A Divine Promise That Changed History," *The Sunday School Times,* XCIX (March 16, 1957), 205-06.
19. Frederick A. Tatford, "Bible Light on Recent Events in the Middle East," *The Sunday School Times,* XCIX (September 28, 1957), 743-44; "The Promised Land in History and Prophecy," *The Sunday School Times,* XCIX (October 12, 1957), 787.
20. *Evangel,* March 3, 1957, p. 2.
21. James C. Dodd, "Israel Today and Tomorrow," *Evangel,* March 31, 1957, pp. 16-17.
22. Oswald T. Allis, "Israel's Transgression in Palestine," *Christianity Today,* I (December 24, 1956), 9.
23. Wilbur M. Smith, "Israel in Her Promised Land," *Christianity Today,* I (December 24, 1956), 7-9.
24. Paul S. Allen, "Arab or Israeli?" *The Alliance Witness,* XCII (May 8, 1957), 2.
25. William L. Hull, *Israel—Key to Prophecy,* p. 35.
26. *Christianity and Crisis,* January 7, 1957, p. 187, as cited in Hertzel Fishman, *American Protestantism and a Jewish State,* p. 150.
27. *Evangel,* November 9, 1958, p. 2.
28. Louis H. Hauff, "Israel's 10th Anniversary," *Evangel,* November 9, 1958, pp. 4-5.
29. *Evangel,* June 10, 1950, p. 10.
30. Coulson Shepherd, "The Unholy Holy Land," *Moody Monthly,* LI (July, 1951), 718.

31. Elmer H. Nicholas, "The Fig Tree Is Budding," *Evangel,* March 22, 1953, pp. 3-4. (Reprinted from *The King's Business*)

32. *Evangel,* May 9, 1954, p. 2.

33. Arnold Toynbee, *A Study of History,* IV, 407-08.

34. Charles E. Pont, *The World's Collision,* p. 215.

35. *Evangel,* April 29, 1956, p. 2.

36. *Evangel,* December 2, 1956, p. 2.

37. Charles L. Feinberg, "Israel—The Apple of God's Eye," *The King's Business,* XLV (October, 1954), 19.

38. *Evangel,* November 5, 1950, p. 5.

39. Leonard Sale-Harrison, "Russia's Militant Opposition to Christianity," *The Sunday School Times,* XCII (October 15, 1950), 867.

40. Milton R. Lindberg, "Regathering Israel," *Evangel,* January 13, 1952, p. 9.

41. F. C. Schwarz, "Red Shadow!" *Moody Monthly,* LI (January, 1951), 306-07.

42. *The King's Business,* XLII (March, 1951), 5.

43. *The Sunday School Times,* XCVII (December 24, 1955), 1029.

44. *Evangel,* September 2, 1950, p. 7.

45. Sale-Harrison, "Russia's Militant Opposition to Christianity," p. 867.

46. Frank M. Boyd, "Russia in Prophecy," *Evangel,* June 17, 1950, p. 5.

47. Wilbur M. Smith, "World Crisis and the Prophetic Scriptures," *Moody Monthly,* L (June, 1950), 679.

48. Louis S. Bauman, "The Russian Bear Prowls Forth to His Doom," *The King's Business,* XLI (September, 1950), 10-12.

49. Douglas Ober, *The Great World Crisis,* p. 75.

50. *The King's Business,* XLII (April, 1951), 4.

51. J. Narver Gortner, "Russia's Origin, Character, and Doom," *Evangel,* September 21, 1952, p. 10. Glad Tidings Bible Institute, Santa Cruz, California, has since been renamed Bethany Bible College.

52. *Our Hope,* LXI (1954-55), 660-61.

53. H. S. Gallimore, "The North and South Prophecy," *Our Hope,* LXII (1955-56), 63 .

54. Edgar Ainslie, "Russia in the Light of Prophecy," *The Sunday School Times,* XCVIII (October 13, 1956), 807.

55. James C. Dodd, "Israel Today and Tomorrow," *Evangel,* March 31, 1957, pp. 16-17.

56. W. W. Kirkby, "Ambitious Russia: Without Doubt Her Greed Will Lead to Her Downfall on the Mountains of Israel," *Evangel,* February 17, 1957, pp. 6-7.

57. Kenneth de Courcy, "World Crisis," *Evangel,* March 23, 1958, p. 3.

58. Merv Rosell, "God Pre-writes the Headlines," *The King's Business,* XLIX (July, 1958), 5. An editorial note on the author said, "An estimated 10 million heard him in person and he is now regularly on radio and TV."

59. John F. Walvoord, "Russia and the Middle East in Prophecy," *Moody Monthly,* LX (December, 1959), 26.

60. *Christianity and Crisis,* November 26, 1956, pp. 158-59, as cited in Fishman, *American Protestantism and a Jewish State,* p. 149.

61. Ober, *The Great World Crisis,* pp. 77-78.

62. Rosell, "God Pre-writes the Headlines," pp. 2-3.

63. Louis T. Talbot, *Russia Mobilizes for Armageddon,* p. 21.

64. Culbertson, "God's Clock," p. 349.

65. C. M. Ward, "Armageddon Ahead!" *Evangel,* September 19, 1954, pp. 1-2.

66. *Our Hope,* LXII (1955-56), 476; Rosell, "God Pre-writes the Headlines," pp. 2-3.

67. Louis S. Bauman, "The Nations Marshalling for Armageddon," *The King's Business,* XLI (December, 1950), 14-15.

68. Ober, *The Great World Crisis,* pp. 77, 82.

69. William Culbertson and Herman B. Centz, eds., *Understanding the Times: Prophetic Messages Delivered at the Second International Congress on Prophecy, New York City,* pp. 185-87.

70. Frank M. Boyd, "Israel and Armagedden" [sic], *Evangel,* December 2, 1956, p. 5.

71. Edgar Ainslie, "Russia in the Light of Prophecy," *The Sunday School Times,* XCVIII (October 20, 1956), 829.

72. Culbertson, "God's Clock," pp. 349-50.

73. H. Palliser, "The Jew and the Coming Crisis," *Evangel,* August 23, 1953, p. 3.

74. L. B. ("Bill") Lewis, "When God Defeats Communistic Russia," *Evangel,* December 12, 1956, p. 5. Talbot, *Russia Mobilizes for Armageddon,* p. 22.

75. Louis S. Bauman, "The Russian Bear Prowls Forth to His Doom," *The King's Business,* XLI (September, 1950), 11.

76. Rosell, "God Pre-writes the Headlines," p. 3.

77. *Evangel,* May 17, 1951, p. 7.

78. Lewis, "When God Defeats Communistic Russia," p. 4.

79. Hull, *Israel—Key to Prophecy,* p. 36.

80. William K. Harrison, "Reminiscences and a Prophecy," *Christianity Today,* I (March 4, 1957), 13-15.

81. Pont, *The World's Collision,* pp. 218-19.

82. *Our Hope,* LXI (1954-55), 221.

83. *Our Hope,* LXI (1954-55), 278.

84. Bauman, "The Nations Marshalling for Armageddon," p. 15.

85. *Our Hope,* LXII (1955-56), 651.

86. Talbot, *Russia Mobilizes for Armageddon,* pp. 24-25.

87. Pont, *The World's Collision,* p. 214.

88. Bauman, "The Nation's Marshalling for Armageddon," p. 30.

89. Hull, *Israel—Key to Prophecy,* p. 32.

90. William K. Harrison, Jr., "Is the United States in Prophecy?" *The Sunday School Times,* CI (May 16, 1959), 383-84.

91. Sale-Harrison, "Russia's Militant Opposition to Christianity," p. 867.

92. Louis S. Bauman, "The Russian Bear Prowls Forth to His Doom," *The King's Business,* XLI (August, 1950), 11.

93. *Our Hope,* LXI (March, 1955), 542.
94. Rosell, "God Pre-writes the Headlines," p. 4.

CHAPTER 10

1. John F. Walvoord, "The Amazing Rise of Israel," *Moody Monthly,* LXVIII (October, 1967), 22.
2. S. Maxwell Coder, "The Future of Russia," *Moody Monthly,* LXIV (October, 1963), 31-32.
3. *Moody Monthly,* LXVII (July-August, 1967), 22-24.
4. *Evangel,* July 9, 1967, p. 4.
5. L. Nelson Bell, "Unfolding Destiny," *Christianity Today,* XI (July 21, 1967), 1044-45.
6. Ralph M. Riggs, "Who Is the Rightful Owner of Palestine?" *Evangel,* July 30, 1967, p. 7.
7. Walvoord, "The Amazing Rise of Israel," p. 25.
8. *Moody Monthly,* LXVIII (October, 1967), 42.
9. Richard Wolff, "God in History," *Moody Monthly,* LXVIII (October, 1967), 30.
10. Arnold T. Olson, *Inside Jerusalem, City of Destiny,* pp. 67, 20, 30.
11. Ibid., p. 120.
12. Ibid., p. 119.
13. *Evangel,* July 26, 1970, p. 26. The earlier studies referred to are Charles Y. Glock and Rodney Stark, *American Piety: The Nature of Religious Commitment and Christian Beliefs and Anti-Semitism* (New York: Harper and Row, 1966).
14. Arnold T. Olson, "Israel After 25 Years," *United Evangelical Action,* XXXII (Spring, 1973), 28, citing *Newsweek* (November 9, 1970).
15. Harold Sevener, "Israel: The World's Timetable," *Christian Life,* XXXV (August, 1973), 28.
16. S. Maxwell Coder, "Jerusalem: Key to the Future," *Moody Monthly,* LXXIV (October, 1973), 32-33.
17. James L. Kelso, "News: Special Report," *Christianity Today,* XI (July 21, 1967), 1051-52.
18. Oral Roberts, *The Drama of the End-Time,* pp. 82-84.
19. Cliff Barrows, "I Walked in His Land," *Christian Life,* XXXII (January, 1971), 22.
20. Robert Flood, "Israel: Land of the Return," *Moody Monthly,* LXXIII (March, 1973), 25.
21. Barrows, "I Walked in His Land," p. 22.
22. Letter from Arnold D. Ehlert, Graduate Studies Librarian, Biola Library, October 12, 1973. The manifesto was circulated by the American Prophetic League, Inc., Los Angeles, California.
23. "A Proclamation Concerning Israel and the Nations," issued by the Board of Directors of Biola Schools and Colleges Inc. in consultation with the faculties of Talbot Theological Seminary and the Bible Department of Biola College, La Mirada, California.

24. Louis H. Hauff, "Israel—The Budding of the Fig Tree," *Evangel,* July 10, 1960, p. 19; *The Prophetic Word in Crisis Days,* p. 116.

25. Louis T. Talbot, "The National Resurrection of Israel and Her Future Glory," *The King's Business,* LV (June, 1964), 21-28.

26. Wilbur M. Smith, "Concluding Words on the Signs of the Times," *Moody Monthly,* LXVII (September, 1966), 50.

27. *Evangel,* July 9, 1967, p. 4.

28. Olson, *Inside Jerusalem,* pp. 83-88.

29. W. D. Cook, "Arabs/Jews: Why They Fight," *Christian Life,* XXXV (August, 1973), 26.

30. *Evangel,* July 14, 1974, p. 31.

31. Harold Sevener, "Israel: The World's Timetable," *Christian Life,* XXXV (August, 1973), 28. Dov Ashbel, *One Hundred and Seventeen Years (1845-1962) of Rainfall Observations,* pp. 118-31.

32. William Ward Ayer, "Anti-Christ: The Nations, the Church, Israel," *The King's Business,* LI (May, 1960), 28.

33. Bernard Ramm, "Behind the Turmoil and Terror in the Mideast," *Eternity,* XVIII (September, 1967), 34.

34. William Culbertson, "Perspective on Arab-Israeli Tensions," *Christianity Today,* XII (June 7, 1968), 6-9.

35. Olson, *Inside Jerusalem,* pp. 50-51.

36. Frank H. Epp, *Whose Land Is Palestine? The Middle East Problem in Historical Perspective,* p. 241.

37. Ibid., pp. 243-44.

38. Charles C. Ryrie, "Perspective on Palestine," *Christianity Today,* XIII (May 23, 1969), 8.

39. Ralph W. Harris, "The Arab-Israeli Conflict," *Evangel,* October 18, 1970, p. 8.

40. *Evangel,* July 9, 1967, p. 4.

41. Louis H. Hauff, "Dry Bones of Israel Come to Life," *Evangel,* August 20, 1967, p. 7.

42. Wilbur M. Smith, *Israeli/Arab Conflict and the Bible,* p. 110.

43. Olson, *Inside Jerusalem,* p. 133.

44. Bruce Shelley, "The Late, Late Great Planet," *United Evangelical Action,* XXXIII (Spring, 1974), 6.

45. Hal Lindsey, *The Late Great Planet Earth,* p. 57.

46. Hal Lindsey, "The Pieces Fall Together," *Moody Monthly,* LXVIII (October, 1967), 27.

47. Walvoord, "The Amazing Rise of Israel," p. 25.

48. "Israel: Things to Come," *Christianity Today,* XII (December 22, 1967), 307.

49. Raymond L. Cox, "Time for the Temple?" *Eternity,* XIX (January, 1968), 17-18.

50. H. L. Ellison, "Israel—A Year Later," *Eternity,* XIX (August, 1968), 38.

51. J. Dwight Pentecost, "Which Comes First the Rapture or the Temple?" *Moody Monthly,* LXXII (October, 1971), 30-31.

52. Malcom Couch, "When Will the Jews Rebuild Their Temple?" *Moody Monthly,* LXXIV (December, 1973), 34-35, 86.

53. William Ward Ayer, "The Arab and the Jew," *Evangel,* July 30, 1967, p. 6.

54. Smith, *Israeli/Arab Conflict,* p. 80.

55. Ibid., p. 85.

56. Charles L. Feinberg, "Isaac and Ishmael," *The King's Business,* LVIII (July, 1968), 23.

57. W. D. Cook, "Arabs/Jews: Why They Fight," *Christian Life,* XXXV (August, 1973), 26.

58. Lindsey, *The Late Great Planet Earth,* pp. 79-80.

59. Shelley, "The Late, Late Great Planet," p. 6.

60. C. M. Ward, "Arab-Israeli Reconciliation Ahead?" *Evangel,* December 27, 1970, p. 18.

61. Martin R. DeHaan, "Russian Communism and God's Timetable," *The King's Business,* LII (October, 1961), 8-9.

62. *The Prophetic Word in Crisis Days,* p. 117.

63. Billy Graham, *World Aflame,* p. 1.

64. S. Maxwell Coder, "The Future of Russia," *Moody Monthly,* LXIV (September, 1963), 74.

65. Richard DeHaan, *Israel and the Nations in Prophecy,* pp. 120-21.

66. Ibid., p. 130.

67. Ibid., p. 135.

68. C. M. Ward, ". . . And World Leaders Tremble," *Evangel,* May 18, 1969, pp. 14-15.

69. C. M. Ward, "Tomorrow's Headlines," *Evangel,* January 10, 1971, pp. 20-21.

70. Ayer, "Anti-Christ," p. 28.

71. Roy L. Aldrich, "Is the United States in Prophecy?" *The King's Business,* LIII (January, 1962), 25. Aldrich was president of Detroit Bible College.

72. Thomas M. Chalmers, "The Future Glory of Israel," *The King's Business,* LV (May, 1964), 16.

73. Talbot, "The National Resurrection, p. 21.

74. Walvoord, "The Amazing Rise of Israel," p. 22.

75. C. M. Ward, "Tomorrow's Headlines," pp. 20-21.

76. C. M. Ward, "Fuses Ignited—Explosion Ahead!" *Evangel,* May 9, 1971, pp. 14-15.

77. Harold B. Light, "Let My People Go," *Christian Life,* XXXVI (May, 1974), 80-83.

78. Edgar C. James, "Armageddon," *The King's Business,* LVII (December, 1966), 28.

79. Lindsey, *The Late Great Planet Earth,* p. 157.

80. Ibid., p. 162.

81. Ibid., p. 168.

82. Charles J. Woodbridge, "Armageddon and the Millennium," *Moody Monthly,* LXIII (September, 1962), 69-75. DeHaan, "Russian Communism," p. 9.

83. S. Maxwell Coder, "The Future of Russia," *Moody Monthly,* LXIV (September, 1963), 74.

84. Wilbur M. Smith, "A Prediction Concerning India," *Moody Monthly,* LXVII (February, 1967), 58-59.

85. DeHaan, *Israel and the Nations in Prophecy,* p. 122.

86. Lindsey, *The Late Great Planet Earth,* p. 72.

87. John F. Walvoord, "Converging Signs of Our Times," *Moody Monthly,* LXIV (July-August, 1964), 22.

88. *The Prophetic Word in Crisis Days,* pp. 122-23.

89. "Russia's Cold War on Christians," *Moody Monthly,* LXV (December, 1964), 16.

90. *Evangel,* July 15, 1973, p. 24.

91. Ayer, "Anti-Christ," p. 25.

92. John F. Walvoord, "End-Time Prophecies," *The Sunday School Times,* CV (August 3, 1963), 548.

93. DeHaan, *Israel and the Nations in Prophecy,* p. 50.

94. Lindsey, *The Late Great Planet Earth,* pp. 94, 96-97.

95. Edgar C. James, "Prophecy and the Common Market," *Moody Monthly,* LXXIV (March, 1974), 24-27.

96. Aldrich, "Is the United States in Prophecy?" p. 23.

97. Frank M. Boyd, "Will Russia Attack Israel?" *Evangel,* September 3, 1967, p. 3.

98. Lindsey, *The Late Great Planet Earth,* pp. 184, 95, 163.

99. *Evangel,* January 17, 1973, pp. 30-31.

100. Flood, "Israel: Land of the Return," p. 23. Nadav Safran, *The United States and Israel,* p. 271.

101. Olson, "Israel After 25 Years," pp. 14-17.

102. Sevener, "Israel: The World's Timetable," p. 32.

103. "Reflections on Israel's Birthday," *Eternity,* XXIV (May, 1973), 12.

104. *Christianity Today,* XVII (May 11, 1973), 27.

105. *Evangel,* November 18, 1973, p. 31. *Christianity Today,* XVIII (October 26, 1973), 119.

106. "Christians and Israel," *Time,* December 31, 1973, p. 57.

107. Judith Banki, *Christian Responses to the Yom Kippur War,* p. 114.

108. Ibid.

109. Earl Raab, "Is Israel Losing Popular Support? The Evidence of the Polls," *Commentary,* LVII (January, 1974), 26-29.

110. Donald Barnhouse, "Worldview," *Eternity,* XXIV (December, 1973), 51.

111. Banki, *Christian Responses to the Yom Kippur War,* p. 42. "Christians and Israel," *Time,* December 31, 1973, p. 57.

112. Malcom Couch, "Let's Not Let Israel Down," *Moody Monthly,* LXXIV (June, 1974), 30.

113. George Otis, *The Ghost of Hagar,* pp. 61, 47.

114. Ibid., p. 76.

115. Ibid., p. 88. Raymond L. Cox, "Will the Real Antichrist Please Stand Up!" *Eternity,* XXV (May, 1974), 15-17.

CHAPTER 11

1. Bruce Shelley, "The Late, Late Great Planet," *United Evangelical Action,* XXXIII (Spring, 1974), 6.

MONOGRAPHS

Aalders, Jan Gerrit. *Gog en Magog in Ezechiel.* Kampen: J. H. Kok, 1951.

Adams, John Quincy. *The Time of the End.* Dallas: The Prophetical Society of Dallas, 1924.

Ammianus Marcellinus. Translated by John C. Rolphe. Four volumes. The Loeb Classical Library. Cambridge, MA: Harvard University Press, 1939.

Anderson, Andrew Runni. *Alexander's Gate, Gog and Magog, and the Inclosed Nations.* Cambridge, MA: The Medieval Academy of America, 1932.

Ashbel, Dov. *One Hundred and Seventeen Years (1845-1962) of Rainfall Observations.* Jerusalem: Hebrew University, Department of Climatology and Meteorology, n.d.

Atlas of Israel. Amsterdam: Elsevier Publishing Company, 1970.

Bailey, Kenneth K. *Southern White Protestantism in the Twentieth Century.* New York: Harper & Row, 1964.

Banki, Judith. *Christian Responses to the Yom Kippur War.* New York: The American Jewish Committee, 1974.

Bauman, Louis S. *God and Gog: or The Coming Meet Between Judah's Lion and Russia's Bear.* N.p.: Louis S. Bauman, 1934.

———. *Light from Prophecy as Related to the Present Crisis.* New York: Fleming H. Revell, 1940.

———. *Russian Events in the Light of Bible Prophecy.* New York: Fleming H. Revell, 1942.

———. *Shirts and Sheets: or Anti-Semitism, a Present-day Sign of the First Magnitude.* Long Beach, CA: Louis S. Bauman, 1934.

Bickersteth, Edward. *The Restoration of the Jews to Their Own Land.* Third edition. London: 1852.

Blackstone, William E. *The Millennium.* New York: Fleming H. Revell, 1904.

Bovis, Eugene H. *The Jerusalem Question 1917-1968.* Stanford, CA: Hoover Institution Press, Stanford University, 1971.

Boyd, Frank M. *The Budding Fig Tree.* Springfield, MO: Gospel Publishing House, c. 1925.

Brookes, James H. *Maranatha: Or, The Lord Cometh.* St. Louis: Edward Bredell, 1870.

Brown, Arthur I. *What of the Night?* Hoytville, OH: Fundamental Truth Store, 1933.

Burton, Alfred H. *The Future of Europe: Religiously and Politically, in the Light of Holy Scripture.* London: Alfred Holness, 1896. Republished Los Angeles: Berean Bookshelf, 1967.

———. *Russia's Destiny in the Light of Prophecy.* New York: Gospel Publishing House, 1917.

Campbell, Faith. *Stanley Frodsham: Prophet with a Pen.* Springfield, MO: Gospel Publishing House, 1974.

Case, Shirley Jackson. *The Millennial Hope: A Phase of War-Time Thinking.* Chicago: The University of Chicago Press, 1918.

Cohn, Norman. *The Pursuit of the Millennium: Revolutionary Millenarians and Mystical Anarchists of the Middle Ages.* New York: Oxford University Press, 1970.

———. *Warrant for Genocide: The Myth of the Jewish World-conspiracy and the "Protocols of the Elders of Zion."* New York: Harper Torchbooks, 1969.

Coleridge, Samuel Taylor. *Notes on English Divines.* London: Bradbury and Evans, 1853.

Coming and Kingdom of Christ. Chicago: Moody Bible Institute, n.d. Report of a Bible Conference, February 24-27, 1914.

Commentary. American Reaction to the Six Day War. New York: Commentary, 1967.

Cooper, David Lipscomb. *The Invading Forces of Russia and of the Antichrist Overthrown in Palestine.* Los Angeles: Biblical Research Society, n.d.

———. *Is the Jew Still First on God's Prophetic Program?* Los Angeles: Biblical Research Society, 1935.

———. *Prophetic Fulfillments in Palestine Today*. Los Angeles: Biblical Research Society, 1940.

———. *The Shepherd of Israel Seeking His Own*. Los Angeles: Biblical Research Society, 1962.

———. *When Gog's Armies Meet the Almighty*. Los Angeles: Biblical Research Society, 1940.

Cross, Whitney R. *The Burned-over District: The Social and Intellectual History of Enthusiastic Religion in Western New York, 1800-1850*. Ithaca, NY: Cornell University Press, 1950.

Crum, Bartley Cavanaugh. *Behind the Silken Curtain*. London: V. Gollancz, 1947.

Culbertson, William, and Herman B. Centz, eds. *Understanding the Times: Prophetic Messages Delivered at the Second International Congress on Prophecy, New York City*. Grand Rapids: Zondervan, n.d.

Cumming, John. *The Destiny of Nations as Indicated in Prophecy*. London: Hurst & Blackett, 1864.

———. *The End: or The Proximate Signs of the Close of This Dispensation*. Boston: John P. Jewett, 1855.

———. *God in History*. New York: Lane & Scott, 1852.

———. *The Great Preparation: or Redemption Draweth Nigh*. New York: Rudd & Carleton, 1860-61.

———. *Signs of the Times; or Present, Past, and Future*. Philadelphia: Lindsay and Blakiston, 1855.

Darms, Anton. *The Jew Returns to Israel*. Grand Rapids: Zondervan, 1965.

Davis, George T. B. *Rebuilding Palestine According to Prophecy*. Philadelphia: Million Testaments Campaigns, 1935.

DeHaan, Martin R. *The Jew and Palestine in Prophecy*. Grand Rapids: Zondervan, 1950.

DeHaan, Richard. *Israel and the Nations in Prophecy*. Grand Rapids: Zondervan, 1968.

Ehlert, Arnold D. *A Bibliographic History of Dispensationalism*. Grand Rapids: Baker Book House, 1965.

Epp, Frank H. *Whose Land Is Palestine? The Middle East Problem in Historical Perspective*. Grand Rapids: William B. Eerdmans, 1970.

Essays on the American Public Opinion and the Palestine Problem. Beirut: Palestine Research Center, 1969.

Faber, George Stanley. *A Dissertation on the Prophecies, That Have Been Fulfilled, Are Now Fulfilling, or Will Hereafter Be Fulfilled, Relative to the Great Period of 1260 years; the Papal and Mohammedan Apostacies; the Tyrannical Reign of Antichrist, or the*

Infidel Power; and the Restoration of the Jews. Second edition. New York: M. and W. Ward and Evert Duyckinck, 1811.

———. *A General and Connected View of the Prophecies Relative to the Conversion, Restoration, Union and Future Glory of the Houses of Judah and Israel; the Progress, and Final Overthrow of the Antichristian Confederacy in the Land of Palestine; and the Ultimate General Diffusion of Christianity*. Boston: William Andrews, 1809.

Finch, Sir Henry. *The World's Great Restauration, or The Calling of the Jews*. London: William Gouge, 1621.

Fisher, H. E. *Soviet Russia and Palestine*. Los Angeles: H. E. Fisher, 1946.

Fishman, Hertzel. *American Protestantism and a Jewish State*. Detroit: Wayne State University Press, 1973.

Frodsham, Stanley H. *The Coming Crisis and the Coming Christ*. Springfield, MO: Gospel Publishing House, n.d.

Froom, LeRoy Edwin. *The Prophetic Faith of Our Fathers: The Historical Development of Prophetic Interpretation*. Four volumes. Washington, DC: Review and Herald, 1946.

Gaebelein, Arno C., ed. *Christ and Glory, Addresses Delivered at the New York Prophetic Conference, Carnegie Hall, November 25-28, 1918*. New York: Revell, 1918.

———. *The Conflict of the Ages: The Mystery of Lawlessness: Its Origin, Historic Development and Coming Defeat*. New York: Publication Office "Our Hope," 1933.

Gartenhaus, Jacob. *The Rebirth of a Nation: Zionism in History and Prophecy*. Nashville: Broadman Press, 1936.

———. *What of the Jews?* Atlanta: Home Mission Board, Southern Baptist Convention, 1948.

Gilbert, Dan. *The Red Terror and Bible Prophecy*. Washington, DC: The Christian Press Bureau, 1944.

———. *Russia's Next Move: In the Light of Prophecy*. Los Angeles: Jewish Hope Publishing House, n.d.

———. *Will Russia Fight America? The Question Considered in the Light of Bible Prophecy*. Los Angeles: Jewish Hope Publishing Co., n.d.

Graham, Billy. *World Aflame*. New York: Doubleday and Company, Inc., 1965.

Gray, James M. *Great Epochs of Sacred History*. New York: Fleming H. Revell, 1910.

———. *A Text-Book on Prophecy*. New York: Fleming H. Revell, 1918.

Guinness, H. Grattan. *The Approaching End of the Age, Viewed in the Light of History, Prophecy, and Science.* London: Morgan and Scott, Ltd., 1918.

———. *The Divine Programme of the World's History.* London: Harley House, 1892.

———. *History of Unveiling Prophecy.* New York: Fleming H. Revell, 1905.

———. *Light for the Last Days.* London: Hodder, 1893.

Haldeman, Isaac Massey. *The Signs of the Times.* Fourth edition. New York: Charles C. Cook, 1913.

Hill, Samuel S., Jr. *Southern Churches in Crisis.* New York: Holt, Rinehart and Winston, 1967.

Hull, William L. *The Fall and Rise of Israel.* Grand Rapids: Zondervan, 1954.

———. *Israel—Key to Prophecy.* Grand Rapids: Zondervan, 1964.

Ironside, Henry Allan. *The Lamp of Prophecy.* Grand Rapids: Zondervan, 1940.

———. *Looking Backward over a Third of a Century of Prophetic Fulfillment.* New York: Loizeaux, 1930.

Janeway, Jacob Jones. *Hope for the Jews: or The Jews Will Be Converted to the Christian Faith; and Settled and Reorganized as a Nation, in the Land of Palestine.* New Brunswick, NJ: J. Terhune and Son, 1953.

Jorstad, Erling. *The Politics of Doomsday.* Nashville: Abingdon Press, 1970.

Kac, Arthur W. *The Rebirth of the State of Israel—Is It of God or of Men?* Chicago: Moody Press, 1958.

Kirk, George. *The Middle East 1945-1950.* Volume V of *Survey of International Affairs, 1939-1946.* Edited by Arnold Toynbee, London: Oxford University Press, 1954.

Kraus, C. Norman. *Dispensationalism in America: Its Rise and Development.* Richmond: John Knox Press, 1958.

Laqueur, Walter. *The Road to War: The Origin and Aftermath of the Arab-Israeli Conflict 1967/8.* Baltimore: Penguin Books, 1969.

Levin, N. Gordon, Jr., ed. *The Zionist Movement in Palestine and World Politics, 1880-1918.* Lexington, MA: D. C. Heath and Company, 1974.

Light on Prophecy: Proceedings and Addresses at the Philadelphia Prophetic Conference, May 28-30, 1918. New York: The Christian Herald Bible House, 1918.

Lindsey, Hal. *The Late Great Planet Earth.* Grand Rapids: Zondervan, 1970.

McCall, Thomas S., and Zola Levitt. *Satan in the Sanctuary.* Chicago: Moody Press, 1973.

McConkey, James H. *The End of the Age.* Fifteenth edition. Pittsburgh: Silver Publishing Company, 1925.

Manuel, Frank E. *The Realities of American-Palestine Relations.* Washington, DC: Public Affairs Press, 1949.

Mather, Increase. *The Mystery of Israel's Salvation Explained and Applyed, or A Discourse Concerning the General Conversion of the Israelitish Nation.* London: John Allen, 1669.

Meyer, Isidore S., ed. *Early History of Zionism in America.* New York: American Jewish Historical Society and Theodor Herzl Foundation, 1958.

Miller, Perry. *Errand into the Wilderness.* New York: Harper and Row, 1964.

Morse, Arthur D. *While Six Million Died: A Chronicle of American Apathy.* New York: Random House, 1967.

Moseley, Edward Hilary. *The Jew and His Destiny.* Berne, IN: The Berne Witness, 1939.

Murray, Robert K. *Red Scare: A Study in National Hysteria, 1919-1920.* Minneapolis: University of Minnesota Press, 1955.

Naish, Reginald T. *The Midnight Hour and After!* Seventh edition. London: Chas. J. Thynne & Jarvis, Ltd., 1928.

Needham, George C., ed. *Prophetic Studies of the International Prophetic Conference.* Chicago: Fleming H. Revell, 1886.

Ober, Douglas. *The Great World Crisis.* Wheaton, IL: Van Kampen Press, 1950.

Olson, Arnold Theodore. *Inside Jerusalem, City of Destiny.* Glendale, CA: Regal Books Division, G/L Publications, 1968.

Otis, George. *The Ghost of Hagar.* Van Nuys, CA: Time-Light Books, 1974.

Owen, Frederick. *Abraham to Allenby.* Grand Rapids: William B. Eerdmans, 1939.

———. *Abraham to the Middle-East Crisis.* Grand Rapids: William B. Eerdmans, 1957.

Palestine: A Study of Jewish, Arab, and British Policies. New Haven, CT: Yale University Press, 1947.

Pankhurst, Christabel. *The Lord Cometh.* New York: The Book Stall, 1923.

———. *Seeing the Future.* New York: Harper and Brothers Publishers, 1929.

———. *Some Modern Problems in the Light of Prophecy.* New York: Revell, 1924.

———. *The Uncurtained Future.* London: Hodder and Stoughton, 1940.

Panton, D. M. *The Panton Papers.* New York: T. M. Chalmers, 1925.

Parkes, James. *Whose Land? A History of the Peoples of Palestine.* Baltimore: Penguin Books, 1970.

Petry, Ray C. *Christian Eschatology and Social Thought: A Historical Essay on the Social Implications of Some Selected Aspects in Christian Eschatology to A.D. 1500.* New York: Abingdon, 1956.

Pont, Charles E. *The World's Collision.* Boston. W. A. Wilde Company, 1956.

Price, Charles S. *The Battle of Armageddon.* Pasadena, CA: Charles S. Price Publishing Company, 1938.

The Prophetic Word in Crisis Days. Findlay, OH: Dunham Publishing Company, n.d.

Riggs, Ralph M. *The Path of Prophecy.* Springfield, MO: Gospel Publishing House, 1937.

Riley, William Bell. *Wanted—A World Leader!* Minneapolis (?): 1939.

Rimmer, Harry. *The Coming War and the Rise of Russia.* Grand Rapids: William B. Eerdmans, 1940.

———. *Palestine the Coming Storm Center.* Grand Rapids: William B. Eerdmans, 1940.

Roberts, Oral. *The Drama of the End-Time.* Tulsa: Oral Roberts, 1963.

Rodinson, Maxime. *Israel and the Arabs.* Translated by Michael Perl. Baltimore: Penguin Books Inc., 1968.

Ryrie, Charles Caldwell. *Dispensationalism Today.* Chicago: Moody Press, 1965.

Safran, Nadav. *The United States and Israel.* Cambridge, MA: Harvard University Press, 1963 .

Sale-Harrison, Leonard. *The Coming Great Northern Confederacy: or The Future of Russia and Germany.* London: Pickering and Inglis Ltd., 1928; Wheaton, IL: Van Kampen Press, 1948.

———. *The Remarkable Jew; His Wonderful Future; God's Great Timepiece.* Thirteenth edition. New York: Sale-Harrison Publications, c. 1940. Reprinted as *God and Israeli.* Wheaton, IL: Van Kampen Press, 1954.

Sandeen, Ernest R. *The Roots of Fundamentalism: British and American Millenarianism, 1800-1930.* Chicago: University of Chicago Press, 1970.

Schor, Samuel. *The Everlasting Nation and Their Coming King.* London: Marshall, Morgan and Scott, 1933.

Scofield, Cyrus Ingerson. *Addresses on Prophecy.* Swengel, PA: Bible Truth Depot, 1910.

———, and Arno C. Gaebelein. *The Jewish Question.* New York: Our Hope, 1912.

———, ed. *The Scofield Reference Bible.* New York: Oxford University Press, 1909.

Scott, Walter. *At Hand: Or, Things Which Must Shortly Come to Pass.* Fourth edition. London: Pickering & Inglis, n.d.

Simpson, A. B. *The Coming One.* New York: Christian Alliance Publishing Company, 1912.

Sims, A. *The Coming War and the Rise of Russia.* Toronto: A. Sims, 1932.

Smith, Ethan. *A Dissertation on the Prophecies Relative to Antichrist and the Last Times.* Charleston, MA: Samuel T. Armstrong, 1811.

Smith, Oswald J. *Prophecy—What Lies Ahead?* London: Marshall, Morgan and Scott, Ltd., n.d.

Smith, Timothy L. *Revivalism and Social Reform in Mid-Nineteenth Century America.* New York: Harper Torchbooks, 1957.

Smith, Wilbur M. *Israeli/Arab Conflict and the Bible.* Glendale, CA: Regal Books Division, G/L Publications, 1967.

———. *Israel, the Bible, and the Middle East.* Glendale, CA: Gospel Light Publications, 1967.

———. *A Preliminary Bibliography for the Study of Biblical Prophecy.* Boston: W. A. Wilde Co., 1952.

———. *World Crisis in the Light of Prophetic Scriptures.* Chicago: Moody Press, 1952.

Spalding, Joshua. *Sentiments, Concerning the Coming and Kingdom of Christ.* Salem, MA: 1796.

Stein, Leonard. *The Balfour Declaration.* New York: Simon and Schuster, 1961.

Strakhovsky, Leonid I. *American Opinion About Russia, 1917-1920.* Toronto: University of Toronto, 1961.

Streiker, Lowell D., and Gerald S. Strober. *Religion and the New Majority: Billy Graham, Middle America, and the Politics of the 70's.* New York: Association Press, 1972.

Talbot, Louis T. *The Judgment of God upon the Russian Confederacy.* The fifth in a series of addresses by Louis T. Talbot, Pastor, The Church of the Open Door, delivered over radio station KMTR, Los Angeles.

———. *Russia: Her Invasion of Palestine in the Last Days and Her Final Destruction at the Return of Christ.* A radio message given over station KMPC, Beverly Hills, CA.

———. *Russia Mobilizes for Armageddon.* Los Angeles: Bible Institute of Los Angeles, n.d.

Talbot, Louis T., and William W. Orr. *The New Nation of Israel and the Word of God!* Los Angeles: The Bible Institute of Los Angeles, 1948.

Taylor, D. T. *The Voice of the Church on the Coming and Kingdom of the Redeemer: or A History of the Doctrine of the Reign of Christ on Earth.* Eighth edition. Scriptural Tract Repository, 1866.

Toon, Peter, ed. *Puritans, the Millennium, and the Future of Israel: Puritan Eschatology 1600-1660.* Cambridge: James Clarke and Co., 1970.

Torrey, Reuben A. *The Return of the Lord Jesus.* Los Angeles: The Bible Institute of Los Angeles, 1913.

———. *What War Teaches; The Greatest Lessons of the Year 1917.* Los Angeles: Biola Book Room, 1918.

Toynbee, Arnold J. *A Study of History.* Six volumes. New York: Oxford University Press, 1939.

Trumbull, Charles G. *Prophecy's Light on Today.* New York: Fleming H. Revell, 1937.

Tuveson, Ernest Lee. *Millennium and Utopia: A Study in the Background of the Idea of Progress.* Berkeley: University of California Press, 1949.

———. *Redeemer Nation: The Idea of America's Millennial Role.* Chicago: University of Chicago Press, 1968.

Vernadsky, George. *Ancient Russia.* New Haven, CT: Yale University Press, 1943.

Walker, William H. *Will Russia Conquer the World?* Miami: Miami Bible Institute, 1960.

Walvoord, John F. *Israel in Prophecy.* Grand Rapids: Zondervan, 1962.

West, Nathaniel. *Daniel's Great Prophecy, the Eastern Question of the Kingdom.* New York: The Hope of Israel Movement, 1898.

———. *Premillennial Essays of the Prophetic Conference Held in the Church of the Holy Trinity in New York City.* Chicago: Fleming H. Revell, 1897.

———. *The Thousand Years: Studies in Eschatology in Both Testaments.* Fincastle, VA: Scripture Truth Book Company, n.d., 1889 reprint.

Williams, William Appleman. *American-Russian Relations, 1781-1947.* New York: Rinehart and Co., Inc., 1952.

Wise, Stephen. *Challenging Years: The Autobiography of Stephen Wise.* New York: G. P. Putnam's Sons, 1949.

PERIODICALS

The Alliance Witness

Annuals of the Southern Baptist Convention 1845-1953 with Index of Convention Proceedings.

"Bible Prophecy and the Mid-East Crisis." *Moody Monthly,* LXVII (July, 1967), 22-24.

Bowman, John Wick. "The Bible and Modern Religions, II, Dispensationalism." *Interpretation,* X (April, 1956), 170-187.

Case, Shirley Jackson. "The Premillennial Menace." *The Biblical World,* LII (July, 1918), 17-23.

Christianity Today.

Christian Life.

Christian Voice for a Jewish Palestine, I (Summer, 1946).

Dawn, an Evangelical Magazine.

Dodge, Bayard. "Peace or War in Palestine." *Christianity and Crisis,* VIII (March 15, 1948), 27-30.

Dollar, George W. "The Early Days of American Fundamentalism." *Bibliotheca Sacra,* CXXIII (April, 1966), 115-23.

English, E. Schuyler. "The Judgment of the Nations," *Our Hope,* LI (February, 1945), 561-65.

Eternity.

Goen, Clarence C. "Jonathan Edwards: A New Departure in Eschatology." *Church History,* XXVIII (1959), 25-40.

Goldberg, Louis. "Dimensions of the Future." *Moody Monthly,* LXIX (December, 1968), 67-72.

Jennings, F. C. "The Boundaries of the Revived Roman Empire." *Our Hope,* XLVII (December, 1940), 386-90.

Karmarkovic, Alex. "American Evangelical Responses to the Russian Revolution and the Rise of Communism in the Twentieth Century," *Fides et Historia,* IV (Spring, 1972), 11-27.

The King's Business.

Kligerman, Aaron J. "Palestine—Jewish Homeland." *The Southern Presbyterian Journal,* VII (June 1, 1948), 17-19.

Ladd, George Eldon. "Israel and the Church." *The Evangelical Quarterly,* XXXVI (October-December, 1964), 206-13.

LaSor, William Sanford. "Have the 'Times of the Gentiles' Been Fulfilled?" *Eternity,* XVIII (August, 1967), 32-34.

Moody Monthly.

Our Hope.

Oxtaby, W. G. "Christians and the Mideast Crisis." *Christian Century,* LXXXIV (July 26, 1967), 961-65.

Parker, T. Valentine. "Premillenarianism: An Interpretation and an Evaluation." *The Biblical World,* LII (1919), 37-40.

The Pentecostal Evangel.

Prophecy Monthly.

The Prophetic Times.

Rall, Harris Franklin. "Premillennialism." *The Biblical World,* LIII (1919), 339-47, 459-69, 617-627.

Revelation.

Ryrie, Charles C. "Dispensationalism Today." *Moody Monthly,* LXVI (November, 1965), 58-59.

"Significant Books About Jews." *Christian Life,* XXXV (August, 1973), 50-54.

Smith, David E. "Millenarian Scholarship in America." *American Quarterly,* XVII (1965), 535-49.

Smith, Wilbur M. "The Prophetic Literature of Colonial America." *Bibliotheca Sacra,* C (January, April, 1943), 67-82, 273-88.

Snowden, James H. "Summary of Objections to Premillenarianism." *The Biblical World,* LIII (1919), 165-73.

The Sunday School Times.

"Two Views of the Arab-Israeli Controversy." *His,* XV (March, 1955), 9-12.

United Evangelical Action.

Watchman Examiner.

Wiersbe, Warren W. "Two Giants of Bible Interpretation." *Moody Monthly,* LXXIV (February, 1974), 61-64. (Partly about Arno C. Gaebelein)

Yost, Charles W. "The Arab-Israeli War: How It Began." *Foreign Affairs,* XLVI (January, 1968), 304-20.

UNPUBLISHED WORKS

Adams, Bobby E. "Analysis of a Relationship: Jews and Southern Baptists." Unpublished Th.D. dissertation, Baptist Theological Seminary, Fort Worth, Texas, 1969.

Adler, Leslie Kirby. "The Red Image: American Attitudes Toward Communism in the Cold War Era." Unpublished Ph.D. dissertation, University of California, Berkeley, 1970.

Cantwell, Emmett Howell. "Millennial Teachings Among Major Baptist Theologians from 1845 to 1945." Unpublished Th.M. thesis, Southwestern Baptist Theological Seminary, Fort Worth, Texas, 1960.

Chenoweth, Maurice Gene. "The Politics of Four Types of Christian Chiliasts." Unpublished Ph.D. dissertation, University of Minnesota, 1965.

Culver, Douglas Joel. "National Restoration of the Jewish People to Palestine in British Non-Conformity, 1555-1640." Unpublished Ph.D. dissertation, New York University, 1970.

Goen, Clarence C. "A Survey History of Eschatology." Unpublished Th.D. dissertation, Southwestern Baptist Theological Seminary, Fort Worth, Texas, 1969.

Harrington, Carrol Edwin. "The Fundamentalist Movement in America, 1870-1920." Unpublished Ph.D. dissertation, University of California, Berkeley, 1959.

Huff, Earl Dean. "Zionist Influences upon U.S. Foreign Policy: A Study of American Policy Toward the Middle East from the Time of the Struggle for Israel to the Sinai Conflict." Unpublished Ph.D. dissertation, University of Idaho, 1971.

Koeppen, Sheliah R. "Dissensus and Discontent: The Clientele of the Christian Anti-Communism Crusade." Unpublished Ph.D. dissertation, Stanford University, 1967.

Leith, D. Malcomb. "American Christian Support for a Jewish Palestine: From the Second World War to the Establishment of the State of Israel." Unpublished senior thesis, Princeton University, 1957.

Mills, Hawthorne Quinn. "American Zionism and Foreign Policy." Unpublished M.A. thesis, University of California, Berkeley, 1958.

Morton, James M., Jr. "The Millenarian Movement in America and Its Effect upon the Faith and Fellowship of the Southern Baptist Convention." Unpublished Th.M. thesis, Golden Gate Baptist Theological Seminary, Mill Valley, California, 1962.

Propst, John Henry, Jr. "The Relation of Pessimism to Millennial Ideas." Unpublished Th.D. dissertation, Southwestern Baptist Theological Seminary, Fort Worth, Texas, 1962.

Snetsinger, John G. "Truman and the Creation of Israel." Unpublished Ph.D. dissertation, Stanford University, 1970.